iOS

App Distribution & Best Practices

First Edition

by Pietro Rea & Keegan Rush

iOS App Distribution & Best Practices

Pietro Rea & Keegan Rush

Notice of Rights

Notice of Liability

Trademarks

ISBN: 978-1-950325-15-3

Dedications

"To my wonderful wife Emily, our daughter Rosita and our son Javier. Thank you for always supporting me in everything I do."

— *Pietro Rea*

"To Caroline, my significant other, without whom I'd never find the time to write this book. To my parents, who selflessly provided for me and set me up for success. To Elad, my first mentor, who forever changed my career by showing me a new world of possibilities."

— *Keegan Rush*

"To my family. Thank you for your unconditional love and support."

— *Jayven Nhan*

"Gratefully dedicated to my wife, Elnaz, and my children, Kian and Nikan."

— *Soheil Azarpour*

About the Authors

Pietro Rea is an author of this book. He is a software engineer, creator, tinkerer and author with a passion for mobile development. Pietro has worked on mobile development since iOS 4. His work has been featured in the App Store across different categories: travel, media, e-commerce and more. He lives in northern Virginia with his wife, two kids and their poodle. He blogs about technology at pietrorea.com and you can find him on Twitter at @pietrorea.

Keegan Rush is an author of this book. Originally from sunny South Africa, he is now based in Poland where he works remotely. He especially loves being able to work on iOS and macOS apps and to provide guidance to others looking to learn Swift and iOS. Keegan is an avid runner and a lifelong learner. He tries to read something interesting every day, but it's obviously not enough, as his 'Books To Read' list is already in the hundreds and shows no signs of coming down.

About the Editors

Jayven Nhan is a tech editor of this book. He is an Apple scholar who contributes his best work to passion, fitness training, and nutrition. Passion makes problem-solving an enjoyment. Fitness training keeps him from staring at his Macbook, unrequited love. Nutrition gives him the epic energy he needs to power his day. He enjoys meeting passionate developers from all around the world. Outside of coding, you may find him listening to audiobooks and podcasts, reading, or watching YouTube videos.

Jordan Osterberg is a tech editor of this book, as well as a full-stack and iOS software engineer and college student in Northern California. He has worked on multiple apps for a variety of businesses, and was a WWDC 2018 Scholarship winner.

Sandra Grauschopf is a freelance writer, editor, and content strategist as well as the Editing Team Lead at raywenderlich.com. She loves to untangle tortured sentences and to travel the world with a trusty book in her hand.

Soheil Azarpour is the final pass editor of this book. He is an engineer, developer, creator, author, and a private pilot. He lives in New Hampshire with his wife and two sons. He is passionate about coding and flying, and a lifelong learner.

About the Artist

Vicki Wenderlich is the designer and artist of the cover of this book. She is Ray's wife and business partner. She is a digital artist who creates illustrations, game art and a lot of other art or design work for the tutorials and books on raywenderlich.com. When she's not making art, she loves hiking, a good glass of wine and attempting to create the perfect cheese plate.

Table of Contents

Book License

Before You Begin

This section tells you a few things you need to know before you get started, such as what you'll need for hardware and software, where to find the project files for this book, and more.

What You Need

To follow along with this book, you'll need the following:

- **A Mac running macOS Catalina 10.15 or later** with the latest point release and security patches installed. This is so you can install the latest version of the required development tool: Xcode.
- **Xcode 12 or later.** Xcode is the main iOS development tool. You need Xcode 12 at a minimum, so that you can use the latest Xcode build system. You can download the latest version of Xcode for free from the Mac App Store, here: apple.co/1FLn51R

  If you haven't installed the latest version of Xcode, be sure to do that before continuing with the book. The code covered in this book depends on Swift 5.3 and Xcode 12 — you may get lost if you try to work with an older version that this book assumes.
- **A paid Apple developer account**, so that you can create new app entries, bundle IDs, generate certificates and so on in the Apple Developer Portal. In order to sign up, you'll need US$99 (or the equivalent fee applicable in your country), a valid credit card, and a browser.
- **One real Apple device**, so you can test your app before submitting it to the App Store. The concepts in the book apply to all Apple devices, however, since some content is geared more toward iOS development and distribution, it's highly recommended that you use at least an iPhone, iPad, or iPod Touch so that you can install the Apple TestFlight app, and download beta versions of your app via TestFlight.

Book Source Code & Forums

Where to download the materials for this book

The materials for this book can be cloned or downloaded from the GitHub book materials repository:

- https://github.com/raywenderlich/pasi-materials/tree/editions/1.0

Forums

We've also set up an official forum for the book at https://forums.raywenderlich.com/c/books/ios-app-distribution-and-best-practices. This is a great place to ask questions about the book or to submit any errors you may find.

About the Cover

iOS App Distribution & Best Practices

Sharks have been known for traveling extremely long distances. Lantern sharks are the smallest ones in the world and they glow in the dark! Great white sharks are recorded swimming around 6,900 miles (11,100 km) from South Africa to western Australia, and then back again within nine months.

If you ever feel lost, chasing and figuring out App Store Connect issues, just think about the shark on the cover of this book. It shines a light on the obscure topics of publishing iOS apps to the Apple App Store and helps you go the extra mile to better understand the ins and outs of submitting apps, and troubleshooting problems.

Introduction

Before the App Store, distributing software was much harder than it is today. There was a time when developers had to put copies of their apps on floppy disks or CDs and literally "ship" them to the stores.

The App Store introduced the next chapter in software distribution. Developers didn't need to worry about hosting, collecting payment or fulfilling orders anymore. Apple ensures that all App Store visitors have a valid payment method on file, eliminating most of the friction from buying apps. Developers can now focus on building great apps and leave the rest to Apple and the App Store.

This book isn't meant to be an all-encompassing App Store distribution manual. It also isn't a replacement for Apple's official documentation. Apple changes its platform every year and many of these changes affect app distribution. The App Store Review Guidelines, the set of rules governing what third-party developers can and can't do, is also a living document that changes frequently.

The purpose of this book is to cover the fundamentals thoroughly so you can build the mental models you need to internalize the hardest parts of App Store distribution. These mental models will help you for years to come.

The book also covers best practices and automation. There is no definitive list of app distribution best practices, but over the last decade, teams have converged on similar practices that you'll read about in this book.

How to read this book

If you've never published an app to the App Store, it may seem like there is an endless list of things you need to do before users can download your app. In this case, you want to start with Chapter 1, "The App Store" and work your way through the first three chapters to learn about the basic concepts related to the App Store and the process of uploading your first app to the App Store.

If you have some experience with App Store release and want to gain more in-depth knowledge about the release process, Chapter 4, "Code Signing & Provisioning" through Chapter 8, "App Approved! (Now What?)" walk you through different phases of app distribution, using the Xcode environment and performing the related tasks via Apple Developer Portal.

Taking things one step further, Chapter 9, "Build Customizations" through Chapter 11, "Managing Secrets" teach you the intricacy of the Xcode build system, such as targets, schemes and build settings, and how you can configure them to create the ideal release pipeline.

The remainder of the book takes you out of Xcode and walks you through the automation process, starting with `xcodebuild` on the command line and, later, using fastlane on a continuous integration server.

Feel free to skip around between chapters. Wherever you need prior knowledge, you'll find cross references to related chapters to help.

Section I: iOS App Distribution & Best Practices

Begin your journey into learning the best practices of the Apple Developer Program, generating the various certificates needed, configuring your app and submitting an app to the App Store for approval, both manually and through automated processes through pipelines. Learn to use Apple TestFlight to add internal and external testers and receive feedback and crash reports. And finally, review some real-world scenarios and learn how this book's lessons apply to them.

Chapter 1: The App Store

By Pietro Rea

Before the App Store, distributing software was much harder than it is today. There was a time when developers had to put copies of their apps on floppy disks or CDs and literally "ship" them to the stores. Once most people could reliably connect to the internet, it suddenly became viable to buy, download and install software from the comfort of your own home. The situation improved, but developers still had to build and maintain bespoke checkout, hosting and payment systems.

In 2008, Apple launched the App Store for its newly released iPhone. The App Store introduced the next chapter in software distribution. Developers didn't need to worry about hosting, collecting payment or fulfilling orders anymore. Apple ensures that all App Store visitors have a valid payment method on file, eliminating most of the friction from buying apps. Developers could now focus on building great apps and leave the rest to Apple and the App Store.

Beyond simpler distribution, the App Store is also the entry point to the most successful personal computing devices in history: the iPhone, iPad, Apple Watch, Apple TV and the venerable Mac. The App Store economy has grown relentlessly over the past decade and it now represents a huge opportunity for developers.

As of this writing, there are over 1.5 billion active Apple devices. Over 500 million people visit the App Store every week across 175 territories worldwide. Developers have also benefited financially during that time. Apple has paid developers over 155 billion dollars and has facilitated billions more in other transactions. Without a doubt, the App Store is a highly successful marketplace that provides great experiences for users and lucrative opportunities for developers. "Getting in" is a worthwhile challenge.

Third-party apps

Apple is arguably one of the most user-friendly companies on the planet. And Apple's philosophy around third-party software comes from this user-centricity. Even though Apple doesn't officially state its philosophy anywhere, the world view that stems from it permeates everything you'll read about in this book. Whether you agree or not, understanding Apple's stance will help you navigate the world of app distribution.

Most Apple devices support two large categories of third-party software. The first category is the open ecosystem of the web. Open web standards govern what kind of software you can build for the web and there are no restrictions on what you can build or how you can build it. If you can use it on a mobile web browser like Safari, Apple supports it.

The second category of third-party software that Apple supports is native apps. Unlike the web, which no single entity controls, Apple controls how to build and distribute native apps. You can do almost anything on the web, but when it comes to native apps, Apple has a strong vision for its app ecosystem.

In a nutshell, Apple believes that part of building good native apps means protecting end-users from bad actors. As a result, third-party apps should always be mediated to encourage and enforce good experiences for the end-user. "Mediation" in this sense means sitting between third-party apps and end-user as a kind of referee.

By default, third-party apps cannot run on a user's device without explicit permission. To be able to run, third-party apps have to match up to officially-supported user needs. The end-user can only install third-party apps for pre-approved reasons on pre-approved devices. This is why third-party developers can only distribute native apps to the public using the App Store.

Apple's vision for its third-party app ecosystem is part of a conscious strategy with many trade-offs. An obvious trade-off is the **complexity of app distribution**. Apple only wants good, safe, user-friendly third-party apps on the App Store, and the controls they have to enforce this can make life difficult for app developers.

App lifecycle

You might think publishing an app on the App Store is like a straight line, going from step to step until you're done. In reality, an app (like any piece of software) needs testing, bug fixes and improvements. As the saying goes, software is never done!

Once you publish the first version of your app, you'll start to receive a stream of feedback — ratings and reviews from the App Store, analytics from your analytics provider, crash reports from Apple and more.

With this feedback, you can decide on the improvements you want to make, the bugs you want to fix and the features you want to add. In terms of app distribution, you have to bundle and distribute these changes into an "app update".

This is why publishing and *keeping* an app in the App Store looks more like a circle than a straight line.

This diagram shows the different steps in the **app development lifecycle**. In more detail, here's what each step represents from a distribution perspective:

1. **Development**: Development just means making the app. Most books about iOS development cover development in detail and leave out the rest of the lifecycle. This book is the opposite. You won't spend much time reading about how to make the app. Instead, the book focuses on distributing your work.

2. **Upload**: Once you're happy with the app, you package it up and upload it somewhere others can download it. Immediately after development, distribution is usually internal, or at least "pre-release". You might need to publish internal versions of the app for a product manager, a business analyst or a QA tester.

3. **Testing**: What to test and how to test is a big topic and also not covered in the book. In the context of distribution, you first need to get your app in the hands of testers before testing can begin. Hopefully, the app passes all testing with flying colors, but if not, you can go back to development, upload a new version of the app and test again.

4. **Product Page**: Marketing is an important part of distribution. You know your app is great, but you also have to tell others what the app does and why they need it. After development and testing, you get to work on your app's App Store product page. This includes setting the app's price, adding screenshots, writing compelling descriptions, and more.

5. **App Review**: Apple requires every publicly distributed third-party app to go through a process called App Review. This applies to the initial version of the app as well as every update you ship afterwards. Real Apple employees look at your app submission to make sure it meets the App Store Review Guidelines. If your app doesn't pass App Review, depending on what the problem is, you might have to go back to development, make some changes, and resubmit to App Review.

6. **App Store**: Once Apple approves your app submission, the approved version becomes available in the App Store! Users around the world can now find it and download it. If you have a paid app, users pay Apple, who then pays you.

7. **Analytics**: Did your users like your app? Does it have bugs you have to fix? After the release, you can look at analytics, app reviews and crash reports and combine those inputs with your product roadmap to determine what changes to make next. Once you decide what to do, the lifecycle beings again.

If you take "app distribution" to mean "giving your app to others", then there's more to distribution than seeing your app on the App Store (step 6). Developers need to install development versions of the app. Internal testers need to install alpha versions of the app. External testers need to install beta versions of the app. Finally, end-users install production versions of the app.

Each type of "distribution" has its own set of rules and needs different things from you. This is what this book is ultimately about. In a nutshell, the book teaches you how to give your app to whoever needs it, whenever they need it, throughout the app lifecycle, in the quickest, most efficient way.

About this book

This book isn't meant to be an all-encompassing App Store distribution manual. It also isn't a replacement for Apple's official documentation. Not only would this be a huge task to read and write, but it would also be a fast-moving target. Apple changes its platform every year and many of these changes affect app distribution. The App Store Review Guidelines, the set of rules governing what third-party developers can and can't do, is also a living document that changes frequently.

What you'll find in this book is a deeply considered sequence of topics, narrative and advice. The book covers the fundamentals thoroughly so you can build the mental models you need to internalize the hardest parts of App Store distribution. These mental models will help you for years to come.

The book also covers best practices and automation. There is no definitive list of app distribution best practices, but over the last decade, teams have converged on similar practices that you'll read about in the second half of the book.

Who this book is for

No single job description perfectly aligns with third-party app distribution. To complicate matters, the entire job of distributing an app might be chopped up into smaller pieces, with some tasks going to developers and the rest going to non-technical team members.

People with wildly different backgrounds routinely handle app distribution. We kept this in mind while writing the book. Some chapters are geared to developers, but we aimed to explain the core concepts from first principles so everyone could learn something new.

When it comes to developers, these three types of developers would benefit the most from this book:

1. **Distribution "novices"**: Being an app distribution novice is not the same as being a software development novice. The most senior iOS developer at Razeware might still be an App Store novice if she doesn't deal with the App Store regularly.

   The book covers the most common distribution workflows so App Store novices can release their first app without getting bogged down with the details. In particular, Chapters 2 and 3 are a "quick guide" suited for novices with simple use cases.

2. **Distribution "expert beginners"**: Some apps only need updates once a quarter or once a year, giving you just enough time to forget everything. There are countless app developers who successfully published an app to the App Store but found the process opaque and frustrating. These developers didn't come out the other side with a good understanding of app distribution, so they're likely to have similar difficulties the next time there's an app release.

   After reading this book, the developers who are regularly frustrated with the opaque process of publishing to the App Store will have an easier time debugging their issues. In particular, code signing seems to trip most people up at some point. If this is you, Chapter 4, explains code signing from the ground up so you can "get it" once and for all.

3. **DevOps and automation engineers**: Many things are unique to the App Store, but at the end of the day, building an app is similar to building any other piece of software. There are well-understood modern practices in software engineering, such as continuous integration (CI) and continuous delivery (CD) that can speed up, and generally improve the app lifecycle.

   Even though each team works slightly differently, there's a real "convergence" of best practices when it comes to App Store distribution and automation. Chapters 10 through 12 dive deeper into setting up a build pipeline so you can distribute apps internally and externally without a lot of manual work.

We've written this book with the hope that we can make it easier for others to share their hard work with the world. We hope you enjoy it.

– Pietro, Keegan, Jayven, Jordan, Manda, Sandra and Soheil.

The *iOS App Distribution & Best Practices* team

Chapter 2: Your First App in the App Store

By Pietro Rea

If you've never published an app to the App Store, it may seem like there is an endless list of things you need to do before users can download your app. In this chapter, you'll learn about the basic concepts related to the App Store and go through the process of uploading your first app to the App Store.

You can think of the first and the second chapters as an overview to get you started as fast as possible. Here are a few things to keep in mind as you work through the first two chapters:

- The chapters assume that you don't have any previous knowledge about App Store publishing. It's perfectly fine if you've only ever interacted with the App Store as an end-user.
- You might already have some prerequisites set up, like an Apple ID or an Apple Developer Program membership. Don't worry — the sections that cover prerequisites are short and you'll have them here if you ever have to do that again. Feel free to skip them if you need to.
- The first two chapters focus on everything you have to do *after you're done coding* so you won't see any code samples. The content is technical but you don't need to be a developer to follow along.

- The first two chapters cover the "happy path" for App Store submission. Your particular situation might include special cases that are covered in later chapters. If you get stuck, you can expect to see "exit ramps" that point to other chapters. Feel free to skip ahead and come back if you need to.
- Automated App Store submissions is a primary goal in this book, but you'll find no automation in the first two chapters. Doing everything manually first helps you understand what to automate later on.

This first chapter walks you through setting up your developer account and uploading your app to the App Store. The next chapter walks you through working with the App Store's "admin interface" to submit your app for App Review.

Without further ado, the first thing you need to do is create an Apple developer account.

Creating a developer account

The App Store's success is built on trust. Trust between Apple and end-users and between Apple and developers. Practically speaking, this means Apple needs to know who you are.

Here are four things you need to do before you can submit apps to the App Store:

1. Create an Apple ID and enable two-factor authentication.
2. Enroll in the Apple Developer Program.
3. Download and install Xcode.
4. Configure your app in the App Store's backend system (covered in the next chapter).

Creating an Apple ID

An **Apple ID** identifies a user in Apple's ecosystem. You use your Apple ID to log into Apple devices, synchronize between devices and pay. If you use an Apple product, you most likely already have one.

Every Apple developer account is also backed by an Apple ID. On top of everything you can do with an Apple ID as an end-user, a developer account also gives you access to tools and resources that are not publicly available. Developer accounts also grant you special privileges, like the ability to publish your work in the App Store.

Since you probably already have an Apple ID, the more relevant question you should answer is, *"should I create a separate Apple ID for my developer account"*?

That depends! There are several setups to choose from. You can have multiple Apple IDs and multiple developer accounts if you work for multiple organizations. Or you can use one Apple ID for everything, or one for your personal apps and one for your professional apps.

An app in the App Store is tied to a developer account and the developer account is forever tied to its Apple ID. It's cumbersome, although possible, to transfer an app to another developer account, but you'll save yourself a lot of headaches if you choose an appropriate setup for your situation.

This decision tree can help you decide if you need to create a new Apple ID.

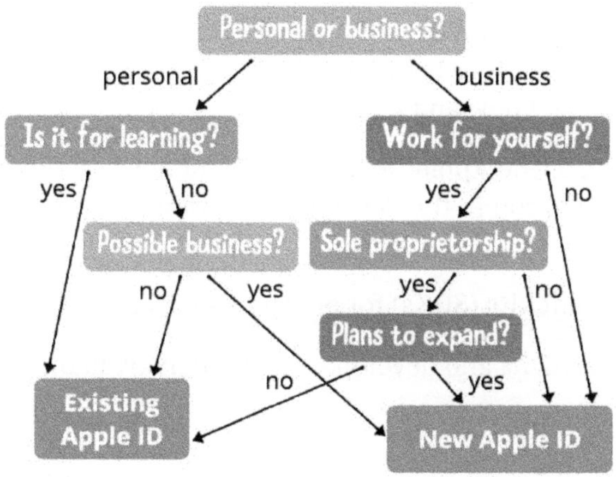

Use your Apple ID if your app's primary purpose is to learn, or if you work for yourself, don't ever see yourself expanding the business past yourself and don't want the hassle of opening a separate legal entity.

In every other case, it's better to create a new Apple ID for your new developer account.

You can create a new Apple ID directly on an iOS, iPadOS or macOS device, or you can also use Apple's web interface at appleid.apple.com. You also need to enable **two-factor authentication** on your Apple ID.

> **Note**: Apple has good documentation on account creation. Keep these links handy if you need to create a new Apple ID.
>
> How to create a new Apple ID: https://apple.co/2S18AzU.
>
> Two-factor authentication for Apple ID: https://apple.co/3kIy1CA
>
> The video course **Publishing to the App Store** on `raywenderlich.com` also walks through the process of creating a new Apple ID if you prefer a video format.

Enrolling in the Apple Developer Program

After you decide which Apple ID to use, the next step is to enroll in the **Apple Developer Program.** As of WWDC 2020, Apple has over 24 million registered developers. This group includes big names like Facebook and Netflix, as well as all the indie developers you know and love.

The best way to think of the Apple Developer Program is as a **bundle of tools and resources**. When you enroll in the developer program, you get access to the following:

- Software development kits (SDKs) for all Apple platforms.
- Beta versions of the SDKs and developer tools when available.
- Advanced app capabilities like In-App Purchases, push notifications and CloudKit.
- Developer relations and editorial support. Entire teams at Apple support developers and feature the best apps on the App Store.
- Code-level support. You can ask two detailed code-level questions per year.
- Special programs and events like the option to attend WWDC.
- App Store distribution.

Enrolling in the Apple Developer Program costs $99 per year and you pay for it using the Apple ID you picked in the previous section.

You only need to enroll and pay **once per team**. If you're joining an organization that has already enrolled in the Apple Developer Program, you don't need to pay separately. Someone in your organization can invite your Apple ID to their existing team and you're good to go.

Note: You need a **paid** Apple Developer Program enrollment to publish apps to the App Store. If you primarily want to learn how to develop on Apple's platforms, Apple also provides a free option.

You can't use advanced platform features like push notifications or CloudKit with free enrollment but at least you can build and install your apps on your devices.

Apple's documentation lays out the benefits for each type of enrollment.

https://apple.co/303Kt8j

Apple provides thorough documentation on how to enroll in the Apple Developer program, so this chapter does not cover it step by step.

You can enroll in the Apple Developer Program either on the web at developer.apple.com or by using the Developer app on iOS, which you can download from the App Store.

Apple supports two types of enrollments. Each has different legal, tax and financial implications, so make sure to pick the enrollment type that best suits you.

1. **Individuals/sole proprietorship**. Publish apps under your personal name or a sole proprietorship. In this setup, you personally enter into legal agreements with Apple. This is a good option if you decided to use your personal Apple ID in the previous section.
2. **Organization**. Publish apps on behalf of a company, non-profit or some other type of organization or legal entity. If you're publishing an app for your employer, you should pick this option. In this setup, a separate legal entity enters into contracts with Apple.

Note: If you're enrolling as an organization, you need to sign up for a D-U-N-S number through Dun & Bradstreet before you can complete your enrollment. Getting a D-U-N-S number is free but requires a verification call.

https://apple.co/308Ikbq

Apple designed the App Store's internal tools to accommodate teams of all sizes — from solo developers to large teams with specialized roles. When you complete the enrollment, you automatically become your team's **Account Holder**.

Here's the full list of roles you can expect to see:

- Account Holder (that's you!)
- Admin
- App Manager
- Developer
- Finance
- Marketing
- Sales

There are certain tasks only the Account Holder can do, like renewing the yearly membership and accepting legal agreements. If you're the Account Holder, be prepared to log into the developer portal periodically to perform administrative chores. Lucky you!

> **Note**: The Account Holder role used to be called "Team Agent". If you come across the older name in forums or blog posts, know that they are the same.

Using the correct developer account

There is one common problem with developer accounts worth mentioning. Whenever you start a new project, make sure you identify the app's publisher and **use the app publisher's Apple developer account**.

This sounds obvious, but sometimes the publisher and the developer are not the same.

Consider this common scenario: National Geographic wants to publish a new iOS app, but they don't have any iOS developers in-house.

They hire your company, Acme Apps Inc., to develop the app for them. You develop the app in record time using your company's developer account. When you submit the app for review, Apple rejects it. Why?

Apple wants to make sure everyone on the App Store is who they say they are. In this made-up scenario, National Geographic and Acme Apps are working together. But, you can easily imagine a scenario where a bad actor tries to impersonate National Geographic. This is why Apple rejects any app that's not submitted by the app publisher's developer account.

Practically speaking, even though you or your employer might already have enrolled in the Apple Developer Program, if you are a contractor or consultant, you have to **use your client's Apple Developer account**. If they don't have one, you need to help them create one.

Installing Xcode

Next, you need to download Xcode. In case you're not a developer or have not worked with Xcode before, Xcode is the de-facto app to develop software for Apple's platforms.

Xcode is primarily a programming tool, but it also uploads apps to the App Store. There are two versions of Xcode to choose from:

1. **The current version**. Xcode is an app just like any other app and Apple publishes the current version on the macOS App Store. If your app doesn't rely on pre-release features of the SDK, download Xcode from the App Store.
2. **The gold master (GM) version**. When Apple is close to releasing new versions of their SDKs, they release a special version of Xcode to upload apps that rely on pre-released SDK features. Most people don't fall into this category. But if you need the GM, you can get it from the developer portal.

> **Note**: There are also beta versions of Xcode that you can download from the developer portal. Beta versions are primarily used for testing and development. You can't upload and distribute apps to the App Store with them.

For this chapter, you'll use the current version of Xcode. Open the App Store on your Mac, search for "Xcode" and click **Download**.

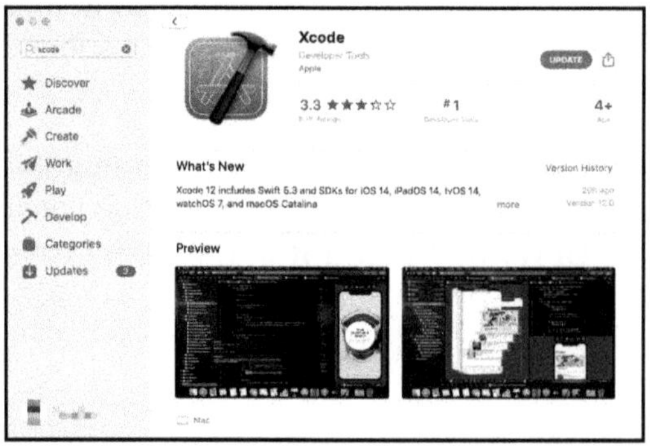

Xcode is a big download, so you might want to grab a cup of your favorite caffeinated beverage while you wait.

In later chapters, you'll work with a production-ready app. In the first and second chapters, however, you start from a brand new project so you can see how to configure everything from scratch.

Open Xcode once the download completes. Xcode asks you if you want to install additional components. You can't move forward without them, so click **Install.**

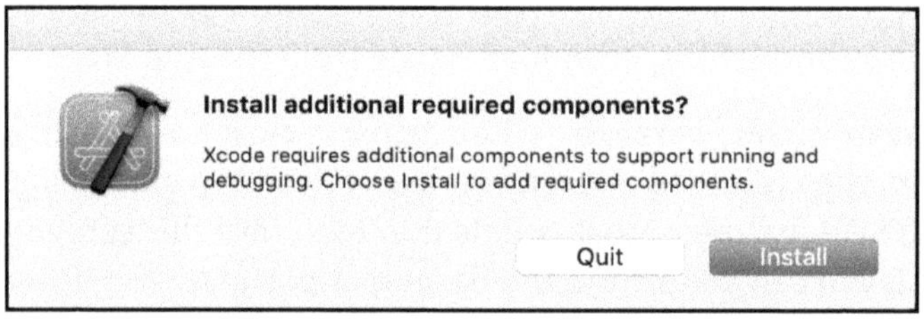

Next, select **Create a new Xcode project** from the Xcode helper screen.

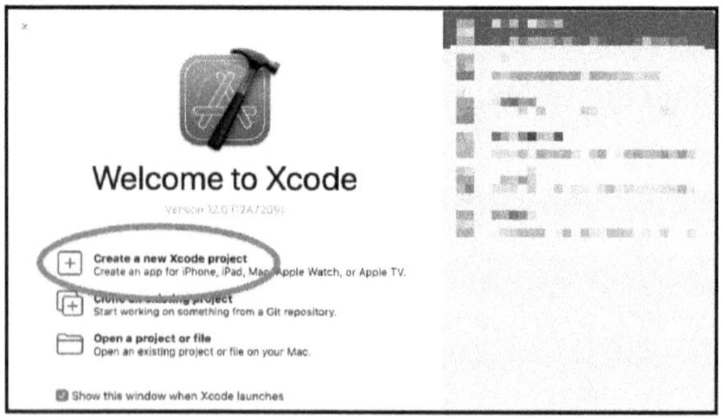

Select the **App** iOS template from the app-modal dialog and click **Next**.

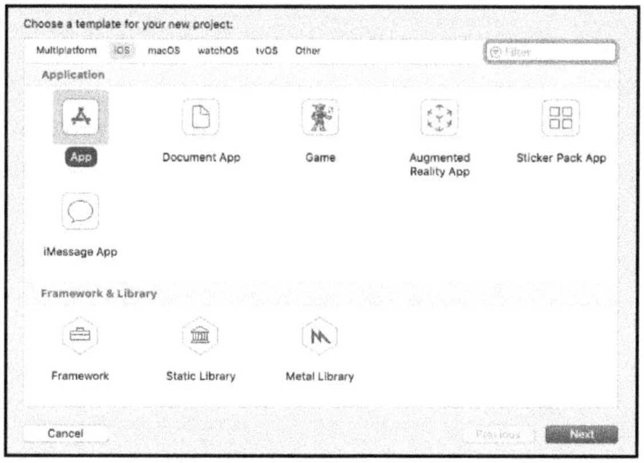

Fill out **raywenderlich** as the **Product Name**. Add your **Organization Name** and **Organization Identifier** and click **Next**.

The Organization Identifier is usually the reverse DNS notation of the app publisher's website (e.g. "com.raywenderlich" in this example).

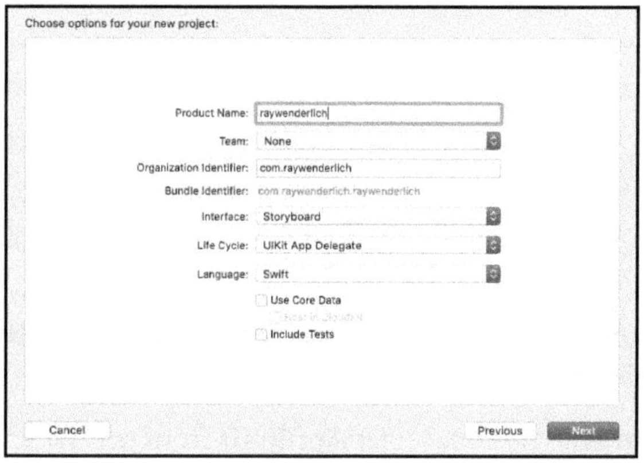

Your Organization Identifier followed by your Product Name represent your app's bundle identifier or **bundle ID**.

In this case, the bundle ID is `com.raywenderlich.raywenderlich`. It'll be different for you since your Organization Identifier is different.

Note: A bundle ID uniquely identifies an app throughout Apple's systems. In other words, no other app on the App Store can currently be using your app's bundle ID.

Also note that you **can't change your app's bundle identifier** later on, even if you sell your app. Don't use your personal name in the bundle ID unless you personally are the app's publisher.

Now that your project is set up, open the Project Navigator and click the blue **raywenderlich** project file. Open the **Signing and Capabilities** tab as shown below.

The checkbox next to **Automatically manage signing** is checked. Leave this default as is.

You'll also notice a warning saying that the app requires a development team. To resolve this issue, you have to sign into Xcode with the Apple ID you enrolled in the Apple Developer Program.

Click on **Xcode ▸ Preferences...** in the menu bar or use the shortcut **Command + ,** to open Xcode's preferences screen.

Click on the **Accounts** tab on top, select **Apple ID** from the list and click on **Continue**.

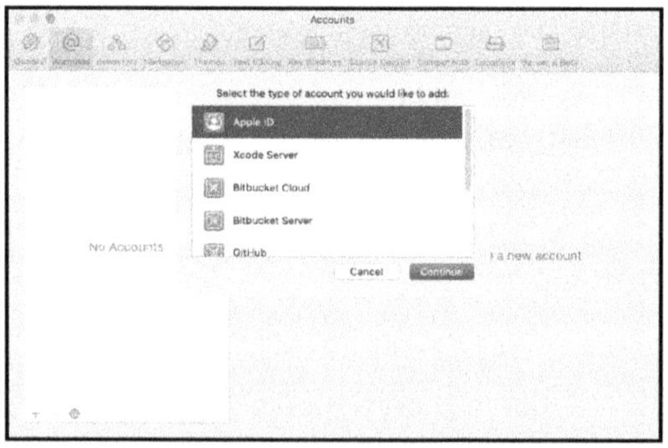

Enter your login credentials.

Once you're logged into Xcode, if you enrolled as an individual your name appears next to the Account Holder role.

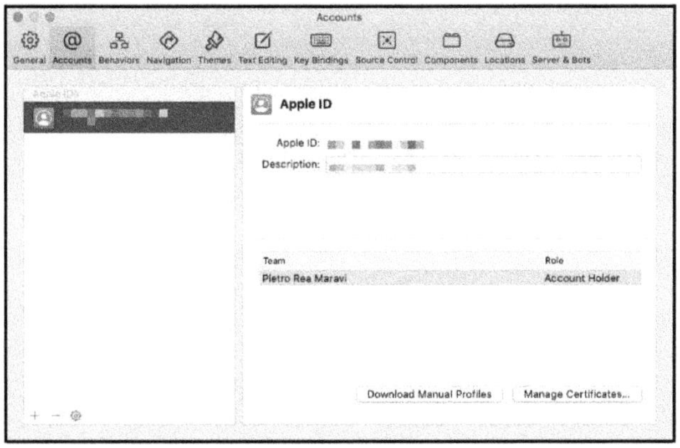

If you joined an existing organization or enrolled as one, you're part of at least two teams.

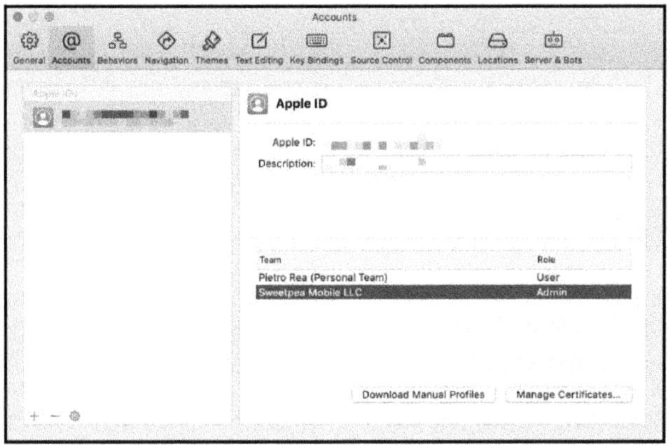

The first team is your personal team, which is the free developer program. The second team is the paid Apple Developer Program enrollment. The role you see next to your name depends on your team assignments. Your Apple ID can be associated with several teams and you can have a different role on each team.

Select your *paid* account. Click **Manage Certificates**. Then, click the **+** button on the lower-left corner. Afterward, click the **Apple Development** option.

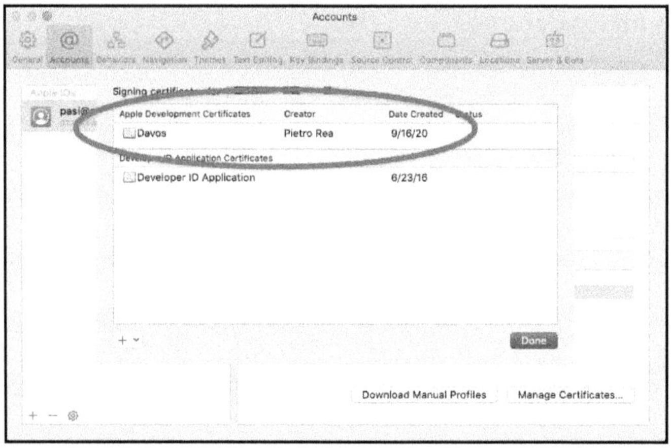

You just created a **development certificate**, which you need to install the app on your personal device.

> **Note**: You'll come across terms you probably haven't seen before, like **certificate** and **code signing**. In broad terms, these are Apple's way of cryptographically verifying you and your app.
>
> If you run into an issue with certificates or code signing, you can refer to Chapter 4, "Code Signing & Provisioning".

In the project navigator, select your project file. Then, click the **raywenderlich** target and open the **Signing & Capabilities** tab.

Now that you're signed in and have a development certificate, select your team from the **Team** dropdown. The warning indicator disappears.

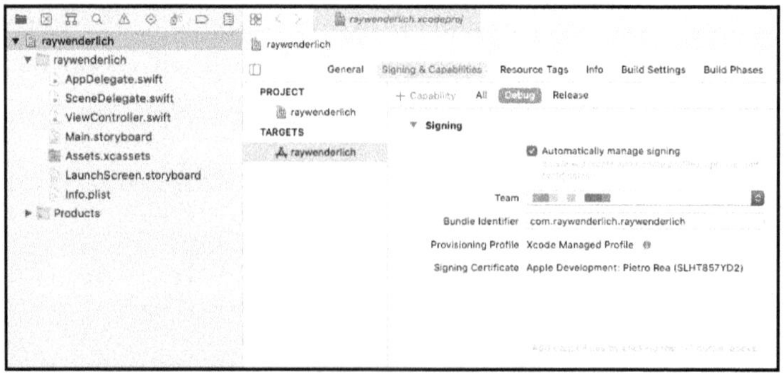

Installing the app on a device

Plug in your Apple device to your Mac. This can be an iPhone, iPad or iPod touch. From this point on, the chapter will use the term "iPhone" instead of "device".

Your iPhone prompts you about trusting the computer to share data with it. Tap **Trust** to continue. If you have set a passcode on your iPhone, you'll be prompted to enter that.

Back in Xcode, click the **Scheme pop-up** menu in the toolbar next to **raywenderlich** and scroll up to Devices. Select your iPhone from the list.

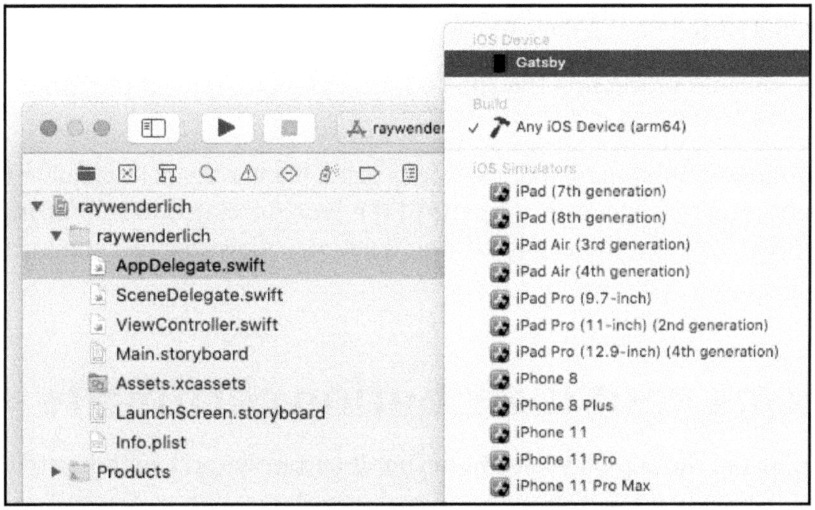

The Scheme pop-up menu lets you select your build destination.

Note: If your iPhone is grayed out with an error message of "OS version lower than the deployment target", update your device's operating system in the iOS Settings app.

With your iPhone selected, click the **Run** button in the toolbar to install the app on your phone. Xcode asks you if you want to register your device with your developer account. Click **Register Device**.

Xcode starts processing your app. Towards the end, you see an alert telling you that an executable called `codesign` needs your keychain password to continue.

This is your Mac's password, not your Apple ID password. Type in your password and click **Always Allow**.

`codesign` adds a cryptographic signature to your app so Apple can make sure no one has tampered with it once a device wants to install it.

Xcode now finishes processing the app and successfully installs it on your iPhone. Hooray!

If you've followed the steps so far, the app is just a blank screen. Remember that the first two chapters only focus on the parts of the process related to submitting an app to the App Store, not on the app itself. You'll get to work with a real app in later chapters.

Creating your distribution certificate

Xcode can install the app on your iPhone, but it currently can't submit it to the App Store. You'll learn to do that next.

The first thing you need to do is to create a **distribution certificate**. The steps are similar to the ones you followed for your development certificate.

To open Xcode preferences, click **Xcode ▸ Preferences...** in the menu bar or press the **Command + ,** shortcut.

With your paid Apple Developer Program team selected, click **Manage Certificates** like before. Click the + button like before. But this time, select **Apple Distribution**.

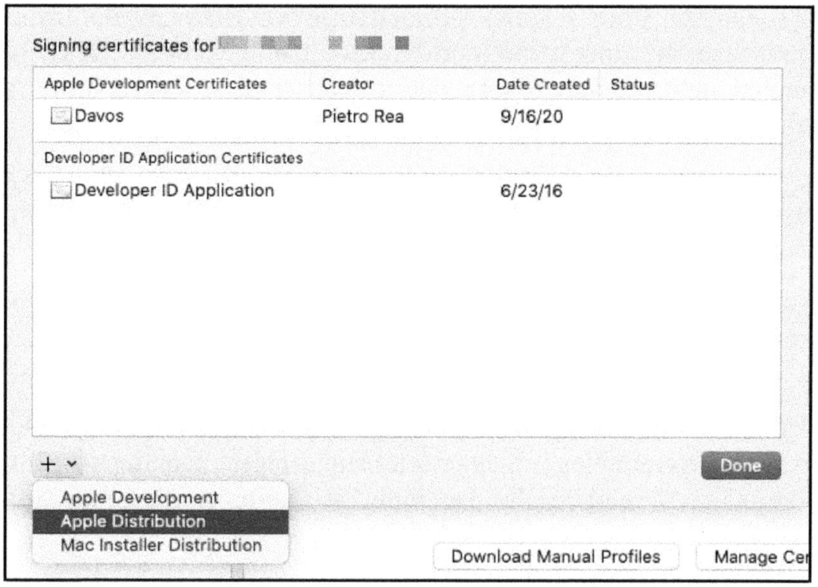

Your new distribution certificate now shows below the development certificate you've already created.

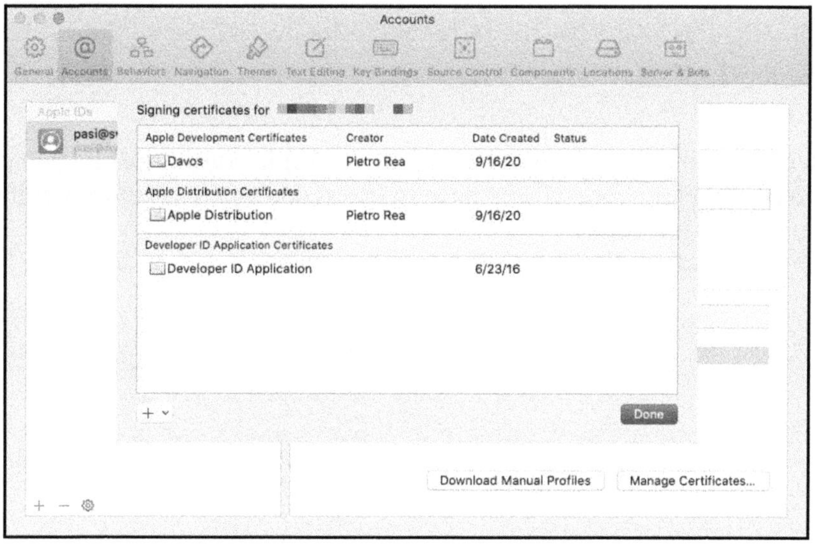

Uploading your app with Xcode

Uploading to the App Store becomes second nature over the years. But if you're doing it for the first time, the process can be unintuitive. Before you begin, it's a good idea to get a general understanding of what you're about to do so you can internalize the steps as you go along.

When you submit an app to the App Store, you're submitting a **build** of the app. Unless you're a developer, you might not have heard this term before, but you'll see it often throughout the book.

In simple terms, a **build** is an executable program that contains everything your app needs to run on a device: the compiled source code, embedded artwork, even the app icon!

It's called a "build" because Xcode goes through a multi-step process, grabbing bits and pieces from different files and directories and cobbles them together into a completed product. Developers also use "build" as a verb: "Xcode builds, installs and runs the build".

> **Note:** Technically speaking, you upload an **archive** of your app. An archive is a build with additional debugging information.
>
> Colloquially, developers use the term "build" for everything, so that's what you'll see in the rest of the book.

Once you create a distribution build using Xcode, Apple doesn't just let you drag this build onto the developer portal. You have to use Xcode again to securely transfer your build to the App Store.

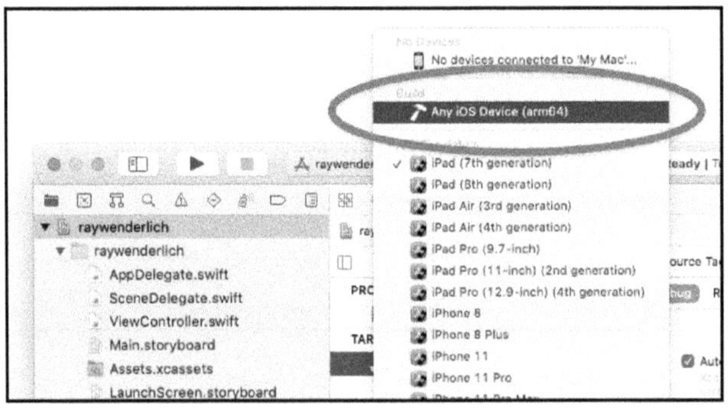

That's enough theory for now. Open Xcode. Set the build destination to **Any iOS Device (arm 64)**. Unlike other options, this build destination doesn't represent a physical device or simulator. It's a special configuration that tells Xcode you just want to create a build, not install it.

Next, click **Product ▸ Archive** in the menu bar.

Once Xcode finishes building the archive, a new window pops to the front. This window is called the **Organizer** and it manages the archived builds of the different apps that you work on.

If this is the only app you've ever worked on, clicking the top-left dropdown menu shows only one entry under **iOS Apps**.

Next, click **Distribute App** on the right-hand side to begin uploading your build. The next screen asks you about the method of distribution.

Select **App Store Connect** and click **Next.** Don't worry if this is the first time hearing about App Store Connect. That's the official name for the App Store's admin interface for developers. The next chapter covers App Store Connect in detail.

Note: You might be surprised that there are so many ways to distribute an app! Apple builds general computing devices that serve all kinds of needs and they're not all served by the App Store.

Chapter 5, "Internal Distribution," covers all the different ways you can distribute your app — the App Store is one of several ways.

The next screen asks you if you want to upload or export your archive. Leave **Upload** selected and click **Next.**

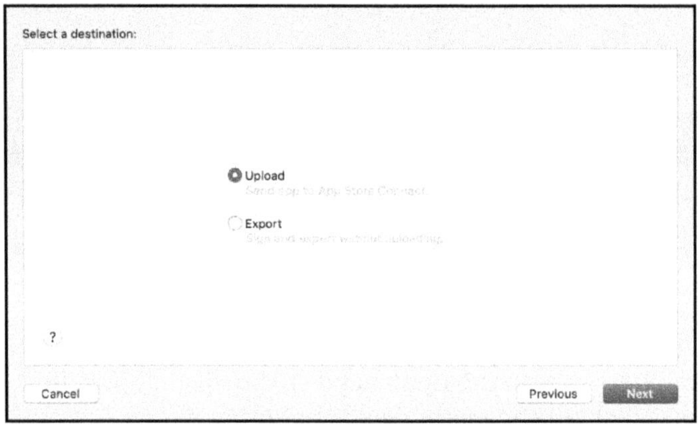

Note: You might be wondering why you'd ever want to export an archive instead of uploading it to App Store Connect. Xcode is not the only way to upload a build to the App Store.

You can also use the command line or Transporter, another app made by Apple. If you want to use these alternatives, you'd need to export a signed archive in this step.

Leave the defaults on for the next screen. You want to include bitcode and upload your app's symbols to Apple.

Turning bitcode on improves the performance of your app. The term "symbols" refers to the human-readable names that developers used in code. You need to upload these "symbols" to make sense of incoming crash reports.

The next screen informs you that your build needs to be resigned for distribution. Leave the default on to let Xcode automatically manage signing.

`codesign` might prompt you again for a password in Keychain Access. Type in your Mac's password to grant `codesign` access.

Verify all your selections on the review screen. If everything checks out, click **Upload**.

And now the moment of truth...you've created a distribution build, signed it, selected all the necessary options. Now, you sit and wait for the upload to...

Wait for a second — the upload failed with the error message, "No suitable application records were found".

There are so many configurations in Xcode and App Store Connect that it's easy to misconfigure or miss some of them. This means you're likely to see errors at least once in your journey to the App Store.

Don't worry — this is normal and Apple usually gives you a detailed explanation about what went wrong.

In this case, you did everything right on Xcode's end but didn't configure App Store Connect. You threw the proverbial ball, but there was no one on the receiving end to catch it!

Even though there's more to do, you've covered a lot of ground in this chapter. You've set up your Apple ID, enrolled in the Apple Developer Program and created your first distribution build. In the next chapter, you'll configure App Store Connect, properly upload your build (finally!) and submit your app to App Review.

Key points

- You need an Apple ID with two-factor authentication enabled to enroll in the Apple Developer Program.
- You can use your existing Apple ID or create a new one depending on your needs.
- You can join the Apple Developer Program as an individual or as an organization. Make sure to use the app publisher's developer account.
- A bundle ID uniquely identifies your app in Apple's ecosystem. You cannot use a bundle ID that another app uses.
- A development certificate lets you install apps on your device.
- A distribution certificate lets you upload builds to the App Store.
- Use Xcode to create a distribution build and upload it to App Store Connect.

Chapter 3: Submitting Your First App for Review

By Pietro Rea

The previous chapter explained how difficult distributing software used to be before the internet and before the App Store. Selling shrink-wrapped software on physical media is now a relic of the past, but it can still be a useful metaphor for explaining software distribution.

In this metaphor, Chapter 2 was about preparing the software to go *inside* the box. Previously, this would have been a CD or a floppy disk. In modern times, what's "inside the box" is the build from Xcode.

This chapter is all about the box itself. If you think about it, the primary purpose of the box is to tell you what's inside! It can answer questions like "what does this software do?" and "will it work with my computer?". Furthermore, good packaging doesn't just tell you what's inside with good copy — it also communicates this to you with compelling images.

In the context of the App Store, the "shrink-wrapped box" is your App Store page. In this chapter, you'll learn about App Store Connect and all the ways you need to configure your App Store page before releasing your app. You'll use the same empty project from Chapter 2 to pick up where you left off.

Introducing App Store Connect

You've heard of the App Store before, but what about App Store Connect?

You can think of App Store Connect as the **administrative dashboard** for the App Store. Practically speaking, it's a website (and a companion iOS app) where you submit apps for review and handle administrative tasks related to your apps.

Wait a minute — you enrolled in the developer program on the developer portal. Is the developer portal the same thing as App Store Connect?

Unfortunately, no. These are two separate systems that you'll have to log into for different things. Having two different systems to manage your apps makes App Store distribution confusing for first-timers. Here's an overview of what you can do in each one.

1. **Apple Developer Portal:** You can access the developer portal at developer.apple.com or via the Developer iOS app. In the developer portal you can create "identifiers" like app identifiers, developer certificates and provisioning profiles. If these don't sound familiar, Chapter 4, "Code Signing & Provisioning," covers certificates and provisioning profiles in detail. You also need the developer portal to download beta versions of Xcode and Apple's operating systems.

2. **App Store Connect:** You can access App Store Connect via appstoreconnect.apple.com or via the App Store Connect iOS app. You typically need to go into App Store Connect to add new "app records" (more on this later), add new versions of your app, submit an app for review, manage users, sign contracts and interact with app reviewers.

Why are these two separate? Apple ran a developer program for decades before iOS and the App Store entered the picture. Also, remember that the App Store is one of many ways to distribute apps. You can still distribute macOS apps outside of the App Store. And on iOS, you can distribute internal apps outside of the App Store using ad-hoc distribution, in-house distribution or "custom apps" distribution.

If you distribute apps outside of the App Store, you'd primarily interact with the developer portal rather than App Store Connect. As the name implies, App Store Connect is directly tied to App Store distribution.

Although Apple has recently moved the developer portal and App Store Connect closer together, the fact the App Store is newer than the developer program means that you need to get used to using two systems. Fortunately, the developer portal links to App Store Connect and vice versa, so it's not hard to navigate between the two.

> **Note**: App Store Connect used to be called iTunes Connect. You might still see the name "iTunes Connect" in old blog posts or forum posts.

Before diving into App Store Connect, you should know that it can do much more than what you're about to see. Keep an eye out for the yearly "What's New in App Store Connect" talk from WWDC to learn about the newest changes to App Store Connect.

The anatomy of an app submission

App Store Connect has so much functionality baked into it that it can easily overwhelm. First get a grasp of the bigger picture.

The following graph represents the different pieces in App Store Connect that make up an app submission.

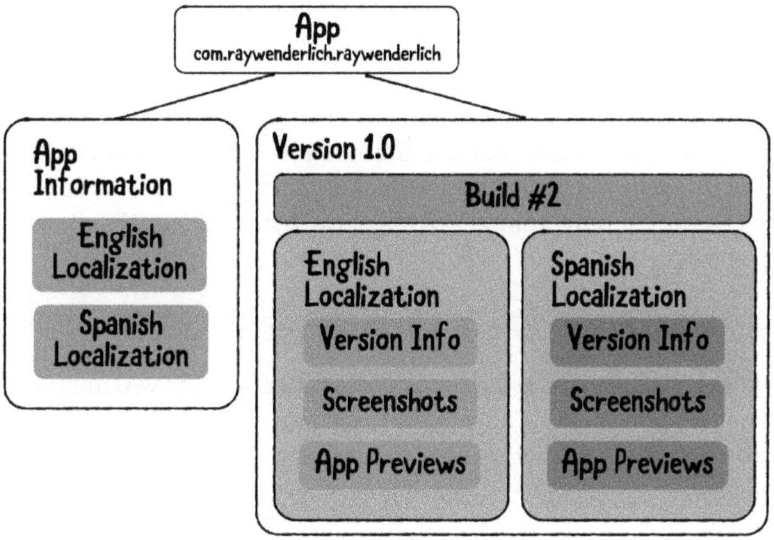

Since this chapter demonstrates the initial submission of a new app, you'll work with every piece of the diagram. But if you just want to update an existing app, you'd only work on the right-most rectangle, which represents a particular version of an app.

App identifier and app record

The top-most rectangle represents the app identifier and the app record. The app identifier, or **App ID**, uniquely describes an app across all Apple platforms. You have to create a new App ID every time you create a new app.

Practically speaking, an App ID is the combination of your team ID and your app's bundle ID. You'll sometimes see the bundle ID as a shorthand for the App ID, like in the diagram above.

An **app record** is an app's headquarters in App Store Connect. The app record holds app-level information, version-level information, as well as builds, pricing information, app review information and much more. You first need an App ID before you can add a new app record to your App Store Connect account.

App information

The left-hand rectangle represents top-level information that applies to the app as a whole rather than to a particular version of the app. What's the app's name? What does the app do? What category is the app in? These are the types of questions that app-level information can answer. You can also localize app-level information into other languages if needed.

When you submit a brand new app for the first time, in addition to creating a new App ID and app record, you also need to fill out app-level information. Keep in mind that app-level information is also subject to App Review. After your app's initial release, you can only submit changes to app-level information when you submit an update to your app.

Version information

The right-most rectangle in the diagram represents a specific version of your app. Each version includes an executable build as well as release notes, screenshots of your app and other metadata. You can also localize version-level information to other languages.

Any time you want to update anything about your app, you need to add a new version and fill out version-level information. Version-level information is also subject to App Review. After Apple approves your app submission, you can't go back to make changes.

Creating a new App ID

Now that you understand the big picture, go ahead and configure the sample app's App ID and app record. Log in to the developer portal and click **Certificates, Identifiers & Profiles** in the sidebar.

From here, click the + button next to **Identifiers**.

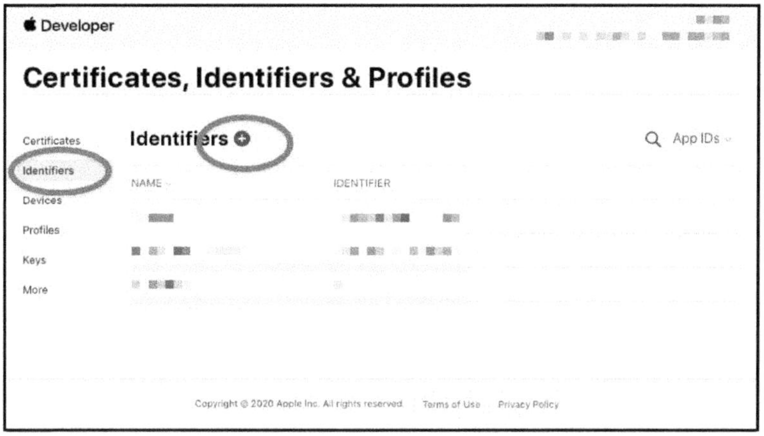

In the next screen, select **App IDs** from the list and click **Continue**. In the following screen, select **App** for type. Click **Continue**.

Next, add a description to your App ID. This is an internal-facing description that only you and your team members can see. For this sample app, type in "Raywenderlich Emitron". In case you were wondering, "Emitron" is the internal codename for the raywenderlich.com iOS app.

Select **Explicit** next to **Bundle ID** and enter the bundle ID from Xcode exactly as it appears in the General tab of the `raywenderlich` target. In this case, it's `com.raywenderlich.raywenderlich` but it should be different for you. Click **Continue** when you're done. Click **Register** to confirm.

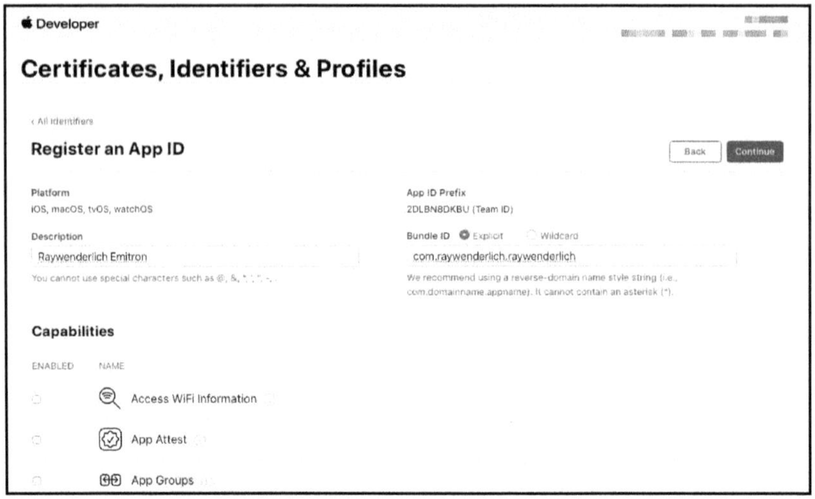

Go back to the **Certificates, Identifiers & Profiles** screen. Click **Identifiers** in the sidebar and verify that your new App ID shows up in the list. Now it's time to use the new App ID to add a new app record to your App Store Connect account.

In this case, you created the Xcode project and its bundle ID *before* the App ID, but the opposite would have also worked. The order of operations doesn't matter — the only thing that matters is that the bundle IDs match exactly in Xcode and the developer portal.

> **Note**: Xcode's automatic signing feature is supposed to create App IDs for you whenever you create a new project, but this feature doesn't work out of the box without additional hand-holding. Fortunately, creating an App ID manually helps you understand how everything works under the hood.
>
> There's more to know about App IDs than this chapter has space for. Here are two links to Apple documentation that explain App IDs in detail.
>
> App ID structure: https://apple.co/3jzDSu1
>
> Explicit vs Wildcard App IDs: https://apple.co/33xdJpU
>
> It's relatively uncommon to distribute apps using wildcard App IDs these days. Some people still find them useful for installing example apps on internal devices without the hassle of creating a new App ID for each new app.

Creating a new app record

Log in to App Store Connect and click **My Apps**.

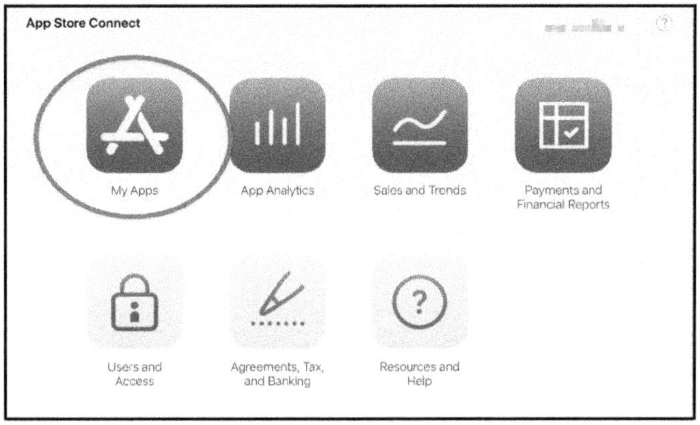

Next, click the + button next to **Apps** and select **New App** from the dropdown menu.

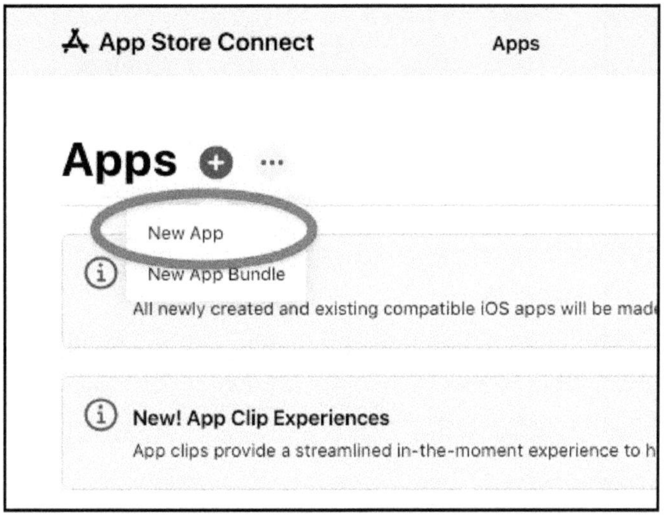

In the next screen, under **Platforms**, check the checkbox next to **iOS**. Type **raywenderlich** for the name and select **English (US)** as the primary language.

Click the dropdown under **Bundle ID** and select the App ID you just created in the developer portal. App Store Connect uses "Bundle ID" as a shorthand to refer to App IDs.

Type in the bundle ID again under **SKU**. The SKU is another internal-facing identifier for your team, so you could fill it with something more meaningful to you.

The **New App** screen should look like the image below. Click **Create** when you're done.

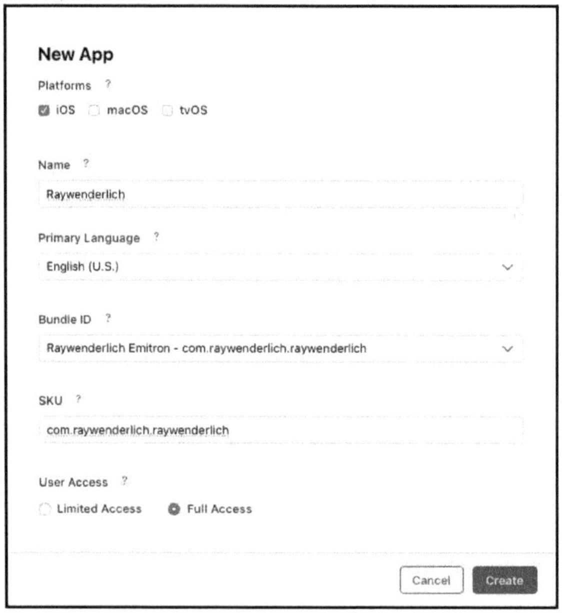

Hooray! Your app record is now configured in App Store Connect. Go back to **Apps** to verify that it is there.

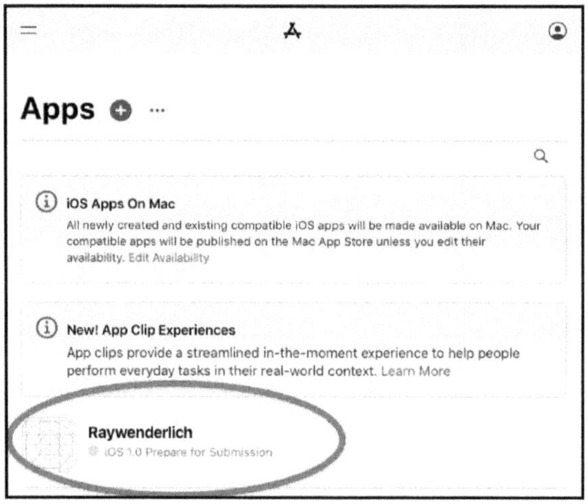

Notice that the status of version 1.0 is **Prepare for Submission**. The status field tells you if Apple accepted or rejected this version of your app, or if your app is live and ready for download.

App Store Connect now knows to expect your build so it's time to upload it. Go back to Xcode and select **Window ▸ Organizer** from the menu bar or use the shortcut **Option + Shift + Command + O** to open the Organizer.

In case you don't see a build because you skipped Chapter 2, use Xcode to open Chapter 3's starter project. Select **Any iOS Device (arm 64)** as the build destination and select **Product ▸ Archive** from the Xcode menu. Once Xcode completes the archiving operation, it'll automatically open the Organizer and show your new build.

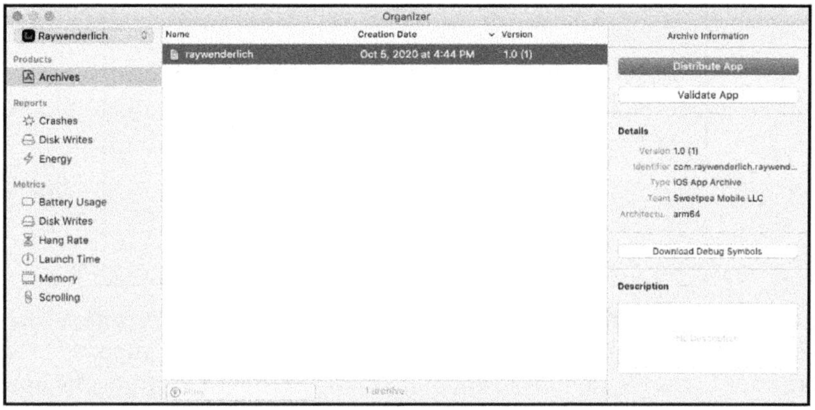

Select the build marked version **1.0 (1)** and click **Distribute App** in the Organizer. You can click through all the screens without modifying the default values. Chapter 2 covers all the pre-upload screens in more detail. Refer back to it if you have questions about an intervening screen.

This time your build goes through and the Organizer shows you a success screen. Great!

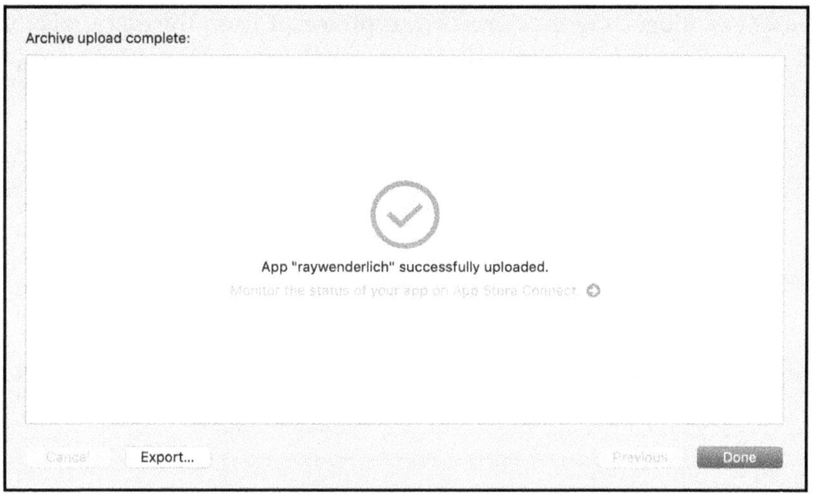

Just when you think you're done, you get a stern-looking email from Apple.

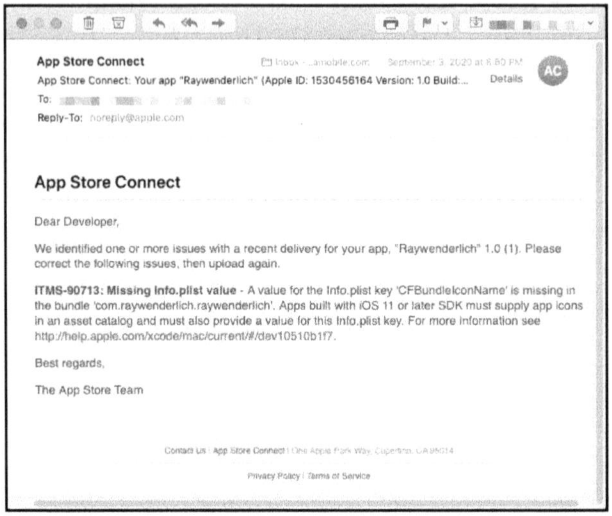

This sentence from the email succinctly describes the problem: `A value for the Info.plist key 'CFBundleIconName' is missing in the bundle com.raywenderlich.raywenderlich`. In layman's terms, you forgot the app icon.

Since this is a new sample project without code or assets, it's not surprising that there's no app icon. Xcode didn't complain about this, but Apple's automated checks caught it and emailed you right away.

Open the materials folder for this chapter. The folder called **AppIcon.appiconset** has all the app icons you need.

Switch to Xcode again. Open the project navigator and click **Assets.xcassets** to open the app's asset catalog. Drag the **AppIcon.appiconset** from the materials folders into Xcode's asset catalog. Remove the existing icon set and rename the one you dragged into **AppIcon**.

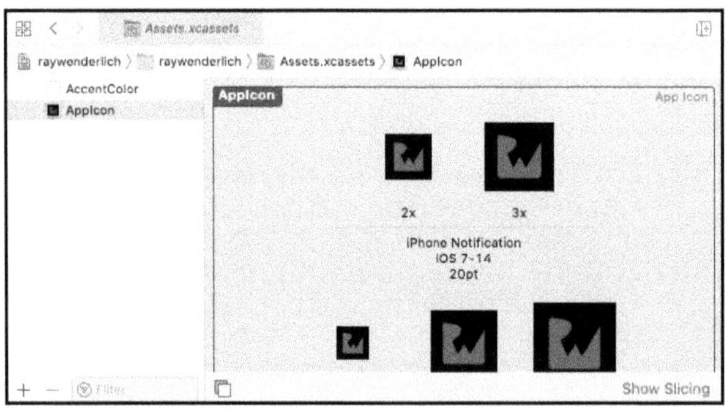

You've now seen two ways Apple can reject your build. Apple built validations into every step of the funnel. Xcode runs validations before and during the upload process. On top of that, App Store Connect also validates your build once you make it past Xcode. App Store Connect also validates your App Store page before you submit your app for review. Not to mention that app review is itself a big list of validations and checks.

In other words, seeing error messages is common. The point of showing you different types of errors is not to frustrate you, but rather to give you the tools and experience to react appropriately whenever you hit a roadblock on your own.

Bumping the build number

A build from Xcode is like a snapshot of your app frozen in time. If you keep making changes after you archive a build, these changes won't be reflected in the snapshot.

Since you made changes to the sample app by adding app icons, you need to generate a new build. The first and second builds both fall under version 1.0 of the sample app, so how can App Store Connect tell the difference between builds?

This is where the **build number** comes in. A version can have any number of builds, each identified by a unique build number. App Store Connect won't accept any upload that uses a build number it has already received.

So, before you generate a new build, increment the build number. Colloquially, this is called "bumping" the build number. In Xcode, click the project file in the project navigator. Next, click the **raywenderlich** target and open the **General** tab. Once here, increment the **Build** number to **2**.

> **Note**: If you are new to **software versioning**, you may want to adopt **semantic versioning**, which is a three-component number in the format of A.B.C, where:
>
> "A" represents a major version, e.g., when you add a new feature.
>
> "B" represents a minor version, e.g., when you enhance an existing feature.
>
> "C" represents a patch, e.g., a bug fix.
>
> In the case of the sample app, the build number represents the patch component. You can learn more about semantic versioning at https://semver.org.

Time to generate a second build. Make sure the build destination is **Any iOS Device (arm64)** and once again click **Product ▸ Archive** in the menu bar. Once Xcode finishes, Xcode opens the Organizer to show the second build.

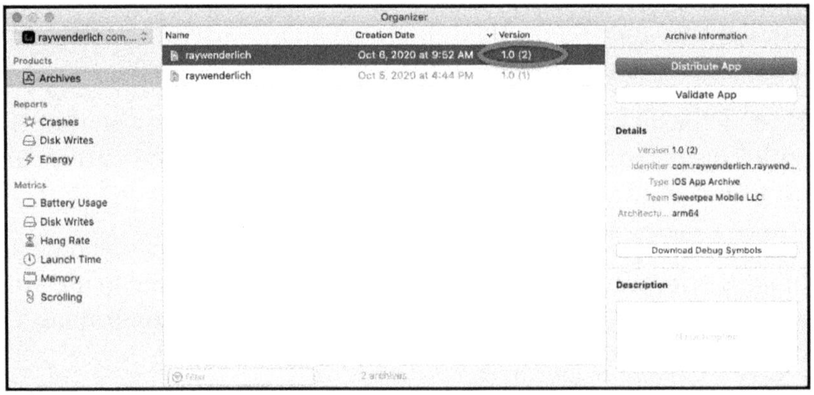

Click **Distribute App** and go through the entire flow again. This is your second time doing this for this chapter, so you should know the steps well by now. You can simply click through every screen without changing the defaults. If you don't remember what to do for a particular screen, feel free to refer to Chapter 2.

This time Xcode uploads your build without any issues and Apple doesn't send you any validation emails after the fact.

Following along with the “shrink-wrapped software” metaphor, the floppy disk is ready to ship but the box is still completely blank. In the next section, you’ll work on the box. In the context of the App Store, this means it’s time to configure your App Store page.

Filling out your App Store page

Switch to App Store Connect on your browser and navigate to the `raywenderlich.com` app. As mentioned before, since this is a brand new app, you have to fill out app-level information as well as version-level information. Review each one in turn.

Adding app-level information

Click **App Information** in the sidebar. Under the heading **Localizable Information** type **raywenderlich - pasi** for the **Name** field. This is the user-facing name that shows up on the App Store page.

The name has to be unique. The real raywenderlich.com iOS app is already using the name “raywenderlich.com”, which is why you added the `-pasi` suffix. The name field in App Store Connect has been the subject of numerous high-profile legal battles. It’s a good idea for the app publisher to hold the trademark for whatever name you type into this field.

Leave the **Subtitle** blank since it’s optional. Under the heading **General Information**, click the **Category** dropdown and select **Education**. You can also have an optional secondary category, but leave it blank for this sample app.

> **Note**: Your app’s category drives different features in Apple’s ecosystem. For example, the new “App Library” in iOS 14 groups apps based on category.
>
> Separately, the App Store’s editorial teams routinely promote the best apps in each category. For example, the Health & Fitness category is currently promoting apps that fall into “Healthy Eating and Dieting”, “Self-Care and Meditation” and “Learn from Fitness Experts”.

The App Information page should look like the screenshot below.

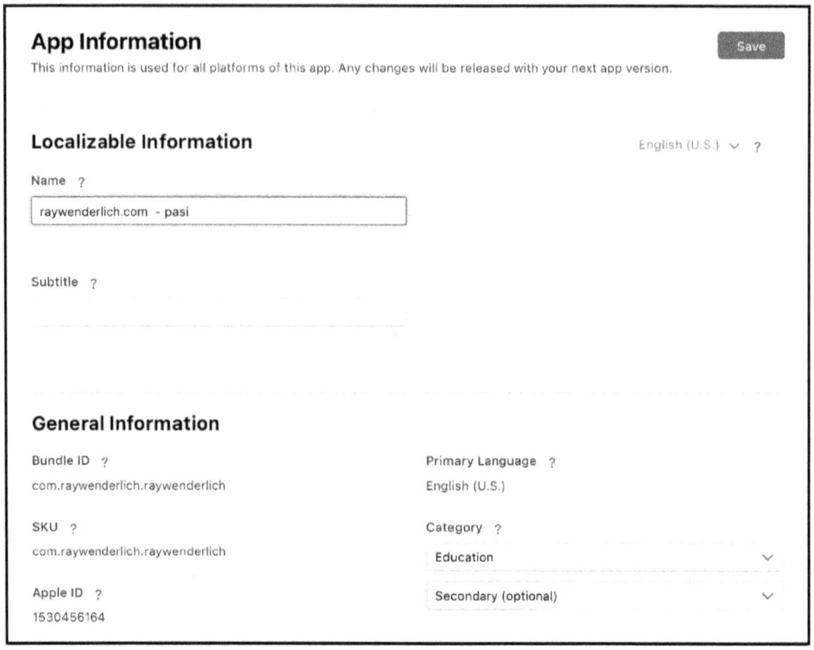

Next, click **Set up Content Rights Information** and select **No, it does not contain, show or access third-party content.**

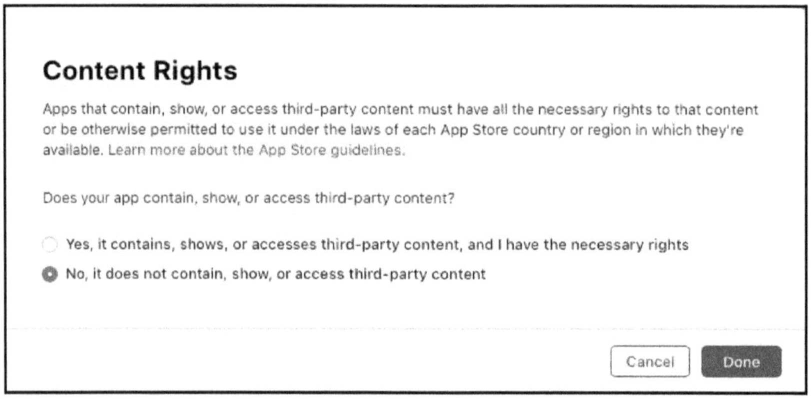

Special App Store rules apply if your app contains third-party content. This is a sample app, so you said the app doesn't contain any. Click **Done** to close the modal and **Save** to save your progress so far.

Next, click **App Privacy** in the sidebar. Next to **Privacy Policy**, click **Edit**. On the ensuing dialog, under **Privacy Policy URL** type **https://help.raywenderlich.com/privacy**.

Every app must have a privacy policy web page. Apple will reject your app if the privacy policy page is blank or inaccessible. Click **Save**.

Before submitting your app for review, you must also answer a series of questions detailing your app's data collection practices as well as those of third-party partners whose code you use. The answers to these questions appear on your App Store product page.

Click **Get Started** to begin. On the modal dialog, select **No, we do not collect data from this app**. Click **Save**. Then click **Publish** in the top-right corner. Click **Publish** again on the modal to confirm your answers are accurate. The App Privacy page should look like the following screenshot.

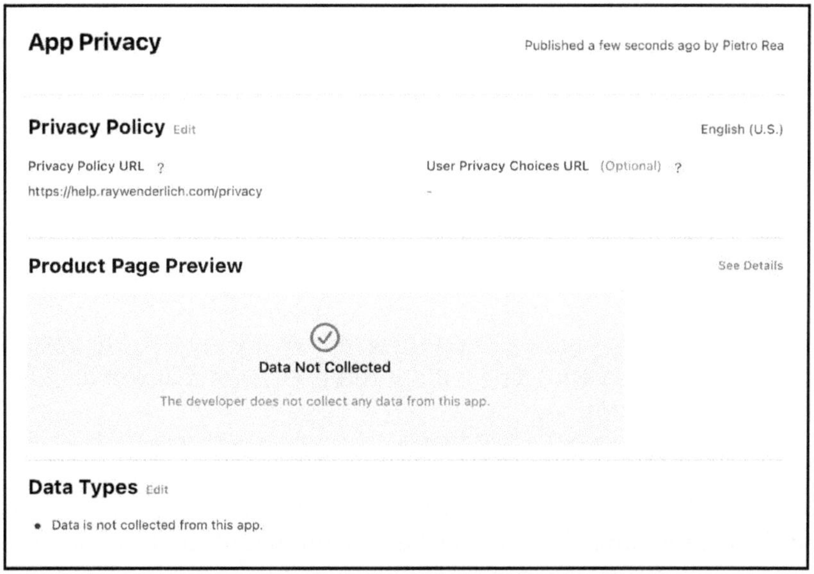

These answers correspond to the empty sample app, which collects no data. Your answers will vary depending on the data you collect and how you use it. If you're unsure how to answer the questions for your app, refer to Apple's documentation on privacy, https://apple.co/3dWzN39.

Now click **Pricing and Availability** in the sidebar. Click the price dropdown and select the **Free** tier. Click **Save**.

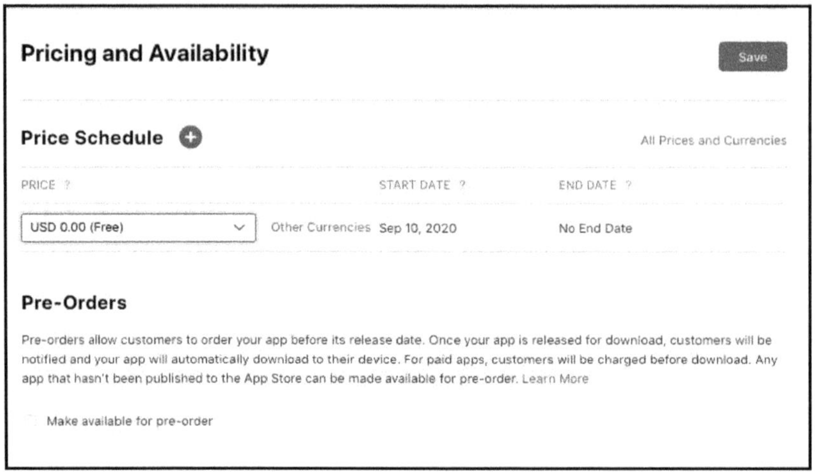

Apple provides over 50 pricing tiers to choose from. If you distribute your app internationally, each pricing tier corresponds to different amounts of money in different currencies. Tier 1 is $0.99 in the United States, €1.09 in the EU and CN¥6.00 in China.

You can only set your app's price to a pre-determined pricing tier. For example, you can set the price to $0.99 with Tier 1 but not to $1.00, since that would fall between Tier 1 ($0.99) and Tier 2 ($1.99).

> **Note**: Setting the price in **Pricing and Availability** only applies if you charge for your app at the time of download. Keep in mind that there are other pricing models available. Some apps are free to download and offer paid In-App Purchases. Other apps charge a recurring subscription.
>
> You can also manage In-App Purchases and subscriptions in App Store Connect, but they fall outside the scope of this book.

Adding version-level information

Click **1.0 Prepare for Submission** in the sidebar. This is where you add version-specific information. Every time you submit a version of your app for review, you'll have the opportunity to update the information on this page.

An image speaks a thousand words, especially on the App Store. If you're an iOS user, you've probably noticed the beautiful screenshots and short videos ("App Previews" in Apple's parlance) on the page where you download an app.

App Store Connect has a fully featured media manager where you can upload screenshots for the sample app. Don't worry — you don't have to fire up Photoshop. The materials folder has all the screenshots you need.

Open the materials folder that corresponds to this chapter and open the **screenshots** folder. Inside you'll find a set of screenshots for the real raywenderlich.com iOS app.

Under **App Preview and Screenshots**, select the first tab, **iPhone 6.5 Display**. Drag the six screenshots in the folder **iPhone 6.5 inch** into the media manager. This is what the result should look like.

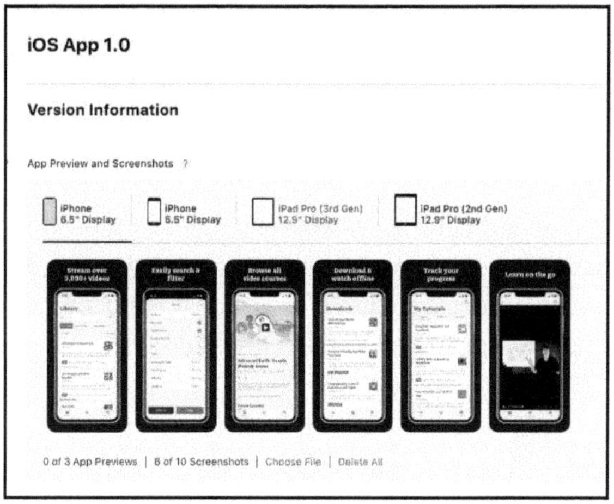

Repeat this process for all the required sizes. As of this writing, they are: iPhone 6.5" Display, iPhone 5.5" Display, iPad Pro (3rd Gen) 12.9" Display and iPad Pro (2nd Gen) 12.9" Display.

You can upload up to 10 screenshots and three app previews per screen size. Size-specific assets make your App Store page more appealing and relevant. Whenever a potential customer lands on your App Store page, Apple displays the assets that most closely match your potential customer's screen size.

> **Note**: App Store Connect's media manager is unforgiving. It only accepts screenshots that *exactly* match the dimensions it expects.
>
> Even if they're only off by 1 pixel, you won't be able to upload them. This is a common source of miscommunication so make sure you keep these documentation links handy.
>
> Screenshot specifications: https://apple.co/30hntCO
>
> App preview specifications: https://apple.co/3kYofN2

App Store Connect needs a few more pieces of information. Below the media manager, type in the following information:

- **Description**: "Take your learning on the go with our new mobile app! Access over 3,000 mobile programming videos right at your fingertips". This is the real description of the raywenderlich app.
- **Keywords**: raywenderlich.com, tutorials, iOS development
- **Support URL**: https://help.raywenderlich.com
- **Marketing URL**: https://www.raywenderlich.com/mobile

The description is also called **release notes**. If you want to communicate something noteworthy to your users for an upcoming version, you can add it here. For instance, does this version include an exciting new feature? Did you squash a long-standing bug? You can sing your praises in the release notes.

The keywords are not visible by the user, but they help your app show up in search results. The support URL and the marketing URL both appear on your App Store page and App Review requires them.

Attaching the correct build

App Store Connect keeps track of all the builds you upload for a particular version. In this section, you can associate the build you want to submit for review — usually the most recent one — with your app version.

Scroll down to the **Build** heading and click the + button. Select **build 2** and click **Done**.

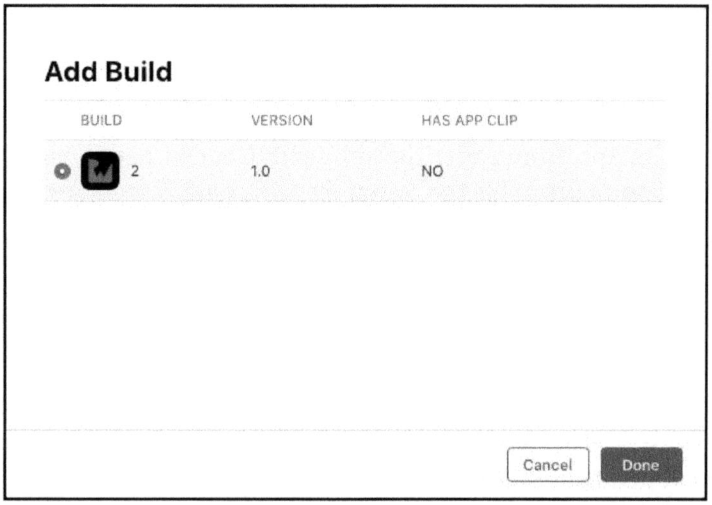

Even though you uploaded two builds, App Store Connect only shows the second one. The first build from earlier in the chapter is not viable because it was missing the app icon.

> **Note**: It's easy to imagine a scenario in which you unwittingly release an outdated build of your app because you clicked the wrong radio button. Don't worry — beta testing with TestFlight eliminates this risk. Chapter 5, "Internal Distribution" and Chapter 6, "TestFlight," cover beta testing in detail.
>
> There's also a "sanity check" you can perform after Apple approves your app but *before* you release it. Chapter 8, "App Approved! (Now What?)," covers this technique.

Wrapping up App Store Connect

Only a few more pieces of information before submitting for review.

1. Under **General App Information**, type "Razeware 2021" for **Copyright**.
2. Also under **General App Information**, click **Edit** next to **Age Rating** and select **None** for every content description.
3. Under **Version Release**, select **Manually release this version**.

Each field is important so review them in detail:

1. An app is creative work subject to copyright law. The App Store displays an app's copyright on its App Store page. The app's publisher, either an individual or an organization, normally holds the copyright. This field is required.
2. Apple assigns an age rating to every app so parents can determine what is appropriate for their children. Apple calculates your app's age rating when you select the frequency of certain types of content like "Profanity or Crude Humor" and "Horror/Fear Themes".
3. Manually release the app after Apple approves it. This is a good option for most people because it gives you time to perform final checks and figure out any coordination that needs to happen.

> **Warning**: Don't submit an empty sample app for App Review using your developer account. The rest of this section is for **demonstration purposes only**.

If you were to submit your real app for review, you'd click on **Submit for Review** on the top right corner of the page. The status of your version 1.0 would then change to **Waiting for Review** as you can see in the next section.

Managing your submission on the go

This is a good time to formally introduce App Store Connect for iOS. You've been doing everything on the App Store Connect website, but there's also a companion iOS app.

Go to the App Store on an iOS device and search for "App Store Connect". Download the app and sign in with the same Apple ID you used to work on the sample app.

After logging in you see that the **raywenderlich - pasi** app also shows up here.

If you enable push notifications for this app, Apple will notify you whenever your app moves into a new phase of the process. You'll also receive emails with the same information, but some people find push notifications more timely.

The iOS app contains a *subset* of the features App Store Connect has on the web. Even though Apple regularly updates this app, what you can do on the web might not be available on the app.

What to expect from App Review?

Apple trains employees to screen every App Store submission that comes through. A reviewer's primary goal is to make sure every app submission follows the App Store Review Guidelines as well as the Apple Developer Program License Agreement. Like any process involving human gatekeepers, parts of App Review are subject to interpretation and can seem inconsistent. What might be ok for one reviewer might not pass muster for another.

Apple holds a high bar for the apps they allow on their platforms. App Review guidelines are *wide-ranging* and *comprehensive*, covering everything from software security to user experience.

Here are a few reasons Apple can reject an app. Some are obvious but others might surprise you.

1. **Crashes**: If your app crashes on launch or in an obvious place.
2. **Inaccurate screenshots**: If your app screenshots don't accurately explain what your app does.
3. **Subpar user interfaces**: If your app wildly deviates from Apple's Human Interface Guidelines and you don't provide a user-friendly alternative.
4. **Incomplete In-App Purchases**: If you don't properly implement IAP functionality (e.g., missing the "Restore" feature).
5. **Disallowed App Category**: Entire categories of apps are not allowed on Apple's platforms. For example, you can't make "launcher" apps that launch other apps.
6. **Private API Usage**: Your app cannot use frameworks built for Apple's internal use. Human reviewers can't catch this but App Review also scans your build for violations.

On average, Apple reviews 50% of the apps within 24 hours and 90% within 48 hours. If there's a problem with your submission, Apple surfaces the issue in App Store Connect. You can interact with app reviewers in App Store Connect using **Resolution Center**.

If you disagree with a rejection, you can contact the App Review Board where you can appeal. Chapter 7, "Preparing for Review", covers disputes and Resolution Center in detail.

> Here are some related links for your reference:
>
> **App Store Review Guidelines**: https://apple.co/36hVYg4
>
> **Human Interface Guidelines**: https://apple.co/3jfeSYS
>
> **Apple Developer Program License Agreement**: https://apple.co/36iA78f

After Apple approves your app and you release it to the public, it can take up to 24 hours to fully go live on the App Store. This is especially true if you publish your app globally. You need to give Apple's content distribution networks (CDNs) and internal systems time to propagate your app all around the world.

Congratulations! If you've made it this far, you've learned how to set up an app record in App Store Connect, upload a valid build from Xcode and submit it for review.

Keep in mind that this chapter represents the manual "happy path". The chapter only covered the simplest case without any automation and assumes nothing goes wrong. In the rest of the book, you'll slowly unwind some of the assumptions from the second and third chapters. In the subsequent chapters, you'll learn how to make your life easier with automation as well as handle more advanced use cases.

Key points

- You need to set up an **App ID** in the developer portal and an **app record** in App Store Connect so you can upload a build from Xcode.
- Select your pricing tier in App Store Connect. Tiers correspond to different amounts of money in different currencies.
- Pricing tiers only apply to up-front pricing models. Apps can also use In-App Purchases and subscriptions.
- You need to add metadata, screenshots and app previews (optional) to make your App Store page as appealing as possible. App Store Connect requires most of these items before you can submit your app to App Review.
- App Review can take up to two days in most cases. Trained human reviewers pore over your submission, checking for compliance with the App Store Review Guidelines as well as the Apple Developer Program License Agreement.

Chapter 4: Code Signing & Provisioning

By Pietro Rea

The previous two chapters took advantage of Xcode's automatic code signing and provisioning feature. In those chapters, the goal was to submit your app for review as soon as possible, so the automatic setting made sense. This feature does a lot of heavy lifting under the hood. You didn't have to pay much attention to certificates, entitlements, provisioning profiles or code signing.

Code signing and provisioning are among the most difficult parts of app distribution — and it's where most developers run into issues. Even the most experienced developers routinely fiddle around with settings until they get something working, without ever understanding how the system should work.

In this chapter, you'll learn how to do what Xcode did on your behalf so far. Automatic code signing is great, but more advanced setups require manual configuration. If something goes wrong, you'll also want to know how the underlying system works so you can troubleshoot effectively.

A historical detour

Before diving into the underlying system, you'll take a brief, historical detour to the 1970s. Apple's platforms are all based on a version of Unix, the operating system famously developed at Bell Labs in the 1970s. Surprisingly, you can trace why code signing is a pain back to Unix's original assumptions!

In Unix, a program has the same access and privileges as the user running it. This made sense back in the 1970s because you had to code and load your own programs using punched cards. But in modern times, this is not a good assumption. Nowadays, the programs you run are typically third-party apps that you didn't write yourself.

For security reasons, your apps should *not* have the same access as you do. Third-party apps shouldn't have free rein over your files, data and hardware. A malicious or compromised app that can do everything you can could wreak havoc on your system.

Consider how you would handle this issue if you were Apple. What kind of system would you build to protect users from the consequences of this decades-old assumption? Are you thinking of a system that separates a user's privileges from those of a third-party app? That kind of system would enforce a strict separation between apps and the operating system's resources, requiring permission for everything.

If that's what you were thinking, congratulations! That's what Apple ended up doing. The resulting system is called **App Sandbox**. On iOS, iPadOS, watchOS and tvOS, apps have been sandboxed from day one. Apple later added sandboxing to macOS. In 2010, Apple announced that sandboxing would be required for all apps distributed on the macOS App Store.

Introducing App Sandbox

The term "sandbox" helps you understand the purpose of the system. You can think of each app being in a restricted, safe space of its own. By default, a sandboxed app only has access to an app-specific section of the file system, plus the data the app itself creates and saves.

Outside the sandbox, the host device has resources that the app might want to use, like the microphone or the camera. However, for security reasons, the operating system closely guards these restricted resources. To use them, the app needs to validate its identity and request permission from the OS and, sometimes, the user.

Broadly speaking, the resources that require permission fall into five categories:

1. **Hardware**: Camera, microphone, sensors, etc.
2. **Network access**: Inbound and outbound traffic.
3. **Data from other apps**: Contacts, calendars, email, etc.
4. **User files**: Files from the file system or the Files app.
5. **Special functionality**: Push notifications, HomeKit access, etc.

> **Note**: This is where terminology gets confusing. In technical documentation, you'll rarely see the word "permission", but you'll see "entitlements", "capabilities" and "resources". In a nutshell, developers request entitlements to add capabilities to their app so it can access system resources.

The diagram below represents how the App Sandbox works. It's not based on the real architecture or implementation of the actual system, but it can help you identify and understand all the big pieces.

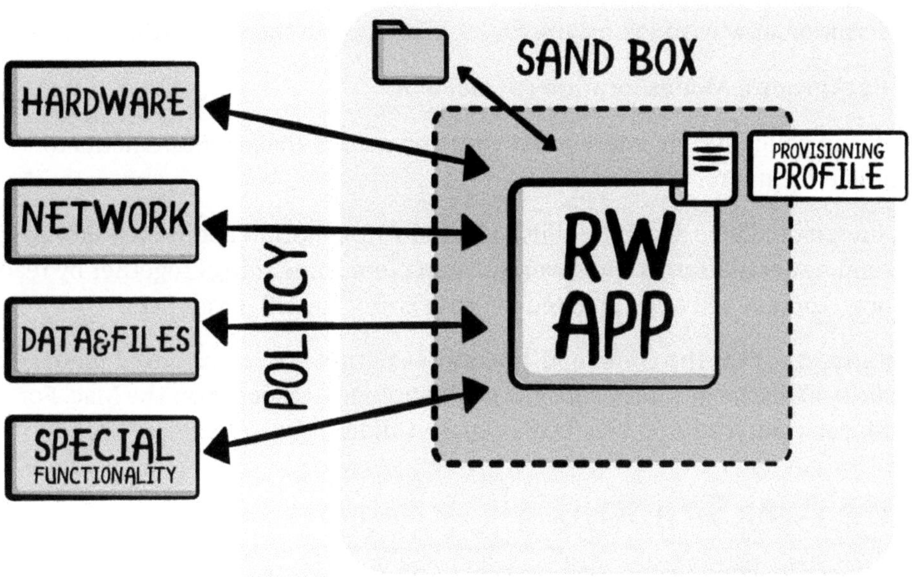

At a high level, there are resources outside the sandbox, components inside the sandbox and a runtime policy system in the middle that grants or blocks access based on the app's entitlements. The following sections describe each in detail.

Outside the sandbox

The left-most column of boxes in the previous diagram represents system resources that require permission from the operating system and the user.

Most resources are **things** you can access, like a user's contacts. Other resources are restricted **roles** you can take on in Apple's ecosystem, like the ability to send push notifications or the ability to integrate with the Health app.

Runtime policy system

At runtime, a sandboxed app might attempt a restricted operation, like getting location updates while the app isn't running. The policy system intercepts this operation and, based on a number of checks, allows or disallows the action.

For example, in the case of background location updates, you need three things:

- The user's explicit consent to start getting location data.
- A description of why you're asking for location data in the app's **Info.plist**.
- The **Background Modes** location entitlement.

The runtime policy system checks that your app met all these requirements to determine if it can proceed.

Apple, understandably, doesn't publish much documentation about its policy system on iOS and newer platforms. However, you can piece some things together by reading about how Apple rolled out App Sandbox to existing macOS developers.

For instance, `spctl` is the command-line tool — part of BSD Unix — that manages the security assessment policy subsystem, including Gatekeeper on the Mac. For more information, read App Sandbox's Design Guide: https://apple.co/2JMJF2u.

Inside App Sandbox

Finally, the right-hand rectangle represents App Sandbox. As mentioned before, each sandbox container has its own file system, which the sandboxed app can access without restriction.

There's a "locked area" in the middle of the sandbox that contains the app binary. It's "locked" because Xcode **digitally signed** it using `codesign`. After code-signing something, it's impossible to change anything about it without breaking the **code seal**, which is easy to check.

The **scroll** icon next to the **app icon** represents the **provisioning profile**, a file embedded in the app's binary. You can think of it as a public declaration that details who the app is, where it can run and what it wants to do.

> **Note**: There's more to code signing and `codesign`. This chapter aims to give you an intuitive understanding of what it does and why, but if you want to learn about the nitty-gritty implementation details, refer to Apple's Code Signing Guide: https://apple.co/36QwNBm.

Working backward

So far, you've read about App Sandbox and why Apple introduced it. This context is important! If you don't have the background context, it's easy to think of code signing and provisioning as a list of unrelated chores.

But once you have a grasp of the system behind it, you begin to think in terms of providing the sandbox with a "plugin" that it can understand and interact with.

To accomplish this, you might find it helpful to work backwards from an end goal. To properly interact with App Sandbox, your goal is to furnish a **code-signed provisioning profile**, represented below.

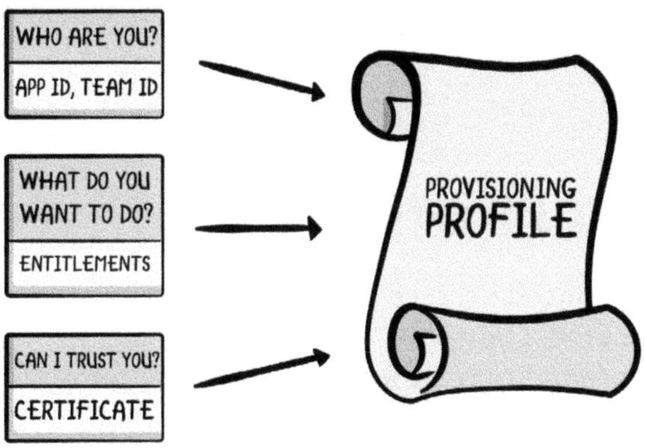

As previously discussed, App Sandbox makes several checks before letting an app complete a restricted operation. The operating system asks questions and a **code-signed provisioning profile** answers them. Here are the basic questions the operating system asks:

- **Who are you?**: A provisioning profile includes an app's App ID, which in turn includes a team ID. Chapter 3, "Submitting Your First App for Review", shows you how to create an App ID in App Store Connect.
- **What would you like to do?**: A provisioning profile also includes the list of entitlements for an app. This is a public declaration of your intentions. When your app starts doing something restricted, App Sandbox checks the app's requests against the intentions in the provisioning profile.
- **Can I trust you?**: You answered who you are and what you intend to do, but these answers are just written in plain files. A malicious actor could overwrite them. How can Apple know that you are who you say you are?

  A provisioning profile also includes a developer identity in the form of a certificate. The certificate includes the public key, which Apple can use to verify that the digital signature was created with its corresponding private key.
- **Where can you run?**: Different rules govern different distribution types. For example, in ad hoc distribution — that is, distribution outside the App Store — you may only install your app on a maximum of 100 devices. If you're using ad hoc distribution, your provisioning profile will also include the list of device IDs that may use the app.

> **Note**: Thinking of a code-signed provisioning profile as the "goal" is useful in practice. But in reality, you copy your provisioning profile's contents to the digital signature. The real source of truth is the digital signature, not the provisioning profile.

Verifying your identity

One of the questions your code-signed provisioning profile needs to answer for the policy system is, "**can I trust you?**". To unambiguously identify the app and its developer, you need to embed a **certificate** in the provisioning profile.

> **Note**: Apple did not invent certificates. The certificates you use to identify yourself are based on the X.509 cryptographic standard. X.509 is also the basis for TLS/SSL and HTTPS.
>
> https://en.wikipedia.org/wiki/X.509

First, inspect the certificates you already have. There are two ways you can do this. The first is to use a built-in app called **Keychain Access**, which stores passwords, secrets and other sensitive data for the OS. It also manages X.509 certificates.

Open **Keychain Access**. Under **Default Keychains** in the left-hand sidebar, click **login**, then click **My Certificates**. Next, search **Apple** in the search bar to filter your certificates. Click the **disclosure indicators** to see the private keys.

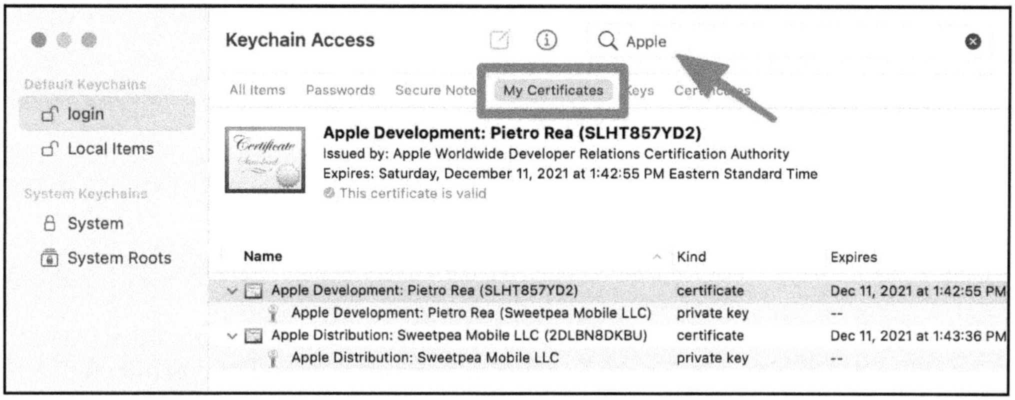

There are two certificates from the previous two chapters: a development certificate and a distribution certificate.

The second way to find your current certificates is by using the `security` command-line tool. Open Terminal and type the following command:

```
security find-identity -v -p codesigning
```

The same two certificates you saw in Keychain Access now print to the console. If you're part of multiple Apple Developer teams, you might see more.

```
1) 51CC49FC309619650FEC581586C7BB21B7467F86 "Apple Development:
pasi@sweetpeamobile.com (PCQP3A43PK)"
2) C2B75ED2E049C4E8B13E2823A493132E0AE41756 "Apple Distribution:
Sweetpea Mobile LLC (2DLBN8DKBU)"
     2 valid identities found
```

Viewing your certificates

Now, go back to Keychain Access and double-click **one of your certificates** to open it.

The modal reveals important concepts related to certificates. You'll go over each in detail.

1. **A certificate authority issues and signs certificates**: Something called "Apple Worldwide Developer Relations Certificate Authority" issued the certificate you're looking at. A certificate authority is part of the X.509 standard. Its role is to tie an entity to a public key. In this case, Apple's WWDR certificate authority ties your Apple Developer Program team ID to your public key.

2. **X.509 certificates rely on public-key cryptography**: In public-key cryptography, a public key and a private key work together. As the name implies, you can give your public key to others while keeping your private key secret.

   In the context of app distribution, Xcode digitally signs your app using your private key. You then give your public key to Apple via the certificate and Apple uses it to verify that the digital signature came from you.

3. **Code signing requires a valid certificate and its private key**: Certificates can become invalid for several reasons. Each certificate has a natural expiration date, usually one year from the time you got it. Separately, either you or Apple can revoke a certificate if it becomes compromised. To create a digital signature in Xcode, the certificate's private key needs to be installed in Keychain Access.

Now that you have some background information on certificates and public-key cryptography, select and delete your **old certificates** in Keychain Access. Keychain Access will double-check that you know what you're doing.

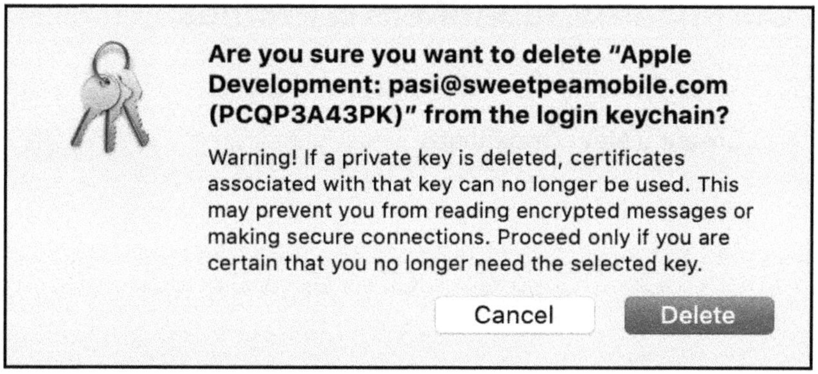

Click **Delete** to confirm.

Next, you'll create new certificates from scratch.

Creating new certificates

Log into **Apple Developer Portal** by opening https://developer.apple.com/ in your browser. Open **Certificates, Identifiers & Profiles.**

Select **Certificates** in the sidebar. Why are the certificates you just deleted here? The developer portal is unaware of Keychain Access on your Mac. It doesn't know you deleted your local copy.

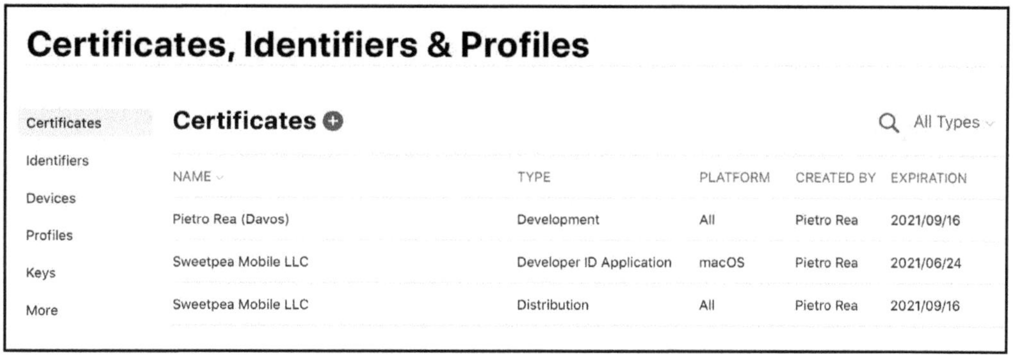

Because you also deleted the private keys in the previous step, you can't use these certificates, even if you download them again. Click each **certificate** and **revoke** it.

Now, click the + button next to the **Certificates** heading. Select **Apple Distribution** on the next screen.

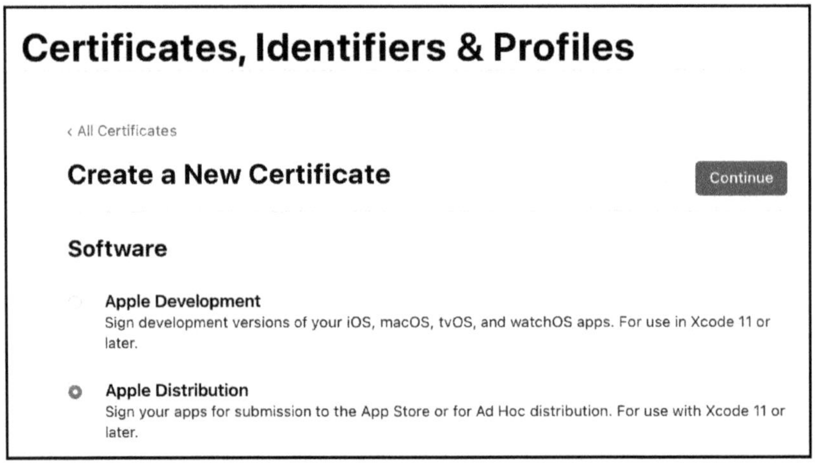

You need a distribution certificate both to distribute apps in the App Store and for ad hoc distribution, which is covered in Chapter 5, "Internal Distribution". In contrast, you need a development certificate to install a build for your development device. You won't create a development certificate in this chapter but the process is essentially the same.

Click **Continue** to move forward. The next screen asks you to upload a **Certificate Signing Request (CSR)**. This is also part of the X.509 standard and the official way to ask Apple to sign your certificate.

Asking Apple to sign your certificate

Open **Keychain Access**. From the menu bar, select **Keychain Access ▸ Certificate Assistant ▸ Request a Certificate from a Certificate Authority**.

In the resulting modal, enter your email address in the **User Email Address** field. Next to **Common Name**, type **Emitron Distribution Private Key**.

Select **Saved to disk**.

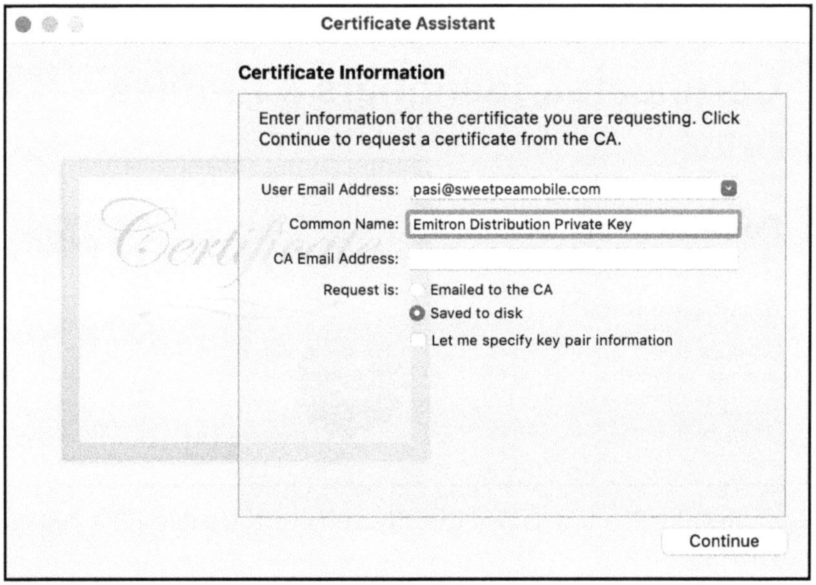

Click **Continue**. Save the certificate signing request somewhere easy to find in a file named **CertificateSigningRequest.certSigningRequest**.

> **Note**: In the time it took to create a **.certSigningRequest** file, Keychain Access already created your public key, private key and certificate. The CSR has all the information in your certificate, as well as your public key.

You just need Apple's cryptographic stamp of approval. That's why the next step is to upload the CSR to the developer portal.

Uploading the CSR

Return to **Apple Developer Portal**. Under the **Upload a Certificate Signing Request** section, click **Choose File**.

Select **CertificateSigningRequest.certSigningRequest** from your computer. Click **Continue** to upload your certificate signing request.

Next, click **Download** on the resulting screen to finally download the signed certificate.

Your browser downloads a file named **distribution.cert**. Double-click it to install it in Keychain Access.

Open **Keychain Access**. Filter by **Apple** certificates to see that your new certificate is there. The certificate expires exactly one year from today.

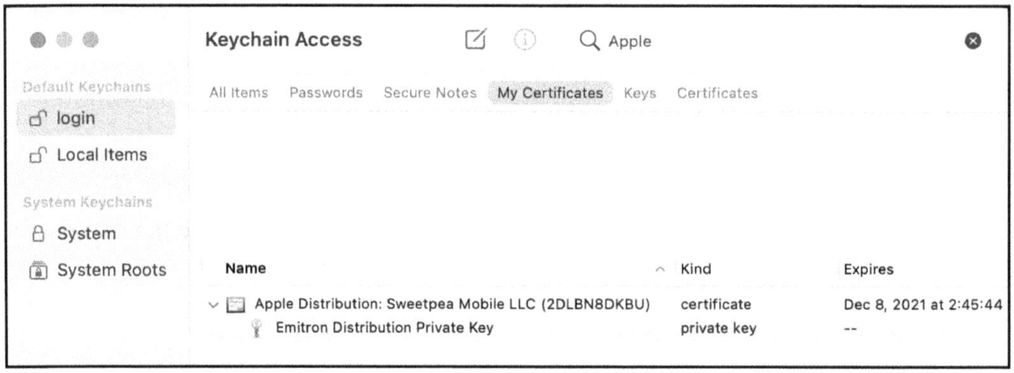

The entry in Keychain Access might not look like much, but it unambiguously identifies you as a developer on your Apple Developer Program team using state-of-the-art cryptographic standards.

Since Apple signed your certificate after you uploaded the certificate signing request, the fact that you have that private key in your possession means there's a direct chain of trust starting from Apple (the certificate authority) to your development team (mentioned in your certificate) to the Mac sitting in front of you.

Once you see the certificate in Keychain Access, you can delete the **.certSigningRequest** file. You no longer need it.

Adding entitlements

To create a code-signed provisioning profile — the end goal! — the next piece of the puzzle is a list of entitlements. To recap, **entitlements** answer the question **"what would you like to do?"** on behalf of your app.

Viewing entitlements

Every sandboxed app uses entitlements, even the ones that Apple makes. Before moving forward, it'll be helpful for you to dig up some entitlements on your Mac to inspect their format.

Open Terminal. Enter the following command to print the entitlements for a built-in app, like Keynote:

```
codesign -d --entitlements - /Applications/Keynote.app
```

`codesign` is the command-line tool for digitally signing binaries that's built into every Mac. Xcode uses `codesign` behind the scenes when you archive a build. The command above will give you a result like this:

```
<!DOCTYPE plist PUBLIC "-//Apple//DTD PLIST 1.0//EN" "http://
www.apple.com/DTDs/PropertyList-1.0.dtd">
<plist version="1.0">
<dict>
  <key>com.apple.security.automation.apple-events</key>
  <true/>
  <key>com.apple.developer.icloud-container-identifiers</key>
  <array>
    <string>com.apple.Keynote</string>
  </array>
...
</dict>
</plist>%
```

That's the beginning of what `codesign` prints to the console. At its core, an entitlement is a key-value pair.

You're looking at the text representation of the entitlements **.plist**, which stores reverse-DNS keys that represent different entitlements. The values can be Booleans (true/false) or other data types, like strings or arrays.

In the **.plist** above, you can see that Keynote has the Mac-only entitlement for sending Apple Events to other apps, `com.apple.security.automation.apple-events`. It also has the entitlement to save documents to iCloud, `com.apple.developer.icloud-container-identifiers`.

Now that you've seen how other apps use entitlements, it's time to add your own.

Creating your own entitlement

Like certificates, entitlements also originate in Apple Developer Portal. Open **Apple Developer Portal**. Click **Certificates, Identifiers & Profiles** followed by **Identifiers**. Then click the **Raywenderlich Emitron** App ID you created in Chapter 3, "Submitting Your First App for Review".

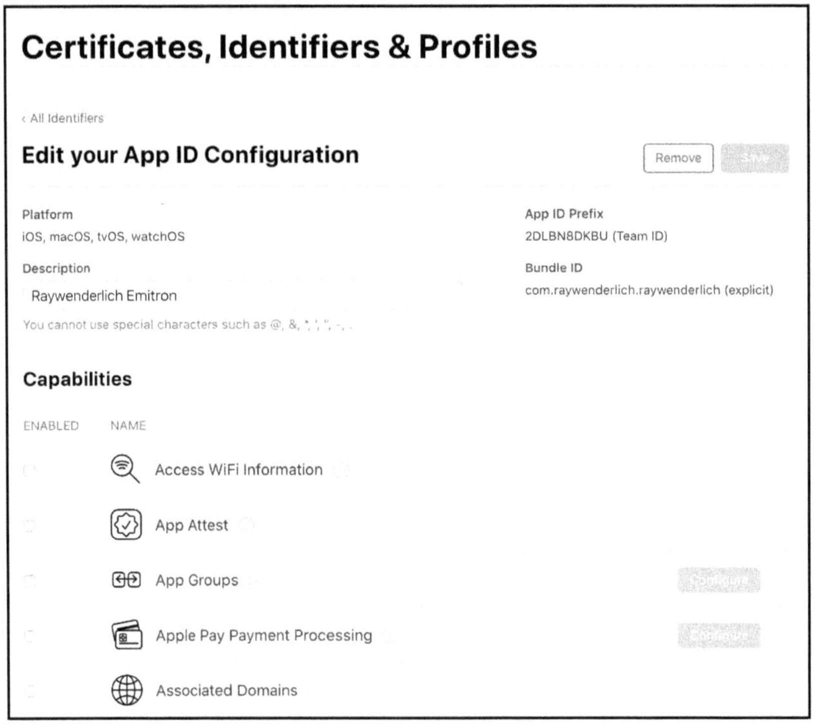

Technically, entitlements are part of an app's App ID. Under **Capabilities**, select the **Associated Domains** checkbox. Click **Save**. Associated Domains let you link an app with a website. The real raywenderlich.com iOS app doesn't use this, but you'll add it here for the sake of practice.

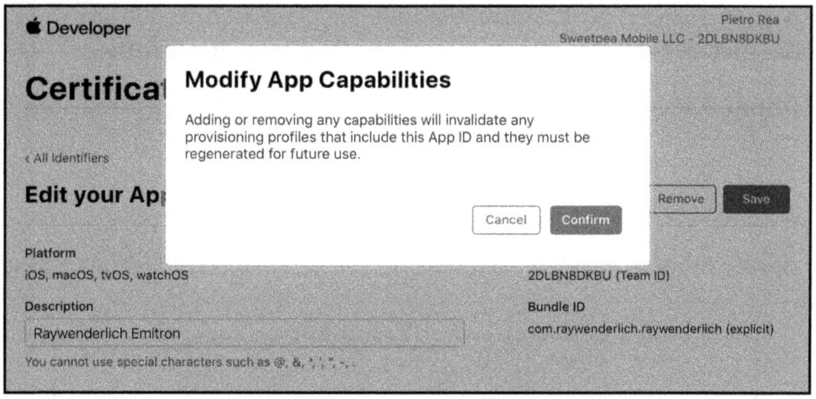

Click **Confirm** to save the change. All provisioning profiles that use this App ID become invalid when you change the ID's entitlements.

> **Note**: You're not technically "adding" an entitlement. All entitlements have a default value at runtime, which is usually set to **off**. Adding an entitlement in Xcode or in Apple Developer Portal merely overrides the default.
>
> Not every entitlement has a checkbox in App Store Connect or is represented in Xcode's **Capabilities** tab. Here's a more comprehensive list of entitlements: https://apple.co/2VT5wrx.

One of the most popular entitlements is **Push Notifications**. Adding push notifications is also the point where many developers realize they don't understand code signing and provisioning as well as they need to.

It takes more than adding an entitlement to send push notifications from a back-end server and display them in your app. If push notifications brought you to this chapter, or if you're generally interested in them, check out *Push Notifications by Tutorials* by Scott Grosch and the raywenderlich.com team: http://bit.ly/3d47yyL.

Generating a provisioning profile

At this point, you have a distribution certificate and an updated App ID with a new entitlement. The next step is to tie it all together in a provisioning profile. Like certificates, provisioning profiles are just files. On your Mac, Xcode stores all provisioning files in **~/Library/MobileDevices/Provisioning Profiles**.

Open **Terminal**. Execute the following command to look at your provisioning profiles:

```
open ~/Library/MobileDevice/Provisioning\ Profiles
```

Terminal opens a Finder window that lists all the provisioning profiles Xcode has ever used.

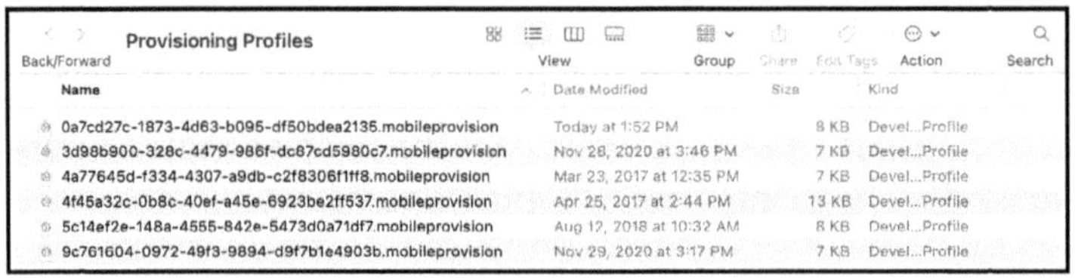

Double-clicking on any row would open Xcode. Instead, select the **first row**. Press **Space** to preview with Quick Look.

> **Note**: Quick Look is a feature in Finder that opens up a **preview** window in Finder. This saves you from having to open the file's designated app. Different file formats do different things with Quick Look previews.
>
> The Quick Look preview for **.mobileprovision** gives you a graphical representation of the provisioning profile. This is often useful for troubleshooting.

A provisioning profile is the combination of a handful of things you've seen before:

1. **App ID**: The App ID uniquely identifies an app on Apple's platforms and ties the app to your development team.
2. **Entitlements**: Technically part of the App ID, but important enough to get their own section in the preview. Notice that there are entitlements that you didn't have to set manually, like `keychain-access-groups` and `beta-reports-active`.
3. **Certificate**: The certificate unambiguously identifies you as the developer and certifies the chain of trust going from Apple to you. Remember that certificates are revokable and have an expiration date. If the certificate on a provisioning profile is invalid or expires, the entire provisioning profile is also invalid.

The list of entitlements on the provisioning profile above doesn't include the **Associated Domains** entitlement you added earlier. That's because you're looking at an old provisioning profile. It's time to generate a new one.

Generating a new provisioning profile

Open **Apple Developer Portal**. Click **Certificates, Identifiers & Profiles**, then click **Profiles**.

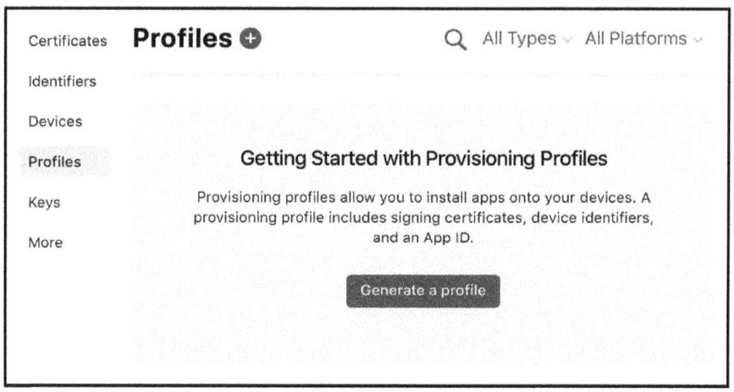

Click the + button next to **Profiles** to add a new profile. On the next screen, under **Distribution**, select **App Store** to register a new distribution provisioning profile.

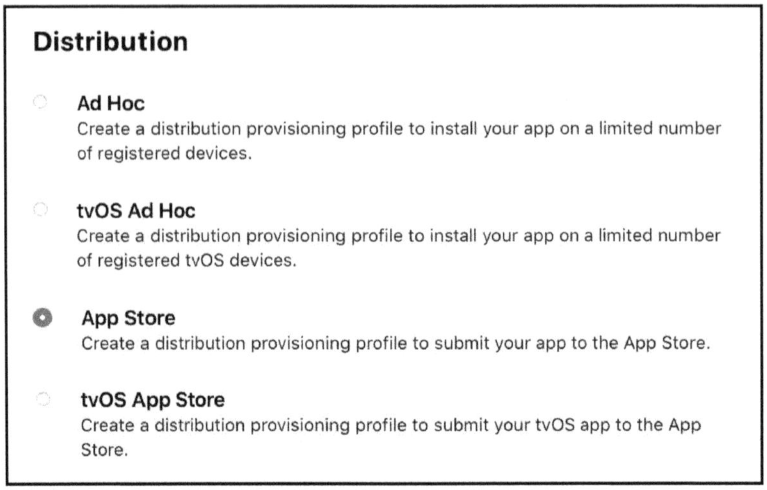

On the next screen, select the **App ID** you created in Chapter 3, "Submitting Your First App for Review". Click **Continue**.

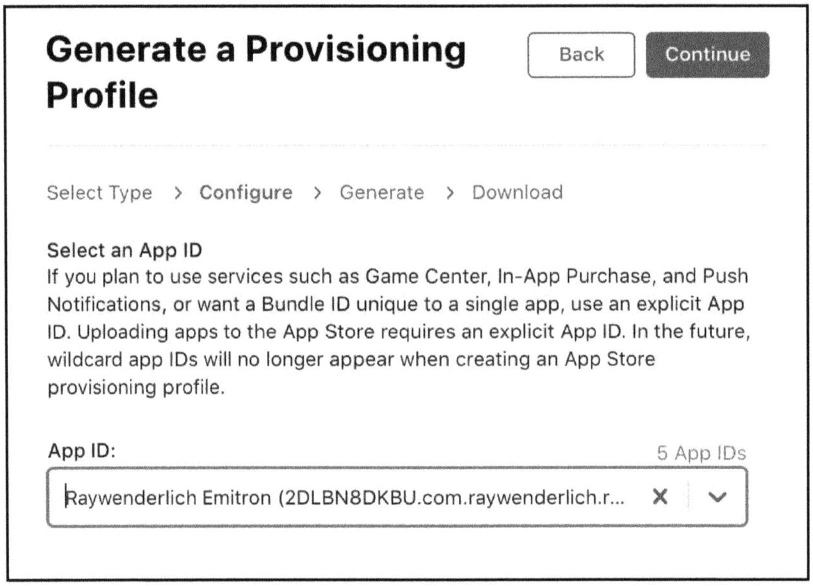

Then, select the **distribution certificate** you created earlier in this chapter. Click **Continue**.

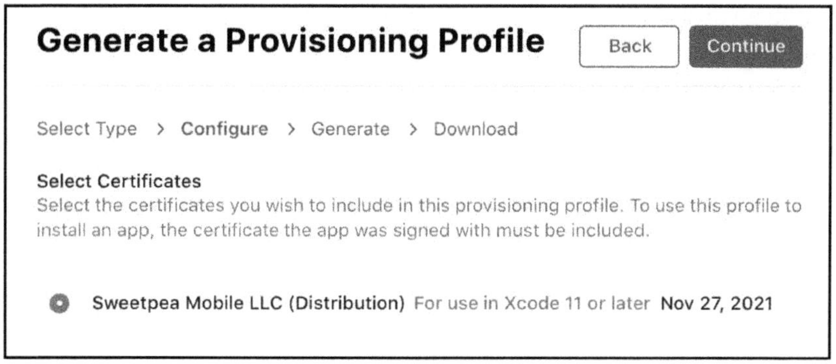

As a final step, App Store Connect asks you to name your provisioning profile. Enter **Emitron Distribution Provisioning Profile**. Click **Generate**.

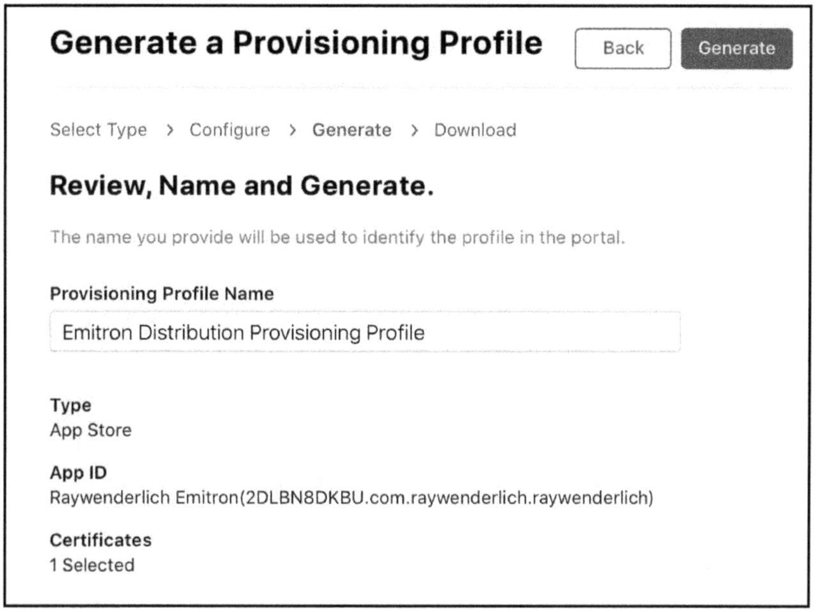

On the next screen, click **Download.** Double-click the resulting **.mobileprovision** file to open it in Xcode. Xcode will acknowledge the file, then move it to **/Library/MobileDevice/Provisioning Profiles**.

Open this folder in Finder and inspect the most recently added **.mobileprovision** with Quick Look to verify that this new provisioning profile does have the **Associated Domains** entitlement you added earlier.

Code signing and distribution

You now have a valid distribution provisioning profile in your possession, along with its associated private key. You'll use these to generate another build, code-sign it and upload it to App Store Connect.

Open the **starter project** in Xcode. Navigate to the **raywenderlich** target.

Click the **Signing & Capabilities** tab, then select the **Release** tab. Under **Signing**, deselect **Automatically manage signing**.

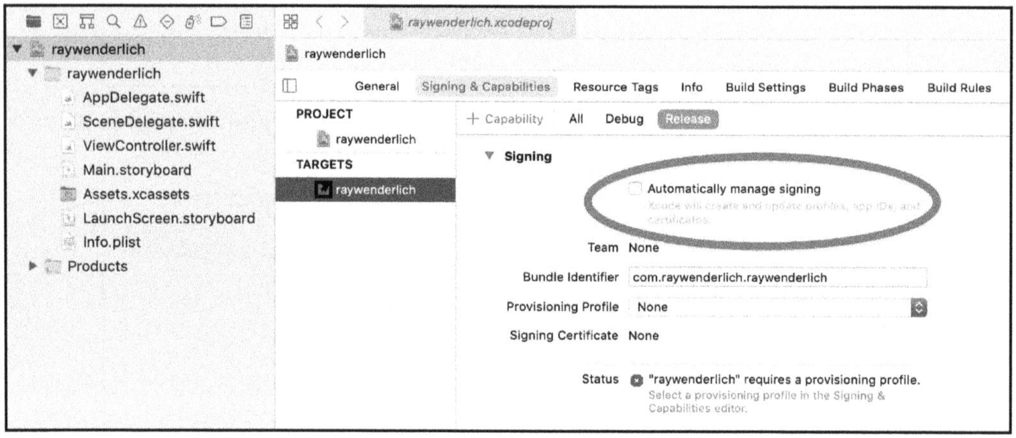

> **Note**: The **Debug** build configuration, which you typically use for development builds, still uses automatic code signing. You can change **Debug** and **Release** configurations separately.
>
> You don't need to know the ins and outs of build configurations to understand code signing and provisioning. Chapter 9, "Build Customizations", covers this topic in detail.

Don't worry that Xcode complains about a missing provisioning profile. You'll fix that next.

Next to **Provisioning Profile**, click the **Drop-down** button. Select **Import Profile...**. Navigate to and select the **provisioning profile** you downloaded in the previous section.

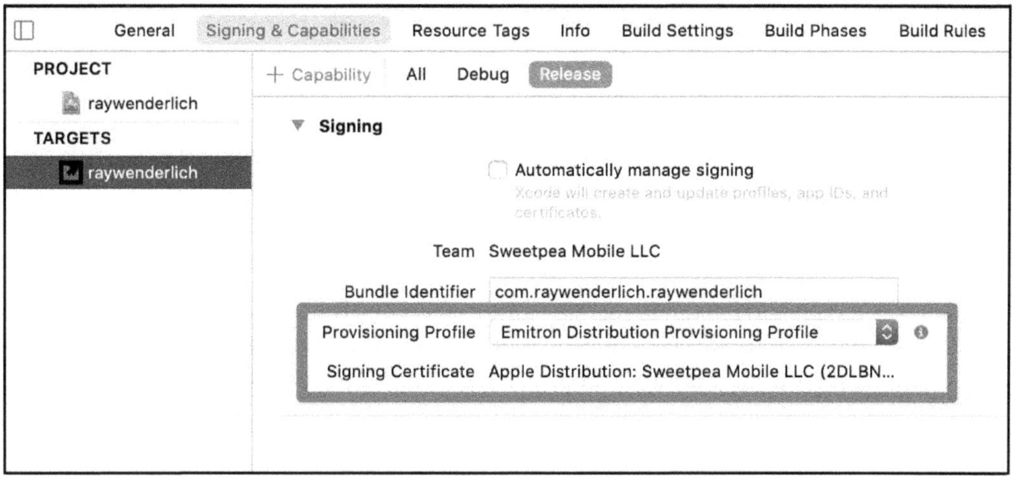

If you missed a step and see an error, double-check your configurations by looking at build settings.

Under the targets list, click **raywenderlich**. Click the **Build Settings** tab, then scroll down to the **Signing** section.

There are four build settings you need to keep in mind if you see any errors with code signing or provisioning: “Code Signing Identity”, “Code Signing Style”, “Development Team”, and “Provisioning Profile”.

Code Signing Identity

Your app's code-signing identity sets the certificate that uniquely identifies you. Even if you choose to manage signing manually, this build setting has a manual option and an automatic option. The values for the automatic option are **Apple Development**, **iOS Developer**, **Apple Distribution** and **iOS Distribution**.

If you use one of the automatic options, Xcode tries to deduce the certificate from the provisioning profile selected below. It can do this because provisioning profiles include certificates. In this case, leave this value set to **iOS Distribution**.

Code Signing Style

This is the same setting you changed earlier in the **Signing & Capabilities** tab. The possible values are **Automatic** and **Manual**. Here, you're managing signing **automatically** for Debug builds and **manually** for Release builds.

Development Team

When you log into Xcode with your Apple ID, your Apple Development Program teams become options you can select. The team you select for this build setting must match the team in your chosen certificate and provisioning profile.

Provisioning Profile

The provisioning profile build setting determines which provisioning profile you'll embed in the build. You can also change this setting in the **Signing & Capabilities** tab you saw earlier.

Uploading a manually signed build

Now that your settings look correct, it's time to generate another build to upload to App Store Connect using your manually created certificate and provisioning profile.

With the **raywenderlich** target selected, click the **General** tab and bump the **Build** number to **3**. If you've uploaded more builds in the meantime, your build number could be higher.

Set Xcode's build destination to **Any iOS Device (arm64)**. In the menu bar, click **Product ▸ Archive**. When Xcode finishes the build process, an Organizer window will open automatically.

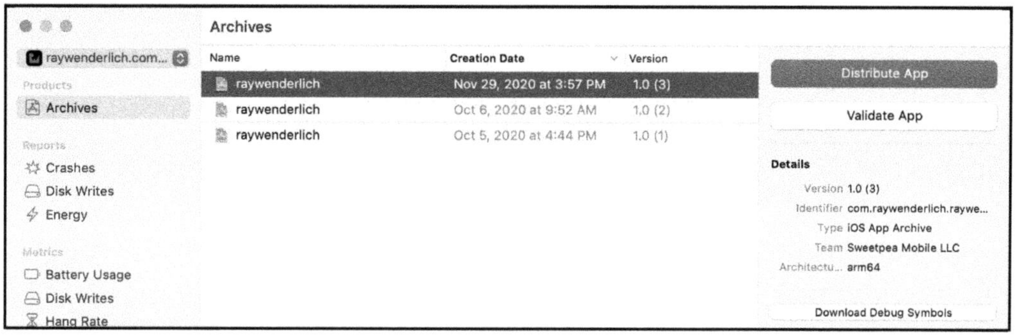

Click **Distribute App**. Go through the Organizer windows using the default values. Since you chose manual signing, Xcode now prompts you to select a distribution certificate and a provisioning profile.

Select **Apple Distribution** as the distribution certificate and **Emitron Distribution Provisioning Profile** as the provisioning profile, as shown below.

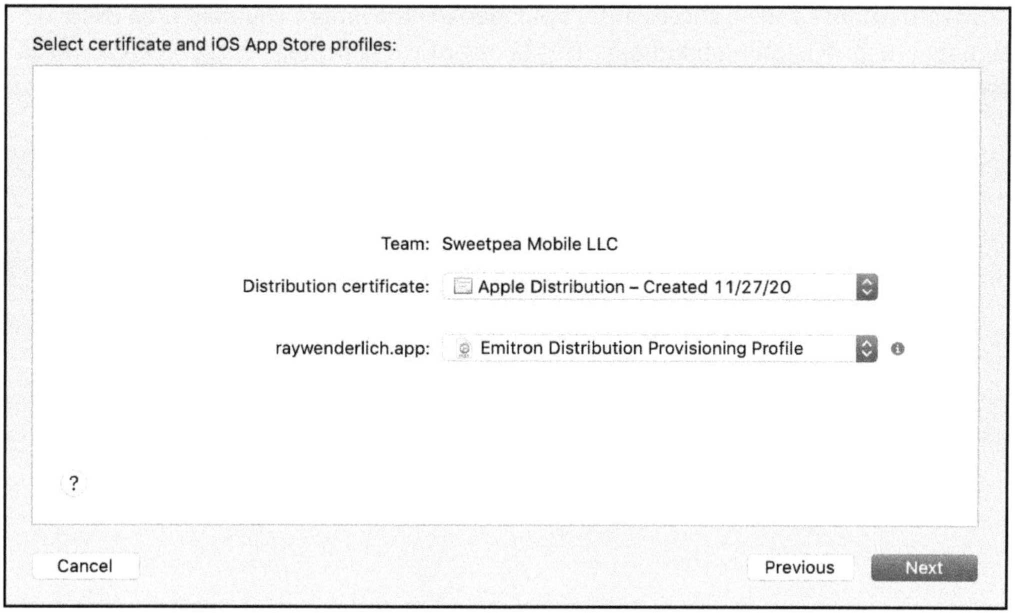

Click **Next** to continue. Xcode then uses the certificate and provisioning profile you selected a moment ago to digitally sign the binary using `codesign`.

Then, click **Upload** to upload the generated IPA file to App Store Connect.

If all goes well, Xcode signs and uploads the binary and you'll see a success screen.

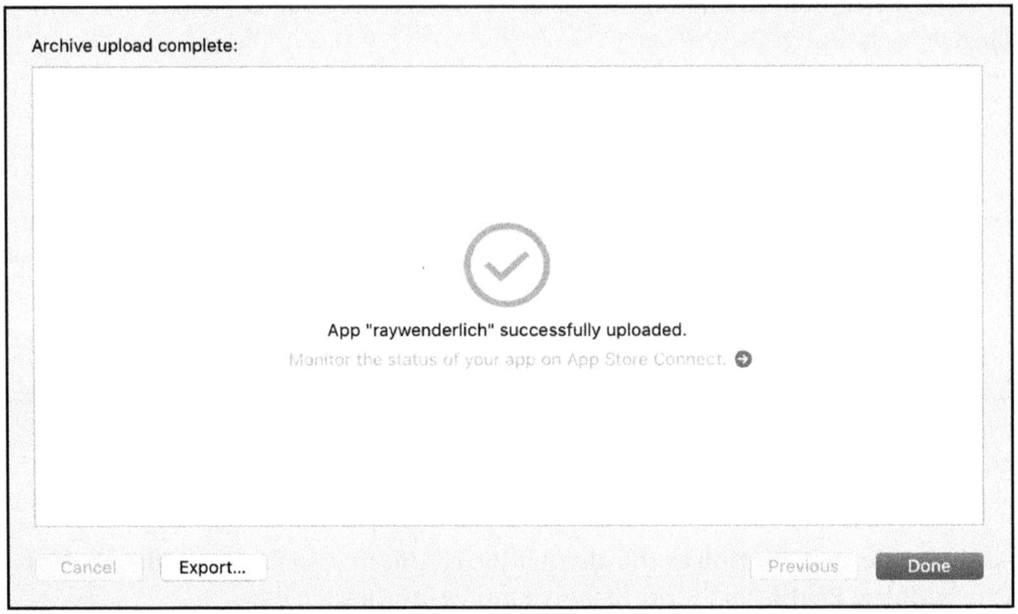

Congratulations! You've successfully uploaded a build where you managed code signing and provisioning manually. This is one of the thorniest things you can do as an Apple developer — and you came out the other end with flying colors.

Key points

- Unix-like systems assume that third-party apps should have the same access and privileges as the user running them. Apple designed App Sandbox as a way to fix this assumption.
- Sandboxed apps need to request permission from the operating system to access hardware facilities, the network, data from other apps, user files and special functionality like push notifications.
- App Sandbox and runtime policy infrastructure make several checks when an app tries a protected operation. You must furnish a code-signed provisioning profile to answer them.
- A provisioning profile comprises several parts: an App ID, entitlements, a certificate and (optionally) a list of device IDs.
- Certificates are based on public-key cryptography and follow the X.509 standard. Certificates contain information about your Apple Developer Program team and are associated with a public key and a private key.
- Entitlements are key-value pairs that describe what an app intends to do at runtime. They're stored in an app's App ID and code-signed with the rest of the binary.
- When it comes to code signing and provisioning, the relevant build settings are **Code Signing Identity**, **Code Signing Style**, **Development Team** and **Provisioning Profile**.

Chapter 5: Internal Distribution

By Pietro Rea

You're on the way to the kitchen at work when you bump into the company's CEO. You chat about your ongoing iOS project, which piques her interest. She'd like to check out the project on her iPhone. What should you do next?

She already has the App Store version, but that doesn't include what you're working on. Unless she's a developer, you shouldn't ask her to download Xcode and build from the source. She may not have a Mac, and even if she does, downloading Xcode is a big time commitment and not a practical option. So how can she see a current snapshot of the app on her own device?

You might remember Apple's third-party software philosophy from Chapter 1, "The App Store": Distribution of any kind of third-party software, even private distribution outside the App Store, has officially-supported distribution methods that Apple expects you to use. Fortunately, you have several options for internal distribution.

This chapter covers **ad hoc distribution**, a manual way of achieving limited distribution to a small group, usually for testing and gathering feedback.

Types of internal distribution

If you're still wondering what internal distribution means, you can mentally substitute *internal* with *private*. Internal or private distribution includes all types of distribution outside the App Store. The App Store remains the only way of achieving *public* distribution on iOS and related platforms.

Internal distribution is a large topic. Before diving into ad hoc distribution, it's worth surveying all the internal distribution methods so you know what the best available method is for you. Which internal distribution method you should choose depends on your end goal, who's going to use the app and who's going to buy the app.

> **Note**: To learn more about officially-supported internal distribution methods, watch the session **App Distribution — From Ad-hoc to Enterprise** from WWDC 2019: http://apple.co/3o3YzjT.

Personal Team distribution

When you register as an Apple developer, you automatically get access to Personal Team, which is a bare-bones version of the full Apple Development Program.

Personal Team allows you to distribute apps to a few devices using Xcode without having to pay for the full enrollment. Personal Team distribution is meant for learning and getting started with the SDKs. Builds you distribute this way expire after a couple of days.

Ad hoc distribution

When you enroll and pay for the full Apple Developer Program, either as an individual or as an organization, you gain the ability to achieve limited distribution to a small group by using ad hoc distribution.

Ad hoc distribution is not a long-term or scalable distribution solution. You can only distribute apps to up to 100 devices per product family per year and builds expire yearly. Developers often use ad hoc distribution to deploy **alpha**, internal-facing builds, usually as part of a build pipeline.

TestFlight

TestFlight is Apple's officially supported method for distributing **beta** — that is, external-facing — builds for testing and gathering feedback. Since Apple makes TestFlight, it's deeply integrated with the App Store and App Store Connect.

With TestFlight, you can have up to 100 internal testers and up to 10,000 external testers, making it a good option if you run into the 100-device limit with ad hoc distribution. Keep in mind, however, that TestFlight builds are only active for 90 days so it's not a long-term solution. Chapter 6, "TestFlight" covers this method in detail.

In-house distribution

In-house distribution allows large organizations to develop and deploy internal-use apps for employees. To use it, you need to apply to the Apple Developer Enterprise Program, which is separate from the regular program, and pay an additional 299 U.S. dollars per year.

In-house distribution also allows large-scale alpha build distribution without having to worry about the 100-device limit. Most of this chapter also applies to in-house distribution of enterprise builds.

Custom App Distribution

For a long time, in-house distribution was the only supported way to achieve large-scale internal deployments. Nowadays, Apple prefers you to use Custom App Distribution. In-house distribution still exists to support edge cases where Custom App Distribution doesn't apply.

Unlike in-house distribution, Custom App Distribution leverages the App Store's tools and infrastructure, like TestFlight and App Store Connect. If you're distributing an internal app for a large organization, Custom App Distribution should be at the top of your list.

Distributing ad hoc builds

This chapter builds on the previous chapter, so feel free to go back to Chapter 4, "Code Signing & Provisioning" if you get stuck on any of the topics from that chapter. In this chapter, instead of creating a distribution provisioning profile to generate an App Store build, you'll create an **ad hoc provisioning profile** to generate an ad hoc build.

Before moving on, make sure you have the following set up:

1. An **Apple ID** enrolled in the Apple Developer Program. You also need to be logged into Xcode with the same Apple ID.

2. An **App ID** registered in Apple's developer portal for the raywenderlich.com app. You should already have this set up from Chapter 3, "Submitting Your First App for Review". If not, go back to that chapter to learn how to create one.

3. A **distribution certificate** registered in the developer portal and saved to Keychain Access on your Mac. If you don't already have one, Chapter 4, "Code Signing & Provisioning", can help.

4. An **iOS device**. This can be any iPhone or iPad running iOS 13.4 or newer, to match the sample app's deployment target.

Registering a device

In ad hoc distribution, you can only distribute builds to a maximum of 100 devices per device family per year. Apple enforces the device limit by requiring you to register each device's **unique device ID (UDID)**, in the developer portal.

Going back to the scenario from the beginning of the chapter, if you want to distribute an internal build to a colleague using ad hoc distribution, the first thing you need to do is collect their device's UDID.

Finding the UDID

A UDID is a sequence of letters and numbers that form a unique identifier. Your iPhone, iPad and all other Apple devices have a UDID that no other Apple device shares.

When faced with the task of retrieving a UDID, a common reaction is to head to the device's Settings app. This is where you find the device's model number, serial number and IMEI number. However, none of those is the UDID. For privacy and security reasons, there's no way to see the UDID on the physical device or in the Settings app.

You can retrieve a UDID by connecting your device to a Mac and using either Finder, Xcode, Xcode Server or Apple Configurator 2. You could also use a hosted Mobile Device Management (MDM) provisioning profile and skip the wired connection, but MDM is out of scope for this book. Using Finder is the simplest option, so this section covers how to get a UDID that way.

First, connect your iOS device to your Mac using a cable. Open Finder on your Mac and click your device's name on the left sidebar. Unless you changed your device's name, the default device name follows the pattern **Your Name's Device Model** (e.g. Ray's iPhone XS Max).

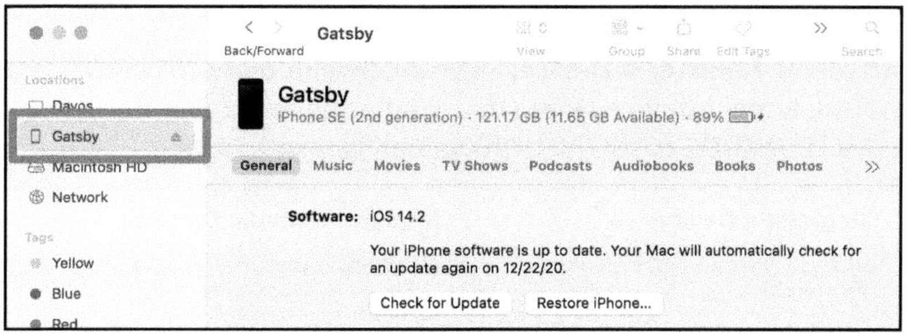

Finder opens a device management pane. Unless you're also a fan of F. Scott Fitzgerald, the device name you see will be different from the one in the screenshot.

Note: Apple moved device management from iTunes to Finder in macOS 10.15 (Catalina). Head to iTunes instead of Finder if your Mac is running 10.14 (Mojave) or earlier.

The text label directly below the device name doesn't look clickable, but it is. Click it.

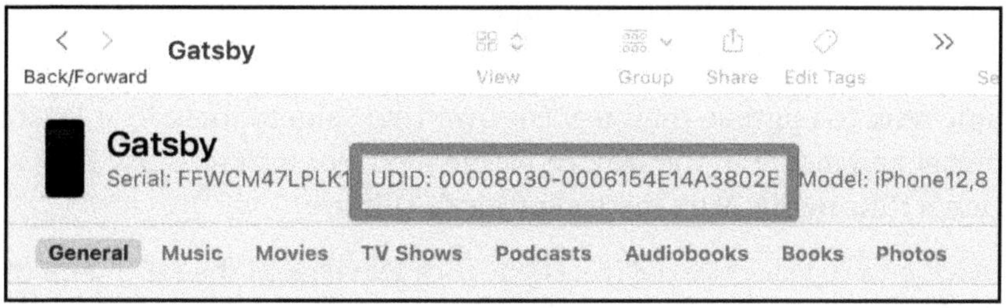

Open sesame! Clicking the text field reveals the information you're looking for. Right-click the text label and select **Copy UDID**.

Typically, the hardest part about registering UDIDs is not anything *you* have to do, but rather getting others to follow these instructions so they can send you their device's UDID. If you're in charge of internal ad hoc distribution, you can save a lot of time by documenting the steps in this section in your own words somewhere easily accessible, like an internal wiki or a Google doc.

Adding a UDID to the developer portal

Now that you've located the UDID, it's time to add it to the developer portal. Log in to the developer portal at developer.apple.com. In the sidebar, click **Devices**. Next to the heading **Devices**, click the + button to register your UDID.

Under the heading **Register a Device**, leave the default platform as **iOS, tvOS, watchOS**. Next, enter a **Device Name** that'll help you remember the device. Finally, under **Device ID (UDID)**, paste the UDID you previously copied.

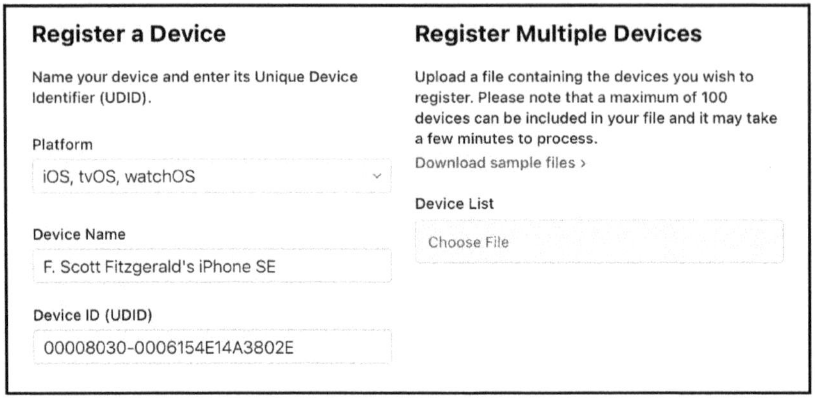

The device name you enter in the developer portal doesn't have to match the device's name in Finder. In fact, it's better to make the device name on the developer portal more descriptive so you can tell devices apart in the future without having to manually compare UDIDs.

Since people tend to upgrade their devices over time, aim to include at least the device's owner and model in the **Device Name** field. For example, use **Ray Wenderlich's iPhone XS Max** instead of **Ray's iPhone**.

Click **Continue** to register the device. Next, click **Devices** in the left menu to verify that the device you just added appears in the list of registered devices.

Creating the provisioning profile

Now that you have a new device registered in the developer portal, it's time to create an **ad hoc provisioning profile**.

You can think of a provisioning profile as a set of answers to questions the system asks about your app. An ad hoc provisioning profile is no different than a regular one, except it answers one additional question.

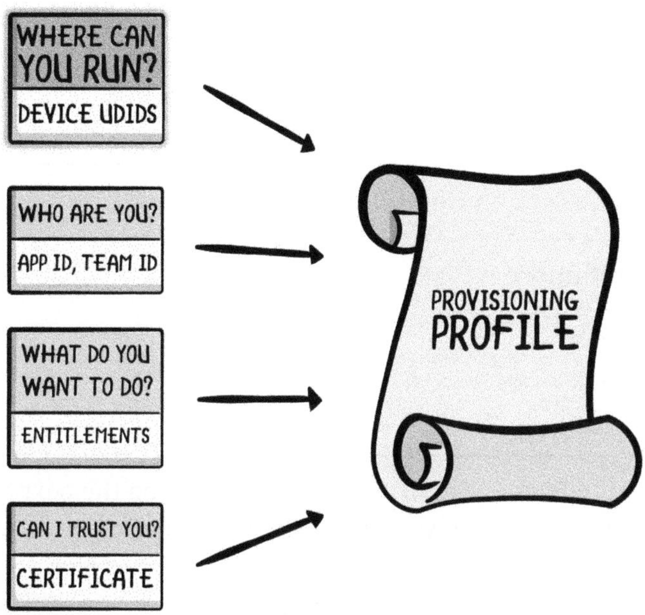

An ad hoc provisioning profile also answers the question **where can you run**? with an embedded list of device UDIDs.

A distribution provisioning profile, like the one you created in Chapter 4, "Code Signing & Provisioning", doesn't need to answer this question because, in this context, the term "distribution" implies distribution on the App Store. If someone can get the app on the App Store, it's allowed to run.

> **Note**: If you need a refresher on provisioning profiles, refer to Chapter 4, "Code Signing & Provisioning".

Go back to the developer portal. In the sidebar, click **Profiles**. Then, next to the heading **Profiles**, click the + button to create a new provisioning profile.

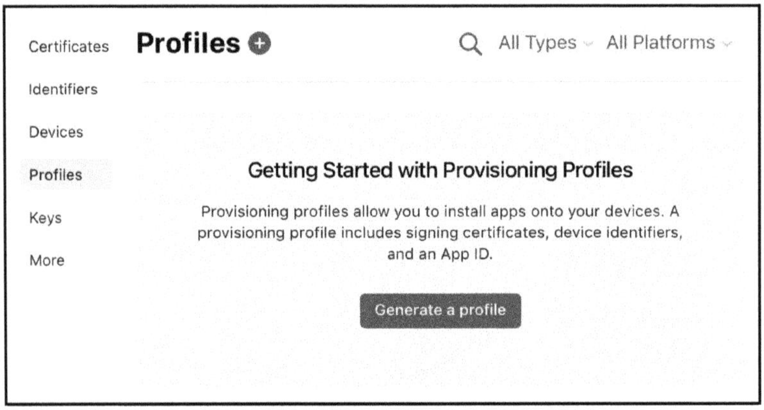

Under **Distribution**, select **Ad Hoc**. Click **Continue**.

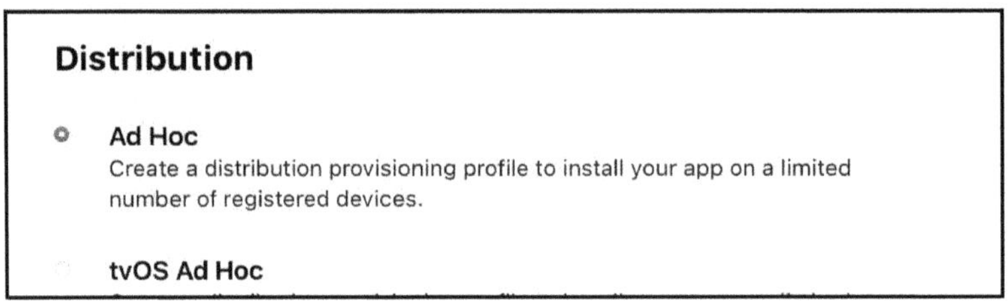

Select Emitron's App ID and your distribution certificate on the next two screens. Once you reach the third step, select the device you registered in the last section.

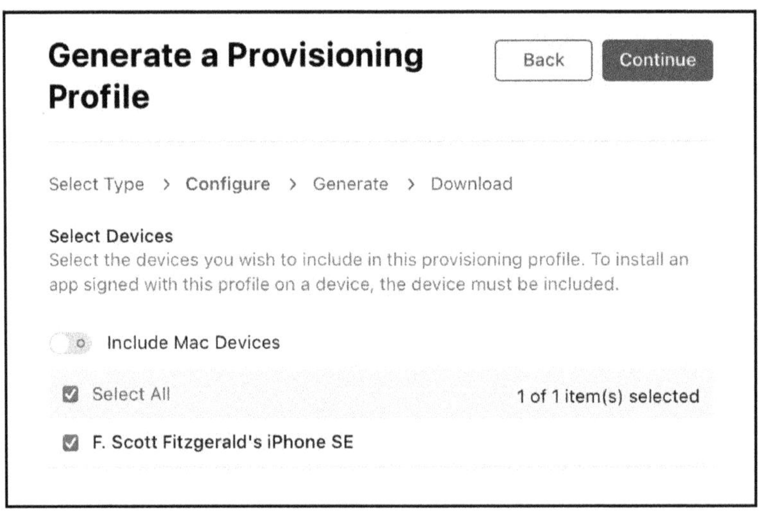

Name your provisioning profile **Emitron Ad Hoc Provisioning Profile**. Click **Generate**.

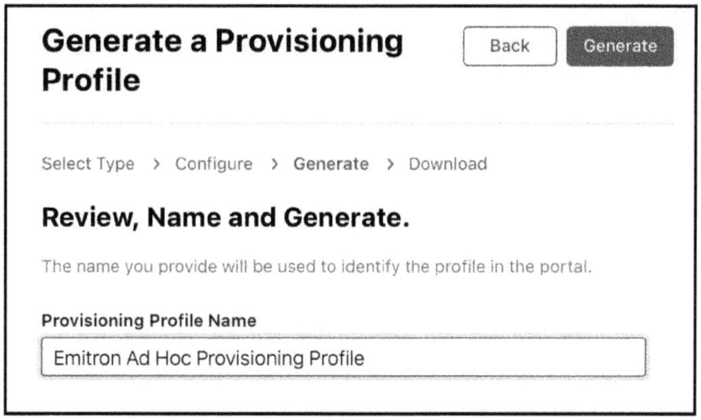

Click **Download**. You can also preview ad hoc provisioning profiles with Finder's Quick Look preview. The only difference is the added **PROVISIONED DEVICES** section, which contains the embedded list of registered UDIDs.

Click the **.mobileprovision file** you just downloaded. Press **Space** to activate the preview.

Now, close the preview and double-click the provisioning profile to install it. This makes it available to Xcode's build process.

The fact that registered UDIDs are part of ad hoc provisioning profiles has an important implication that developers often overlook: Every time you register a new UDID, you need to create a new internal build.

How so? Unfortunately, you can't simply swap the provisioning profile in past builds. So if you need to distribute an internal build to someone new, you need a brand-new provisioning profile that includes all previously registered devices, plus any new ones from the new person. You then need to create a new build using the new provisioning profile. Only then will the new person be able to install the app.

Creating an ad hoc build

So far in this book, you've used an empty shell as your sample project. In this chapter, you'll upgrade to the real raywenderlich.com iOS app, codenamed **Emitron**, and use that to create an ad hoc build for internal distribution.

Open this chapter's resources folder and double-click **/emitron/Emitron/Emitron.xcodeproj** in the **starter** folder to open the project in Xcode.

You're not part of the raywenderlich.com development team, so you don't have access to the real App ID. Instead, swap it out for the App ID you created in Chapter 3, "Submitting Your First App for Review".

In Project navigator, click the **Emitron** project file. Make sure the **emitron** target is selected and open the **Signing & Capabilities** tab. Scroll down to **Signing (Release)** and change **Bundle Identifier** to the one you registered in the developer portal back in Chapter 3, "Submitting Your First App for Review".

The next screenshot has **com.raywenderlich.raywenderlich** as the bundle identifier, but this value will be different, in your case.

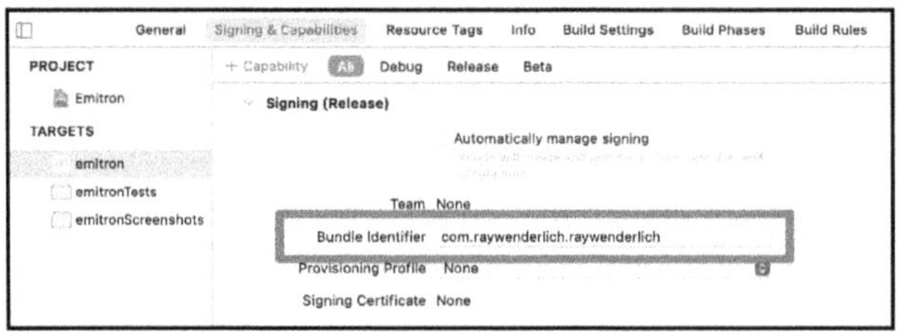

Now, open the **Build Settings** tab. Scroll down to the **Signing** section. Click **Combined** below the tabs to see a simpler version of build settings.

This project has two build configurations: Debug and Release. Ad hoc distribution always uses the Release build configuration. For the following three build settings, click the **disclosure** indicator and only modify the build setting for the **Release** build configuration.

Next:

1. Change **Code Signing Identity** to **Apple Distribution**.
2. Change **Development Team** to the team you're logged into. Your distribution certificate and App ID should both be registered in this team's developer portal.
3. Change **Provisioning Profile** to **Emitron Ad Hoc Provisioning Profile**, which is the same profile you downloaded and installed earlier.

Verify that your build settings look like those in the next screenshot. Your team name will be different from the one you see.

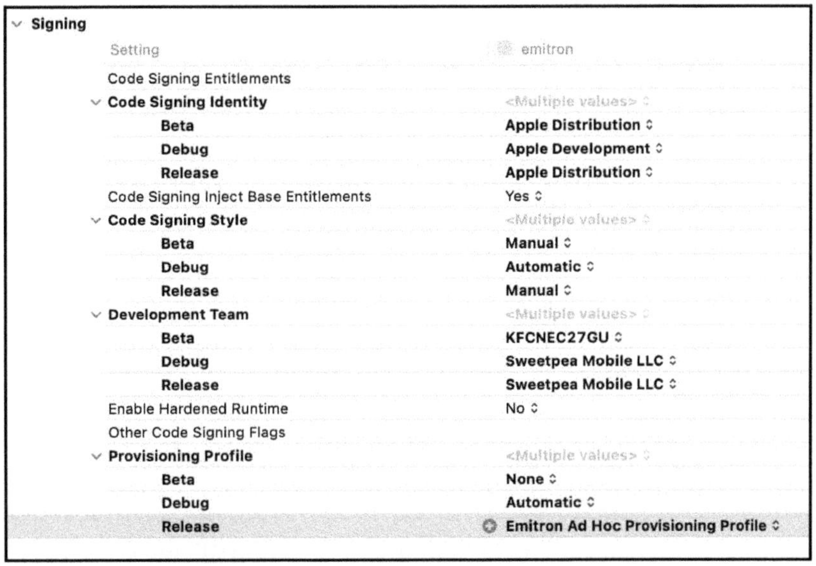

Select **Any iOS Device (arm64)** as the build destination, then select **Product ▸ Archive** from the menu to start the build process.

Once Xcode finishes archiving, it shows you Organizer. The top entry is the archive you just finished building.

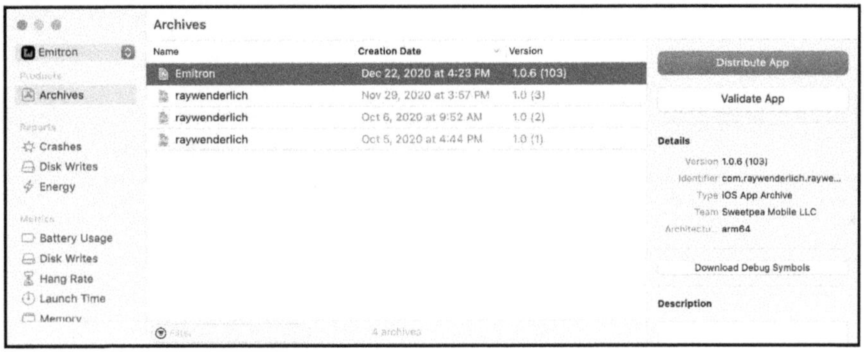

Click **Distribute App**. On the next screen, select **Ad Hoc** as the method of distribution

On the following screen, leave the default distribution certificate selected. Next to **raywenderlich.app**, click the drop-down and select **Emitron Ad Hoc Provisioning Profile**.

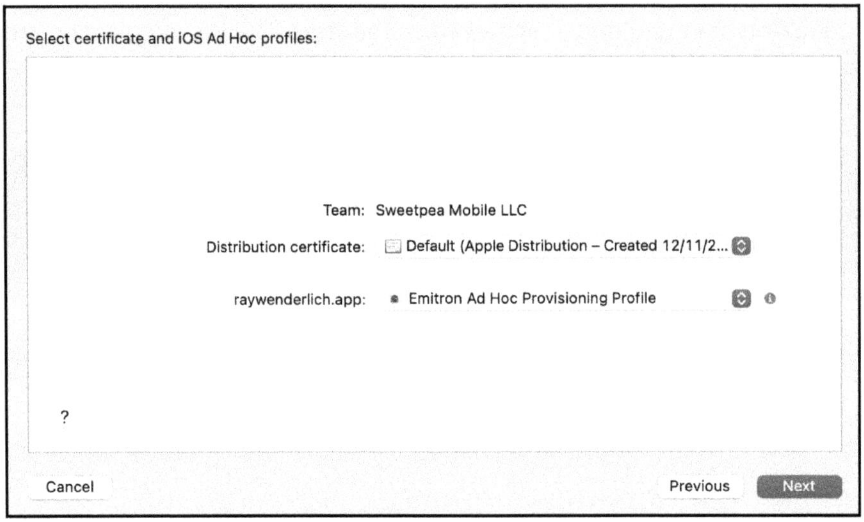

Click **Next**. On the review screen, click **Export**. On the modal that appears, give your export a name and a destination. Once saved, open the **archive** folder to inspect its contents.

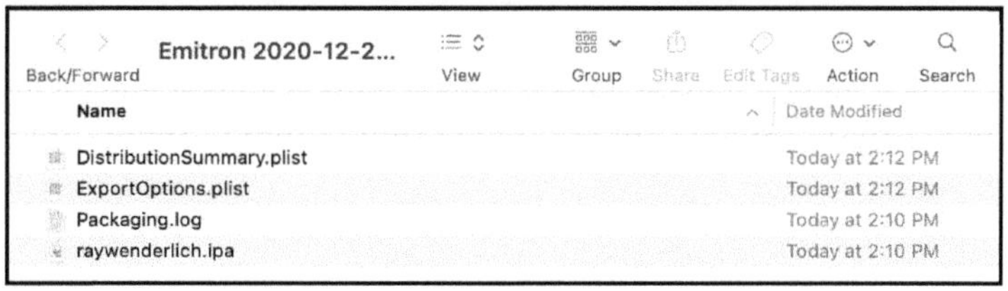

For all intents and purposes, the .ipa file *is* the app. **IPA** stands for **iPhone Package Archive** and it contains the app binary and all the resources it needs to run. You can ignore the other three files in the **archive** folder, for now.

Apple supports two methods for installing ad hoc builds on registered devices: manually and wirelessly.

Installing the app manually

Installing an ad hoc build manually is similar to retrieving a device's UDID. You need physical access to the device. You also need to connect the device to a computer.

You can either borrow the registered device and do it yourself or you can distribute the IPA along with some instructions. Since the IPA is just a file, you can share it as you would any other file: by attaching it to an email, copying it to a USB drive, uploading it to Dropbox and so on.

Regardless of how you choose to share the IPA, it's worth re-emphasizing that **only registered devices** can install ad hoc IPAs. A common source of frustration is sharing an ad hoc build to someone who doesn't show up in the list of registered UDIDs, so make sure you're clear on who's in and who's out.

Installing the IPA with Finder

For this section, imagine you're on the receiving end of the ad hoc IPA. Plug the device you registered earlier into a Mac running Catalina or newer. Use iTunes instead of Finder if you're running macOS 10.14 (Mojave) or older.

Open Finder. In the left menu, click your device's name. Even if you search through every tab on the Device Management screen, you won't see anything that mentions installing IPAs. So how do you do it?

Much like finding a UDID, installing an IPA is a bit of a hidden feature. Simply drag **raywenderlich.ipa** onto the device management screen. Once a green plus icon appears, drop the file to begin installation.

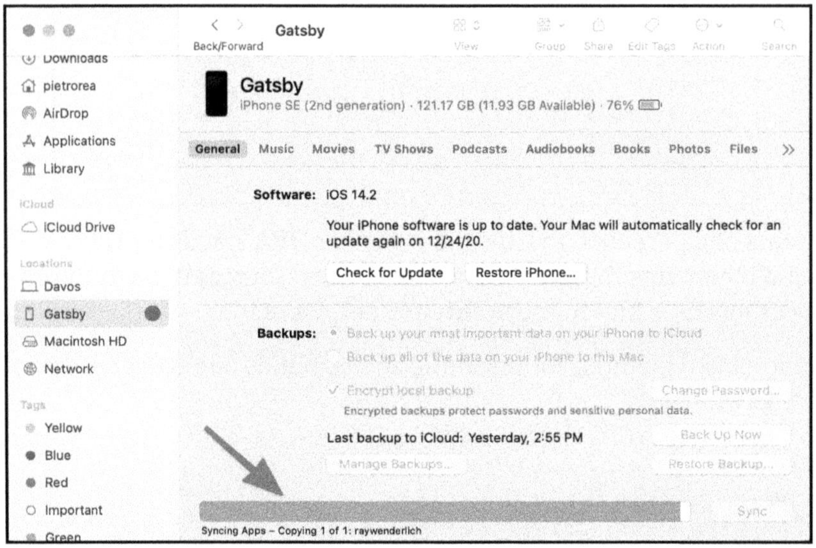

Unlock your device after installation completes. Tap the new **raywenderlich** icon on your home screen to verify that you can launch the app without any issues.

If the app finished copying but you can't find it on your home screen, try restarting your device. There's a caching issue that affects IPA installations on devices running iOS 14.

> **Note**: Similar to retrieving a UDID, you can also install an IPA manually using Xcode, Xcode Server or Apple Configurator 2.

You've learned how to collect a device's UDID, how to register it on the developer portal, how to create an ad hoc provisioning profile and how to install an ad hoc IPA manually using Finder. It all technically *works* but there's one problem: Your internal users have to jump over hurdle after hurdle just to try out your internal builds.

When you're using ad hoc builds to gather feedback, that kind of friction directly translates to low usage and little feedback. Luckily, there's one more thing you can try: Apple also supports over the air (OTA) internal distribution.

Installing the app wirelessly

You can think of OTA internal distribution as a bespoke App Store that you build and maintain yourself. You handle uploading builds, hosting the IPAs and creating the App Store front end. All a user has to do is point a mobile web browser to your web page and click a link to begin the download.

OTA distribution requires an HTTPS-enabled web server. Setting one up is out of scope for this book, so this section uses GitHub Pages for demonstration. However, you should use your own web server whenever possible.

GitHub Pages is a free way to host your own website. GitHub statically generates and hosts a website based on the files you push to a GitHub repo. All you need is a GitHub account and some basic knowledge of Git.

To get started, create a new repository in GitHub named **USERNAME.github.io**, where USERNAME is your GitHub user name. You can read more in GitHub's guide, **Getting Started with Github Pages**: http://bit.ly/2WPWnk2. Before moving on, make sure you can access your web page at https://username.github.io.

Exporting for OTA distribution

Go back to Xcode's Organizer window. Select the last archive you built. Click **Distribute**, select **Ad Hoc** as the method of distribution and click **Next**.

On the second screen, select the same options as before, except this time also click the checkbox next to **Include manifest for over-the-air installation**.

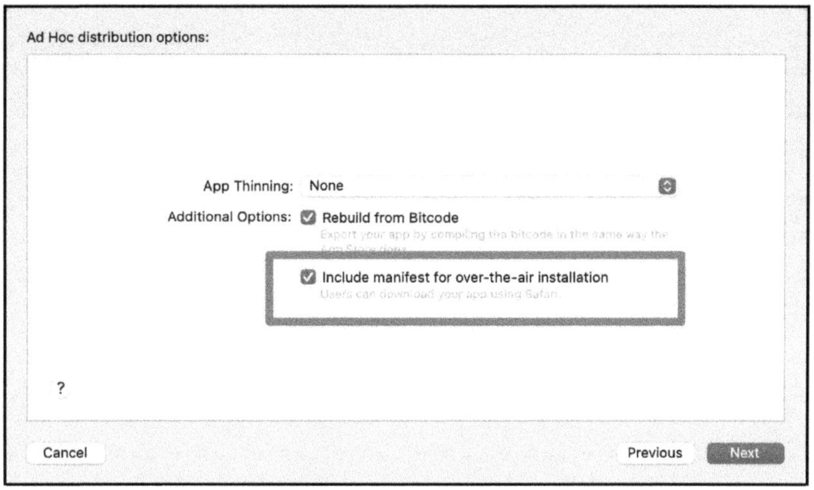

The next screen asks you to fill out three different URLs. The first one specifies the location of the IPA on your web server. The second and third URL specify the location of images of different sizes.

Fill out the URL fields like this:

- Next to **App URL**, enter **https://USERNAME.github.io/raywenderlich/raywenderlich.ipa**.
- Next to **Display Image URL**, enter **https://USERNAME.github.io/raywenderlich/images/icon57x57.png**.
- Next to **Full Size Image URL**, enter **https://USERNAME.github.io/raywenderlich/images/icon512x512.png**.

Don't forget to replace **USERNAME** with your GitHub username.

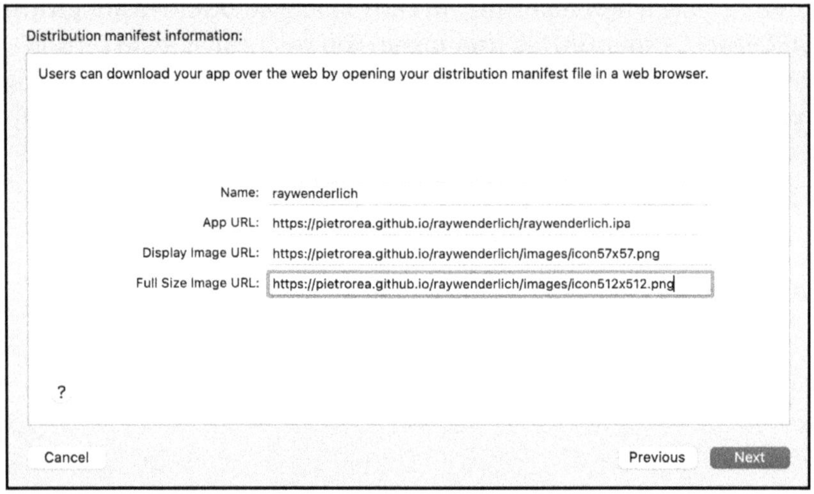

Click **Next**. Specify the same distribution certificate and provisioning profile as before. Click **Next** and save the archive to your computer.

The archive folder is almost identical to the one from earlier in the chapter, except now it also includes a file named **manifest.plist**. You need to host this XML file alongside the IPA so iOS can find, download and install the internal build.

Building a web page for OTA distribution

If you followed the Github Pages guide, you should have an HTTPS-enabled website at **https://username.github.io** powered by a folder on your computer. Navigate to this folder and create a folder named **raywenderlich**.

Next, copy the **images** folder from this chapter's resources into the new **raywenderlich** folder. Also copy **raywenderlich.ipa** and **manifest.plist** into the same folder.

Now, open your favorite text editor and create a file named **index.html**. Save it in the **raywenderlich** folder and add the following HTML:

```
<!DOCTYPE HTML>
<html lang="en-US">
    <head>
      <meta charset="UTF-8">
      <title>Internal Ad hoc Builds</title>
    </head>
    <body>
      <h1>raywenderlich iOS app</h1>
      <h2>Version 1.06 (Ad hoc)</h2>
        <li>
          Publish Date: Dec 27, 2020
        </li>
        <li>
          <a href="itms-services://?action=download-
manifest&url=https://USERNAME.github.io/raywenderlich/
manifest.plist">Install Build</a>
        </li>
        <li>
          <a href="https://github.com/razeware/emitron-iOS/
releases/tag/v1.0.6">Release Notes</a>
        </li>
    </body>
</html>
```

Replace **USERNAME** in the second **<li>** tag with your GitHub username.

This short HTML snippet is a simple, yet complete, webpage. It lists out build details for version 1.06, along with a link to download the app (second <li> item) and a link to the release notes (third <li> item).

The most important piece is the URL in the second list item: **itms-services://?action=download-manifest&url=https://USERNAME.github.io/raywenderlich/manifest.plist**.

This special URL uses the custom scheme **itms-services** instead of **https**. iOS intercepts this URL scheme and looks for the manifest file specified in the URL parameter `url`. The manifest at this location then tells iOS where to find the IPA.

When you're done, the structure of the **raywenderlich** folder should look like this:

Time to test if your internal App Store works! Commit and push your changes to GitHub, then wait a few minutes for GitHub to publish your new webpage.

Next, open **https://USERNAME.github.io/raywenderlich/index.html** in mobile Safari on your registered device, replacing **USERNAME** with your GitHub username.

It's not the most avant-garde web design in the world, but it gets the job done. Click **Install Build** to install the internal ad hoc build.

Distributing builds with third-party services

OTA wireless distribution is easier than distributing and installing IPAs manually. You simplified everything for the end-user, but at the price of making more work for yourself. Now, you have to maintain a web server. If you add features over time, you can quickly find yourself supporting a non-trivial web app.

Enterprising readers might see an opportunity. Doesn't everyone have the same problem? Couldn't you create a web app to help others distribute their IPAs internally?

That's exactly what started happening over a decade ago. Two of the most popular third-party OTA solutions were TestFlight and HockeyApp. Apple acquired TestFlight in 2014. Likewise, Microsoft acquired HockeyApp in 2014 and integrated it into Visual Studio App Center, or App Center for short.

In the following section, you'll use App Center to see how OTA distribution works with a third-party solution.

OTA distribution with AppCenter

The first thing you need to do is register for a new App Center account. Head to appcenter.ms/sign-in on your browser.

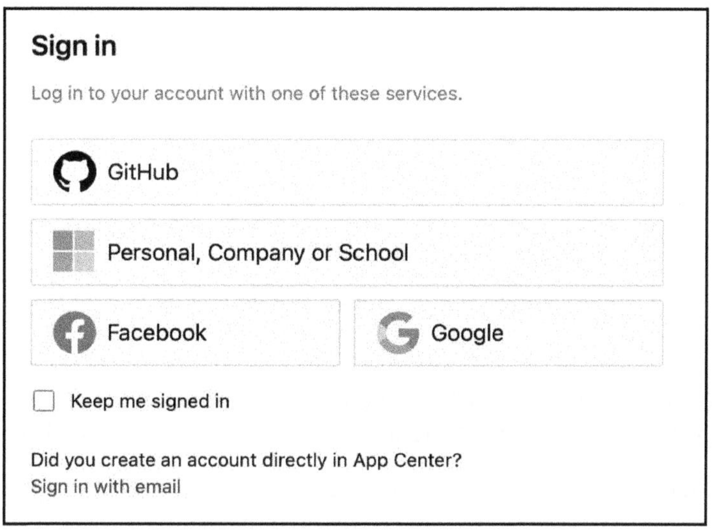

You can register and log in with the same GitHub account from the previous section or you can register using an existing Facebook or Google account. If none of those options suit you, you can also create a new Microsoft account.

After successfully logging in, click **Add new app**. Fill out the details for the raywenderlich app.

Under **App name**, type **raywenderlich.** Under **Release Type**, click the drop-down and select **Alpha**. You can leave OS and Platform set to the defaults.

Click **Add New App**. In the left menu, click **Distribute**. Next, click **New Release.**

On the following screen, click **Upload .ipa file** and select the **.ipa** file from earlier.

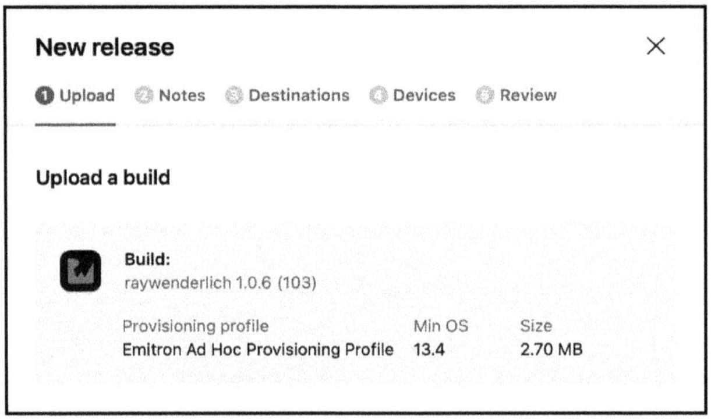

App Center guides you through a five-step process to finalize your internal release. Don't worry, you're almost done. Here are the settings you need to choose:

1. **Notes**: You can optionally add release notes, which will show up in App Center and in your build notifications. Leave the field blank for now. Click **Next.**

2. **Destinations**: Select the default **Collaborators** distribution group, which currently only includes you. The users in your distribution group should always match the registered devices in the developer portal. Click **Next.**

3. **Devices**: You don't need to do anything in this step. Click **Next.**

4. **Review**: Review your release's details. Click **Distribute**.

Notifications are one of the many benefits you get with a third-party service like App Center. Check the email you used for your new account — App Center notified you of the new release.

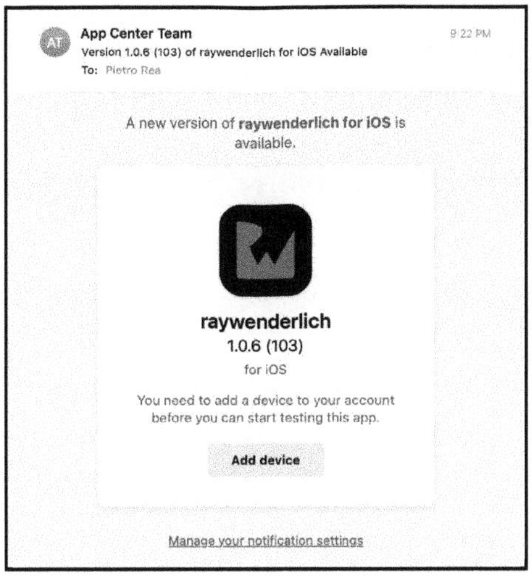

You might be wondering why the button says **Add device**. Third-party services like App Center try to be helpful by offering device management separate from Apple's developer portal. As long as you know which devices you registered, you don't need this feature.

Open this email on your registered device. Tap **Add device**, which takes you to App Center. Log in and dismiss the modal that asks if you want to register your device. Tap **emitron** under **My Apps**.

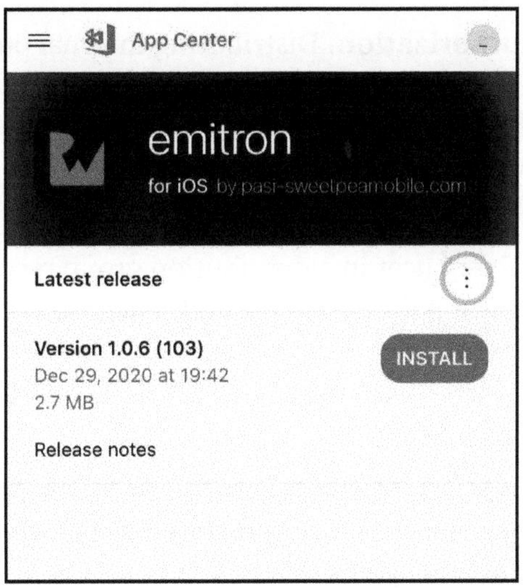

Tap **Install** to begin downloading the build. An alert shows up telling you that App Center would like to install Emitron. Tap **Install.**

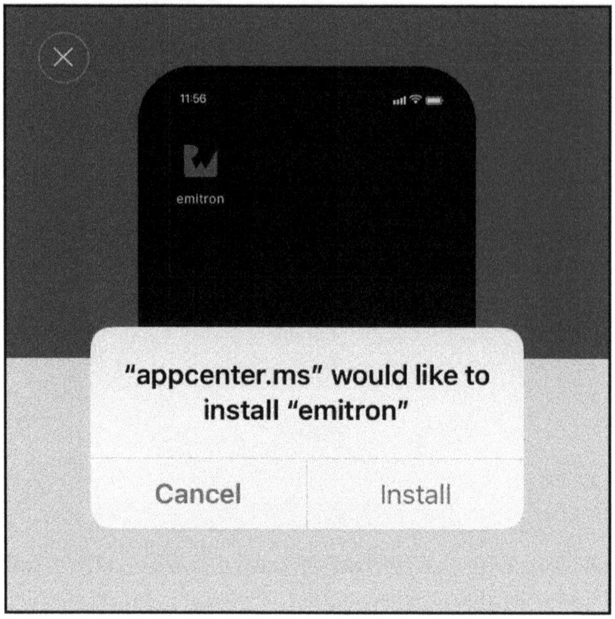

The download begins and you soon have the raywenderlich app installed on your registered device.

Getting internal builds via App Center might not seem like a significant upgrade from your GitHub Pages OTA web page. However, App Center actually did a lot on your behalf:

- **Authentication & authorization**: Distributing internal builds on a publicly-accessible web page is generally not a good idea. A bad actor could break your code signature, run your IPA on jailbroken devices or disassemble your binary to inspect your code. A third-party service like App Center limits the distribution of your ad hoc builds to users you trust.
- **Build notifications**: Every user in a distribution group receives an email notification whenever you publish a new build. There's no need to handcraft emails and attach IPAs anymore. Integrating with App Center's iOS SDK also lets you receive in-app build notifications. For more details, refer to the official documentation: http://bit.ly/3pyifg7.
- **Zero maintenance**: You don't have to write or maintain any HTML. App Center is a fully-featured web app that can accommodate diverse workflows without having to write or maintain any code yourself.

App Center's API, which you didn't get to see in this chapter, is also one of App Center's primary benefits. You can use App Center's API to programmatically upload builds as part of your build pipeline. Refer to Chapter 14, "Continuous Integration", to learn more about setting up your build pipeline.

Choosing a distribution method

You've now seen three different methods to distribute ad hoc internal builds: manually, wirelessly with your own solution and wirelessly with a third-party service. It's tempting to think that third-party services always win on features.

That's not necessarily the case, however. Each distribution method has advantages and disadvantages. Understanding how ad hoc distribution works lets you make an informed decision based on your particular use case.

For example, if you're building a side project and don't need internal testing, managing a third-party service is overkill. You might be better off sharing one-off IPAs manually, should you ever need to.

If you're deciding between different internal distribution options, wait until you read Chapter 6, "TestFlight", before finalizing your decision. TestFlight is tightly integrated with Apple's system. It doesn't offer as much flexibility as ad hoc distribution, but it could be a good fit for your app.

Key points

- Apple supports several internal distribution methods: personal team, ad hoc, TestFlight, in-house and Custom Apps.
- Ad hoc distribution lets you distribute internal builds to a maximum of 100 registered devices per device family per year.
- You can register a device in Apple's developer portal using the device's UDID.
- Generating an ad hoc provisioning profile requires an App ID, a distribution certificate and a list of registered UDIDs.
- You can distribute an ad hoc build by manually sharing the .ipa file with registered users. They can install it by connecting a registered device to a Mac and using Finder, Xcode or Apple Configurator 2.
- You can also distribute an IPA wirelessly by hosting it yourself on an HTTPS-enabled web server. You need a manifest .plist specifying the location of the IPA on the server, as well as a special **itms-services** URL.
- Third-party services like App Center and Firebase can make OTA distribution easier by providing authentication, build notifications and API integrations.

Chapter 6: TestFlight

By Pietro Rea

Ad hoc distribution is a good option for distributing internal apps to a limited audience. However, there's a catch: You can only install ad hoc builds on a maximum of 100 devices. If you work for a large organization with lots of internal users or need to accommodate numerous testers, you can quickly hit this limit.

Historically, you could get around ad hoc distribution's device limit by applying to be in the Apple Developer Enterprise Program or, more recently, by using Custom Apps distribution. With those distribution methods, you can install internal apps on an unlimited number of devices. However, you can only use them to distribute apps to employees or associates. So how could you get *external testers* to test your app and not worry about the device limit?

This is where **TestFlight** comes in. TestFlight is Apple's solution for testing apps — and it can accommodate both internal and external testers. As of this writing, TestFlight is the only officially-supported way to conduct large-scale external testing, commonly known as a **beta test**, on iOS.

TestFlight is unique among all other internal distribution methods. Before diving into specific features, it's worth going over some key differences:

- **Users instead of devices**: TestFlight follows a user-centric model instead of a device-centric model. In practice, this means you can onboard users directly instead of having to collect and register their device UDIDs. TestFlight keeps track of which users have access to which apps, so you don't have to spend time creating and managing provisioning profiles, either.
- **Two types of tester**: TestFlight supports 100 internal testers per app. Each internal tester can test on up to 30 devices. TestFlight also supports 10,000 external testers per app. You can add external testers with an email address — no Apple ID required — or with a shareable invite link.
- **System integrations**: TestFlight is so deeply integrated with the operating system and the App Store that it's difficult to know where TestFlight begins and where it ends. At the most obvious level, "TestFlight" refers to the app on the App Store that testers need to install beta apps. TestFlight also covers all related user management, build management and feedback management in App Store Connect. On top of that, TestFlight includes the system integrations that power its user-facing features, like crash reporting and analytics.
- **Regular updates**: From a developer's point of view, other types of internal distribution don't change much year to year. TestFlight is different. Apple wants TestFlight to be the de facto way to test apps. Whenever there's a new product or platform, Apple is quick to add TestFlight support. You can also expect Apple to improve TestFlight and add new features regularly. The yearly WWDC session named "What's New in App Store Connect" always covers what changed with TestFlight that year.

For this chapter, you'll use the raywenderlich.com iOS app to upload a **distribution build** to App Store Connect.

You did something similar in Chapter 5, "Internal Distribution", except you used an ad hoc provisioning profile instead of a distribution provisioning profile. The steps are almost identical, so this chapter omits them. You can refer to **Appendix A** if you need them. Make sure to upload a distribution build before moving on.

Getting started with internal testing

You need to be a registered App Store Connect user to be considered an "internal" tester. Fortunately, you don't need to register someone new for this section. You can (and should!) always add yourself as an internal tester.

Note that not all App Store Connect users can become internal testers. Only the roles of Account Holder, Admin, App Manager, Developer or Marketing are eligible. To add a new user or change an existing user's role, refer to App Store Connect's documentation: https://apple.co/3nV8pUp.

Registering testers

Now, it's time to add yourself as an internal tester. Log into **App Store Connect**. Click **My Apps**. Click the **raywenderlich.com** app record you created in Chapter 3, "Submitting Your First App for Review". Next to the main header, click the **TestFlight** tab.

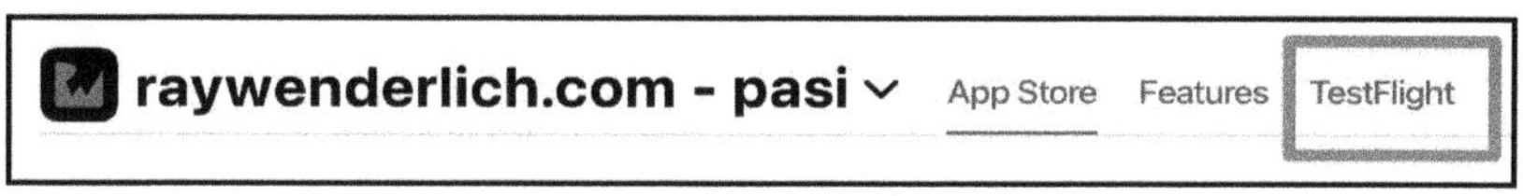

The TestFlight tab lists all the builds you've ever uploaded to App Store Connect, organized by version and build number.

> **Note**: If you're unsure where version numbers come from, a build's version and build number come from the target's **Info.plist** in Xcode. Version corresponds to the key `CFBundleShortVersionString`. Likewise, the build number corresponds to `CFBundleVersion`.

Under **Version 1.0.6**, click the **build number**. The version and build number should match the build you uploaded earlier.

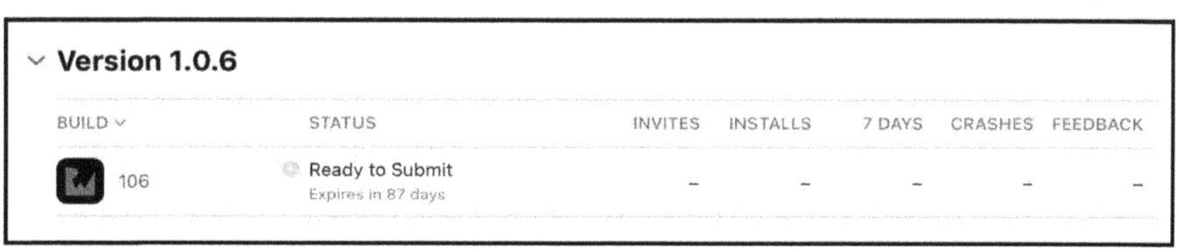

External testing supports groups of testers as well as individual testers. But when it comes to internal testing, you can only add testers to the default **App Store Connect Users** group.

Under **Internal Group**, click **App Store Connect Users.** Surprisingly, the group is empty. Shouldn't you at least see yourself?

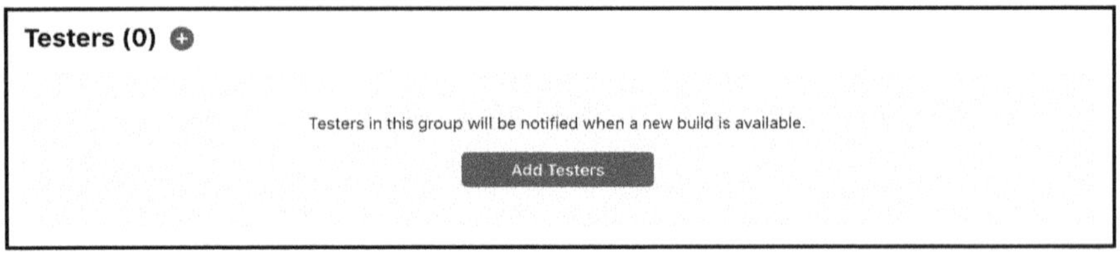

Adding internal testers is a two-step process. First, you have to register new users in App Store Connect. Second, you have to add them to the default group of internal testers.

Click **Add Testers**. On the next screen, select the checkbox next to your name. Click **Add**.

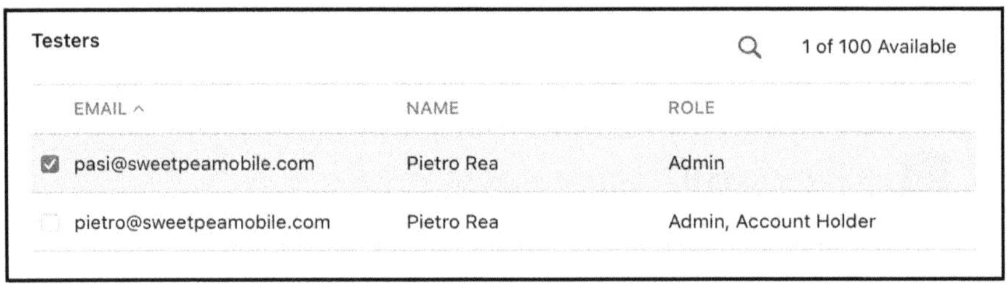

On success, App Store Connect navigates you back to the previous screen. Here, you can verify that you're now part of the default App Store Connect Users group.

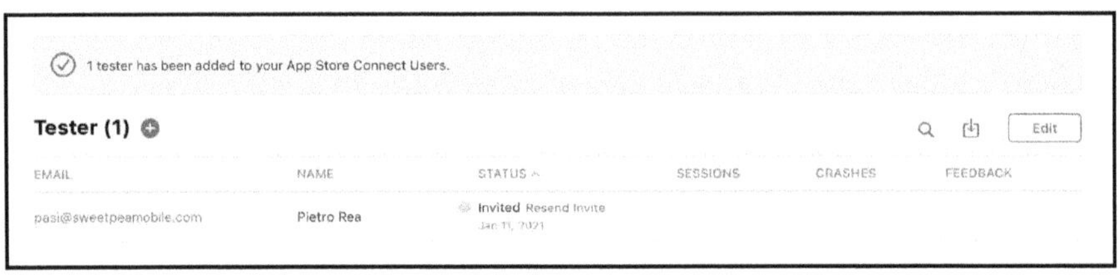

Testing an app

When you add an internal tester, Apple sends an email invite to the user's email address. Next to the user's name, the **Status** column keeps track of which users haven't accepted their invites so you can resend the invites to them. For each user, you can also see the number of times they've opened this build (sessions), as well as the number of crashes and feedback they've sent back.

Under the **Builds** section, click a **build**.

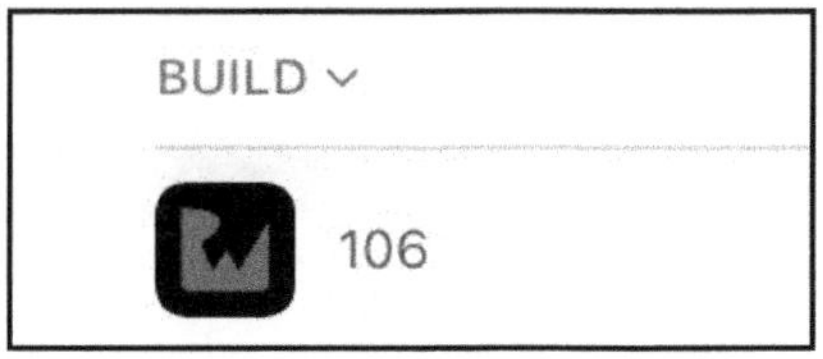

On this page, you can add notes for your testers so they know what to test. Under **Test Details**, enter something short. Click **Save**.

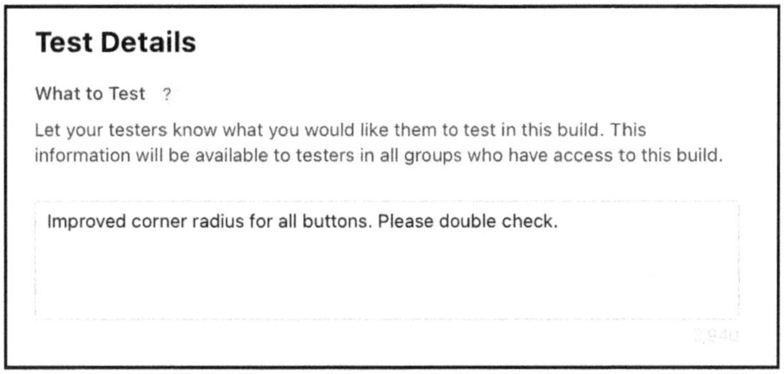

On your iOS device, open the email invite you received from TestFlight.

Tap **View in TestFlight**. If you don't have the TestFlight app, doing so takes you to the App Store. Download it and come back. If you already have the TestFlight app installed, the email link opens TestFlight directly.

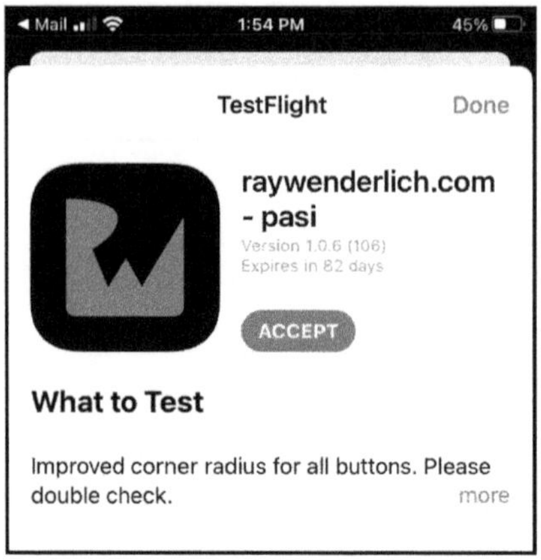

Tap **Accept**. Then tap **Install**. Tap the **Back** button to go back to the previous screen. You'll see the raywenderlich.com app listed on the main screen.

Exit the TestFlight app. Once the raywenderlich.com app finishes installing, the name of the app appears next to an orange dot.

The orange dot means that this is a TestFlight-managed app. If you've enabled App Library (iOS 14 and above), apps managed by TestFlight also show up in an app group named **TestFlight**.

TestFlight features

TestFlight supports different features to help you and your testers, which are all available for both internal and external testers. Before moving on to external testing, here are the most important ones:

1. **Redemption codes**: In case you can't access the invite email on your test device, TestFlight also supports accepting invites with a redemption code. To use redemption codes, have the tester open the invite link on a desktop computer. Opening an invite link on a web browser displays its redemption code. The TestFlight app has a **Redeem** button on its main screen.

2. **Using a different Apple ID**: The way people set up their devices can get complicated. Some users may have a personal device and a work device. Others may use one device for everything. To accommodate as many setups as possible, testers can redeem TestFlight invites even when they're logged into a different Apple ID than the one that you invited. As long as they have access to the email link or redemption code, they're good to go.

3. **Automatic updates**: In TestFlight, automatic updates are turned on by default. Whenever there's a new build available, it will download automatically and replace the old one. Testers can turn off automatic updates for a particular app in the TestFlight app.
4. **Build notifications**: TestFlight supports push and email notifications out of the box. Every time a new build becomes available for testing, testers receive email and push notifications. Testers may change their notification settings in the TestFlight app.
5. **Previous builds**: TestFlight builds are available for 90 days from the date the developer uploads them to App Store Connect. Testers can install a previous build if it falls within the 90-day window and if the developer hasn't manually expired it in App Store Connect. This is helpful when trying to determine if a bug is new or if it existed in previous builds.

TestFlight also supports rich features for reporting bugs and submitting feedback. These are also available to internal and external testers. Internal testers, however, often prefer internal channels of communication for submitting feedback. The chapter covers feedback-related features in the next section, along with external testing.

Using TestFlight for internal testing is not radically different from other internal distribution methods, such as ad hoc distribution. If you're deciding between TestFlight and ad hoc distribution for internal testing, the second to last section of this chapter covers the advantages and disadvantages of each.

Beta testing with TestFlight

In addition to internal testing, TestFlight can also help with external testing, which is also known as **beta testing**. Beta testers are closer to being "real users" than internal testers. In many cases, they are real customers that you recruited to test a future software release.

Unlike internal testers, who might literally sit next to you, beta testers have less incentive to submit feedback. To make a round of beta testing meaningful, the number of beta testers has to be much greater than the number of internal testers. TestFlight supports 10,000 beta testers per app.

Running a successful beta test is hard work. Furthermore, the technical work is minuscule compared to the coordination and communication work that needs to happen. If you want to run a beta test, expect to spend a lot of time doing the following:

- **Recruiting users**: If you have an existing customer base, you could put out a call for testers. Otherwise, you can use a public link, covered in the next section, to recruit testers from social media and the general public. Some beta tests use an intake or application process if there's a lot of interest. It's not uncommon to offer an incentive for participating, like a free copy of the app.
- **Onboarding users**: Using TestFlight isn't straightforward to everyone. Some testers might have trouble accepting the invite or downloading the TestFlight app. Others might be confused by your app. Someone on your team needs to field questions from beta testers and help them get started.
- **Triaging feedback**: Receiving feedback and bug reports is the whole point of the beta test. Once you start receiving feedback, someone needs to make sense of it. If the feedback isn't clear, someone needs to follow up with questions. If you're receiving bug reports, someone needs to reproduce the bugs and communicate with your development team.

Ongoing communication with your beta testers is key to running a successful beta test. You need to answer questions from testers, make sense of incoming feedback and work with your development team to make any improvements.

Finally, you should close the loop and ask testers to retest after you ship improvements.

TestFlight helps you by providing some tools to do this, but it cannot do the work for you.

Onboarding beta testers

After you've found a group of interested testers, there's a series of steps you have to take to give them a build to test. First, you have to add them to App Store Connect — not as full App Store Connect users, but as external testers. Dealing with so many beta testers can get unruly, especially if you're testing multiple apps at once. You can organize testers into groups or add them individually.

Before adding any beta testers, create a group. In App Store Connect, click the raywenderlich.com app's **TestFlight** tab. Next to **External Groups** in the navigation bar, click + to add a new group. Type **Beta Testers** as the Group Name. Click **Create**.

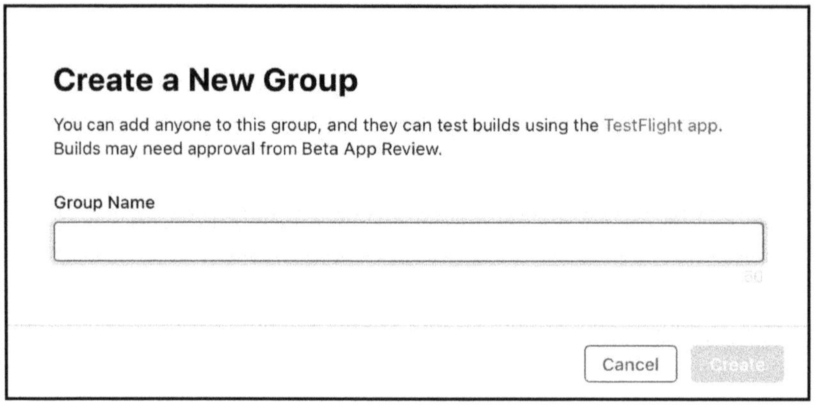

There are two ways to add beta testers. If you have a list of names and email addresses, you can add them yourself in App Store Connect. You can also let testers sign up by themselves with a public invite link.

Adding beta testers in App Store Connect

If you only have a few testers, you can add them manually by entering their names and email addresses in App Store Connect.

As you can imagine, this takes a long time when you have a lot of testers to enter. To help, App Store Connect supports adding multiple testers at once with a CSV upload.

For now, just add yourself. Under the **Testers** section, click **Add Testers**.

From the drop-down, select **Add New Testers**. Fill out the **Email** field with a secondary email address you can access. If you use a service like Gmail, you could use an email alias like **username+ailas@gmail.com**. Fill out the **First Name** and the **Last Name** fields. Finally, click **Add**.

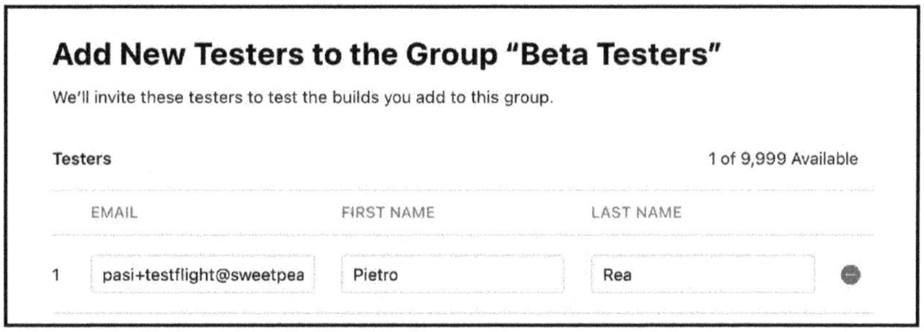

Like internal testing, you can tell if a beta tester accepted your email invite. You also have access to basic metrics for sessions, crashes and feedback.

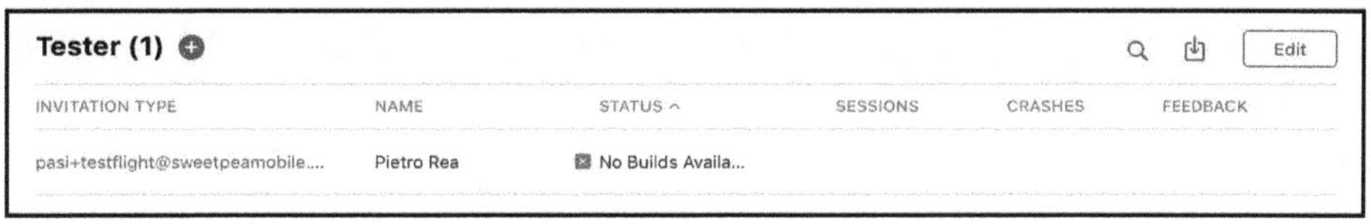

Although the build you uploaded is available to internal testers, the **Status** column for your beta tester says **No Builds Available**. Why?

Apple requires beta builds to pass **Beta App Review** before beta testers can use it. Beta App Review ensures that beta builds adhere to the App Store Review Guidelines.

Furthermore, if you check your secondary email, you won't find a TestFlight invite. TestFlight doesn't send email invites to new users until there's a build available. Once your beta build passes Beta App Review, you'll attach it to a group and TestFlight will send out invites to any beta user that needs one.

Another significant difference with internal testing is the Apple ID requirement. All internal testers need to first register as App Store Connect users, which requires an Apple ID. You can invite external testers even if they don't have an Apple ID.

> **Note**: Internal testers and external testers can test different builds at once. While a build goes through Beta App Review, and even after you distribute it to external testers, internal testers in the default **App Store Connect Users** group will continue to receive the latest builds as you upload them.

Adding beta testers with a public link

In addition to adding beta testers yourself, you can also create a shareable public link that allows anyone to join your beta test. If you don't already have a pool of users to draw from, opening your beta test to the public can help. Keep in mind that the testers that join your beta program count against your limit of 10,000 external testers.

There are some drawbacks to using a public link. Most obviously, you lose some control. You can't control how others share the link once you publish it, nor can you control who signs up or vet them in any way before they do.

Additionally, when someone joins a Testflight beta through a public link, they're added as anonymous testers. You won't know these testers' names or email addresses unless they choose to share their contact information when they submit feedback via TestFlight.

> **Note**: You can only create public links if you have at least one build approved by Beta App Review.

Click the **Beta Testers** group name. Under **Public Link**, click **Enable Public Link**.

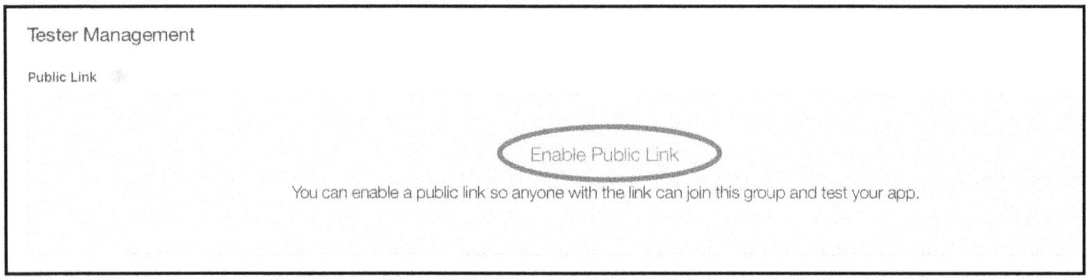

App Store Connect confirms you want to proceed. Then, under **Public Link**, a link with this format appears: `https://testflight.apple.com/join/{identifier}`.

If you're worried that your beta build might get a lot of attention, you can cap the number of testers that can sign up using the public link by clicking **Set limit**. Once you have enough beta testers, you can also disable a public link altogether by clicking **Disable Link**.

Submitting for Beta App Review

Adding beta testers won't do any good if they don't have a build to test. A build needs to pass Beta App Review before it becomes available to external testers.

Only the first build of a version needs a review. Subsequent builds don't need a review as long as the version is the same. For example, if version 1.1 (1) passed Beta App Review, version 1.1 (2) won't need one. Beta review times vary but they're generally shorter than going through the full, non-beta App Review.

Submitting a build for Beta App Review is part of adding a build to a group. Back in App Store Connect, navigate to the **Beta Testers** group. Under the heading **Builds**, click **Add Build**.

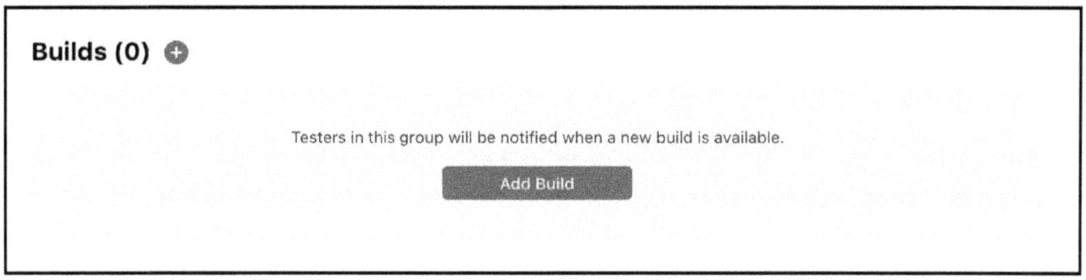

Select the radio button next to **Build 106**. Click **Next**.

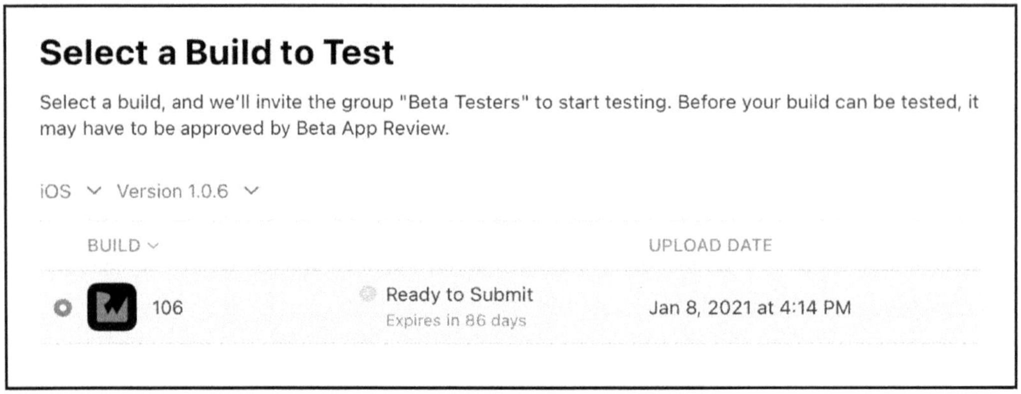

Fill out the **Test Information** form, including the **Feedback Email** and **Contact Information** fields. Click **Next**.

On the next screen, under **What to Test**, type in short release notes. Leave the checkbox next to **Automatically notify testers** selected.

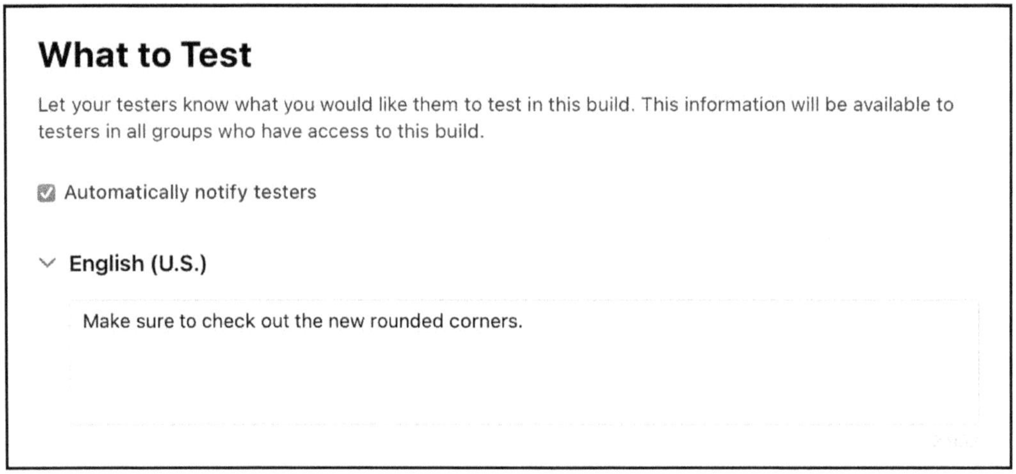

If you were doing this for a real app, the next step would be to click **Submit for Review**. However, real Apple employees go over Beta App Review submissions, so **don't submit** this build for review.

Once the app has passed Beta App Review, you'll receive an email confirmation. If you selected **Automatically notify testers**, your beta testers will also receive notification emails. If you didn't select this option, you have to go back to App Store Connect to start testing. Your beta testers will receive an email at that point.

Collecting TestFlight feedback

Collecting tester feedback is the whole point of testing. TestFlight supports different ways to submit feedback, but some of them are so deeply integrated into the operating system that they're easy to miss. You can save a lot of time by documenting the next few sections in your own words for your testers.

Sending feedback

If you see a bug in an app and want to it show someone else, what's the first thing you do? You take a screenshot. That's exactly how the first way to submit feedback from a TestFlight app starts.

Try it now. Open the **raywenderlich.com** app. Take a **screenshot**. Then quickly tap the **screenshot preview** to open it in Markup. Here, you can mark up the screenshot with the built-in tools.

> **Note**: How you take a screenshot depends on the device you have. Some testers might need help figuring out how to do it. It helps to keep Apple's documentation handy so you can share it with your testers: http://apple.co/3qhXHck.

There are two ways to send feedback from Markup. To see the first way, tap **Done** in the upper-left corner. Doing so opens an action sheet with options. Tap **Share Beta Feedback...**.

To see the second way to send feedback from Markup, tap the **Action** button in the upper-right corner. You can submit feedback from here as well. Tap **Share Beta Feedback**.

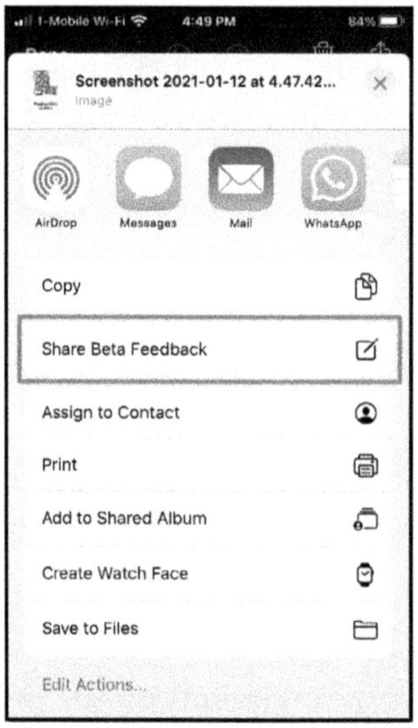

Doing so brings up a feedback screen that includes your screenshot. Tap the area above the screenshot to start typing. Enter something short and tap **Submit**.

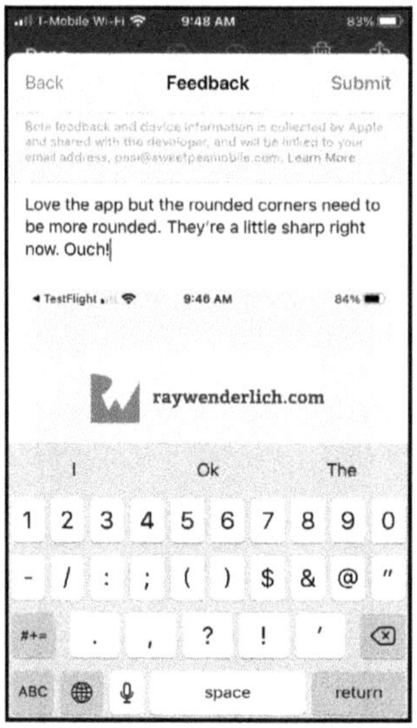

If you took a screenshot but forgot to send it, you can do it later from the TestFlight app.

Try that now. Open the **TestFlight** app. Tap **raywenderlich.com**. Tap **Send Beta Feedback.**

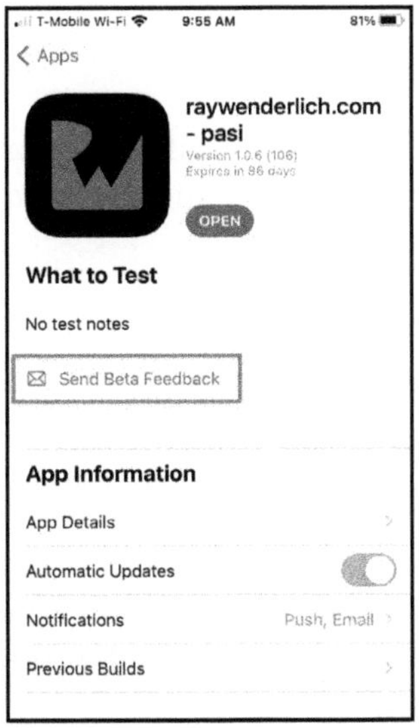

TestFlight asks you if you want to include a screenshot. Say yes, and you can choose any photo from your photo library. You can also send feedback without a screenshot. Tap **Don't Include Screenshot** in the action sheet to try that.

Enter something short in the text field. Tap **Submit**.

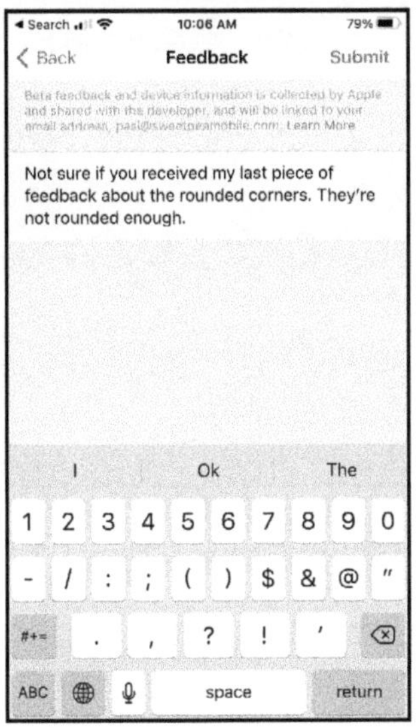

All the feedback that testers submit via TestFlight ends up in App Store Connect, where you can view it or export it.

Sending crash reports

Despite your team's best efforts, your app will crash sometimes. Every time this happens, some unlucky user is summarily and unceremoniously kicked out of your app and onto their home screen.

Beta testing is a great way to find crashes that you overlooked during development or internal testing. Fortunately, TestFlight also supports crash reporting.

Unbeknownst to you, the starter project you used to create and upload a build is *not the exact* copy of version 1.0.6. It has a defect that makes the app crash every time you try to sign in. Whoops!

Try it now. Open the **raywenderlich.com** app. Tap **Sign In**. The app exits and you're faced with an alert asking if you want to share additional information with the developer. Tap **Share**.

On the feedback screen, enter something short. Tap **Submit**.

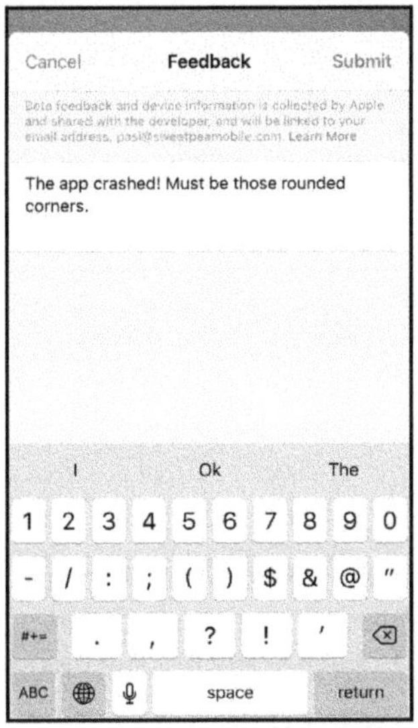

Sharing crashes with developers is optional, so when you onboard beta testers, instruct testers to share crash reports as often as possible.

Collecting feedback

App Store Connect has a section that aggregates all feedback and crash reports. In the previous two sections, you submitted feedback with and without a screenshot, along with a crash report. Now, you'll see where you can find this information.

Open the app's page in **App Store Connect**. Click the **TestFlight** tab. On the left menu, under **Feedback**, click **Screenshots**.

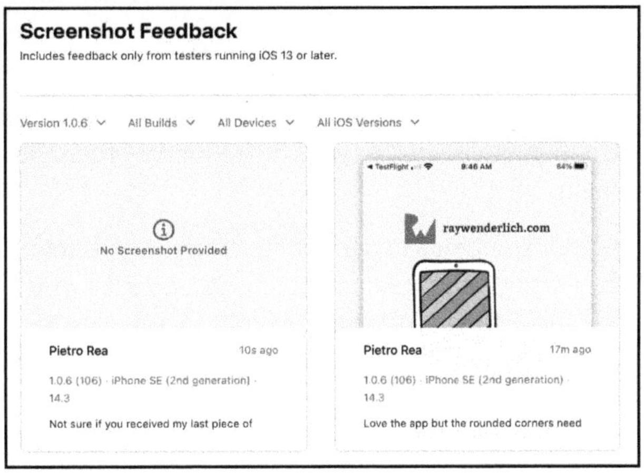

This page aggregates all feedback sent from the TestFlight app as well as feedback sent immediately after taking a screenshot. Note that the name of the page is slightly misleading. Even feedback that doesn't contain a screenshot ends up here.

Now, turn your attention to the crash you experienced earlier. On the left menu, under **Feedback**, click **Crashes**. The crash feedback page is where you can find all crash reports.

Click the single **crash report** for version 1.0.6. The crash detail page has useful troubleshooting information about the device that sent the crash report. Click the **Download** button in the top-right corner.

Unzip **testflight/_feedback.zip**. The resulting folder contains two files: **crashlog.crash** and **feedback.json**. Open **crashlog.crash**.

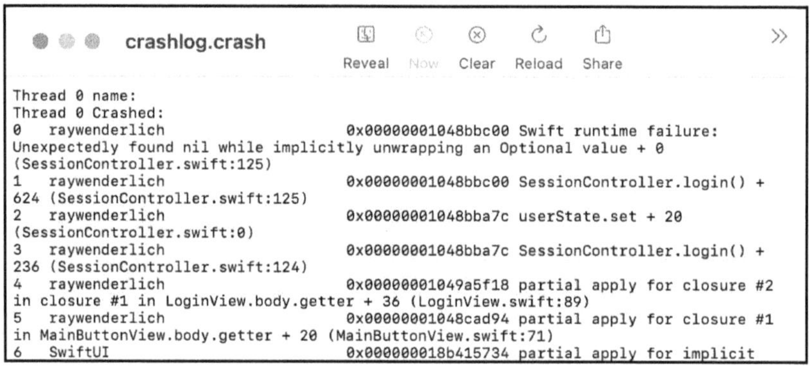

This is a symbolicated stack trace. It's like a trail of breadcrumbs that the app left before it crashed. Sending .crash files to your development team helps diagnose and, eventually, fix the crash.

As a developer, you can also open a .crash file in Xcode. Try it now. Right-click **crashlog.crash**. Select **Open With**. Select **Xcode**. Xcode asks which project it should use to open the .crash file. Select **emitron**.

Doing so opens a debugging session in Xcode's Debug navigator, as if you had crashed while running the app locally. It even highlights the line where the crash occurred.

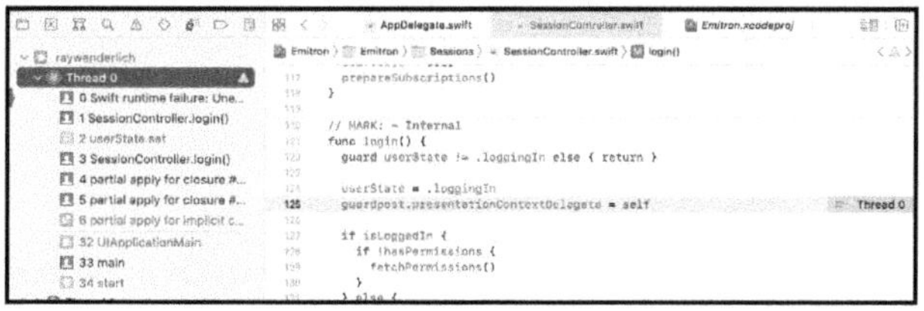

You can also download TestFlight and App Store crash reports from Xcode's Organizer window. As of this writing, downloading them manually from App Store Connect is the most reliable way to collect them.

TestFlight versus ad hoc

TestFlight is the only option if you want to run a large beta test on iOS, but when it comes to internal testing, you have more choices. The previous chapter covered ad hoc distribution and this chapter did the same for TestFlight. If you're deciding which one to use for internal testing, here are three things to consider:

1. **Flexibility**: Ad hoc distribution wins on flexibility. With ad hoc distribution you can use a third-party solution like Firebase or AppCenter, which support a wide variety of use cases, or you can build your own over-the-air (OTA) solution tailored to your specific needs. TestFlight has a growing set of features and APIs, but you're always constrained by what Apple provides.

2. **Speed**: Ad hoc distribution wins again. With ad hoc distribution, you're only constrained by Xcode build times. As soon as you have an IPA, you can upload it to a third-party service or host it yourself and you're done. With TestFlight, there's an additional processing step once your build reaches Apple's servers. It usually takes only a few minutes, but it can sometimes take longer. The size of your team and the frequency of your builds will determine how much this matters to you.

3. **Simplicity**: TestFlight wins the medal for simplicity. It's simpler to add users to TestFlight than it is to collect, register and manage device UDIDs. TestFlight is also the simplest option for developers. In fact, TestFlight doesn't require *any* additional development work to use — not even linking against a new framework in Xcode. This also means TestFlight requires zero ongoing maintenance.

Smaller teams tend to prefer TestFlight for its simplicity. As your internal distribution needs grow, larger organizations tend to prefer third-party ad hoc distribution solutions. The largest organizations typically benefit the most from building and maintaining custom OTA solutions.

Key points

- TestFlight is a good solution if you hit the device limit in ad hoc distribution or want to run a beta test with external testers.
- Internal testers need to be registered App Store Connect users on your account.
- Internal and external testers receive an email invite. Tapping the email's invite link prompts them to download the TestFlight app and install the build.
- Running a successful beta test requires a lot of time to recruit and onboard testers, triage feedback and manage ongoing communications.
- You can add external testers manually in App Store Connect. Another option is to create and share a public link, which anyone can use to sign up for your beta.
- Unlike internal testing, Apple requires beta builds to pass Beta App Review before external testers can use the build. Beta builds must also adhere to the App Store Review Guidelines.
- Testers can submit feedback by either taking a screenshot while using the TestFlight build or using the TestFlight app. TestFlight also supports sharing crash reports.
- You can use TestFlight or ad hoc distribution for internal testing. Ad hoc distribution is faster and more flexible, but TestFlight is simpler to use, implement and manage.

Chapter 7: Preparing for App Review

By Pietro Rea

Getting through App Review is one of the most confusing and stressful things about publishing an app to the App Store. Even a decade later, App Review continues to be shrouded in mystery. Apple is prolific about *how* to pass App Review but publishes almost nothing about *what* it is.

Here's what we do know: Apple hires and trains employees whose main responsibility is to review incoming app submissions. These reviewers make sure submissions adhere to the App Store Review Guidelines. If something falls in a gray area, which is not uncommon, they make a judgment call. App Review also includes automated checks to catch things that would be hard for a human to detect, such as the use of private APIs.

If you do get slapped with a rejection, you can use the Resolution Center in App Store Connect to work it out with Apple. If you have broader disagreements with the guidelines, you can also make an appeal to the App Review Board.

It's difficult to internalize all the guidelines you need to follow. App Review is based on long documents that change frequently and are sometimes hard to understand. The good news is that you don't have to be an expert. Understanding the guiding principles behind them can help you sail through App Review, even as the specific guidelines evolve over time.

Apple doesn't publish its guiding principles, so the following comes from real-world experience and a close reading of the guidelines:

1. **Provide value**: Apps need to be useful, unique and provide lasting value. Apple won't accept your app if it's simply a wrapper around a static website. You might also run into trouble if you're building an app in a category that's already saturated — think flashlight apps — without adding anything new.

2. **Ensure quality**: App Review rejects apps that crash, don't work correctly or look incomplete. All metadata must include fully-functional URLs. Scrub all placeholder content, like "Lorem Ipsum", and stock images. Also, make sure you keep up with the latest SDKs and platform requirements. From time to time, Apple purges old apps that don't work anymore from the App Store.

3. **Don't cheat**: Don't try to circumvent or cheat the App Review process. Use Apple's platform capabilities in the way Apple intended. If you do get creative, don't do it maliciously. Don't take advantage of users, harm them or profit from them unfairly.

4. **Respect users**: Beyond the mandate not to cheat or harm your users, Apple also wants you to respect their data and privacy. Properly ask for permission when requesting sensitive information. Assume they don't want to see offensive or questionable content. Don't track them if you don't need to. Be extra careful if you build apps for kids.

5. **Assume full responsibility**: You're responsible for everything that happens in your app, even if it's driven by back-end systems or third parties. As an example, if you show user-generated content, Apple expects you to provide some measure of content moderation. Ensure that all software frameworks and dependencies also adhere to the App Store Review Guidelines.

At the end of the day, Apple wants the App Store to be a safe and healthy ecosystem. Apple wants users to feel safe as they discover and download any of the nearly two million apps in its App Store catalog. Doing so keeps users coming back, which benefits Apple as well as third-party developers (that's you!).

Following the App Store Review Guidelines

The guiding principles mentioned above help you understand the guidelines and anticipate changes, but they can only take you so far. Sometimes you can't predict what Apple's guidelines have to say about your particular use case. The only way to find out is to read them.

For example, did you know that you cannot use Location Services to control an aircraft?

> **5.1.5 Location Services**
>
> "Location-based APIs shouldn't be used to provide emergency services or autonomous control over vehicles, aircraft, and other devices, except for small devices such as lightweight drones and toys, or remote control car alarm systems, etc."

However, most developers have never read the App Store Review Guidelines. When most people think about them, they picture a dense legal document. That's not the case at all. They're written in plain, easy-to-understand language. Sometimes the language is so direct it's funny. For example, here's what Apple has to say about non-essential apps:

> **4.3 Spam**
>
> "... the App Store has enough fart, burp, flashlight, fortune telling, dating, and Kama Sutra apps, etc. already. We will reject these apps unless they provide a unique, high-quality experience."

If you're in the business of making apps, particularly if you decide *what* to make, it behooves you to read the App Store Review Guidelines. That gives you an intuition about what's possible on Apple's platforms.

You should also read the guidelines if you plan on doing something that no one's ever done before on the App Store. Before you invest time and money into a project, wouldn't you like to know in advance if Apple will accept your app?

Unfortunately, Apple never gives you pre-approval. They tell you to develop your app and submit it for review. A close reading of the App Store Review Guidelines is your only recourse if you want to do something radically different.

Reading the guidelines

The App Store Review Guidelines contain the bulk of the information you need to know, but it also links to a handful of other documents. There seem to be guidelines for everything. Some tell you what you shouldn't do, while others amount to gentler recommendations about how you should build your app. Here's a list of the most important documents:

App Store Review Guidelines

https://apple.co/36hVYg4

This document is the holy grail for all App Review questions. The structure of the document gives you an idea of the breadth and reach of App Review. There are five big sections: Safety, Performance, Business, Design and Legal. Apple also provides guidance about what to do before and after you submit to App Review.

Apple Developer Program License Agreement

https://apple.co/36iA78f

You accepted the license agreement when you joined the Apple Developer Program. The license agreement covers more ground than just App Review. The sections that deal with App Review often include more details than the review guidelines themselves. The license agreement reads more like a legal document, but it's accessible even if you're not a lawyer.

Human Interface Guidelines

https://apple.co/3jfeSYS

The App Store Review Guidelines and the license agreement largely outline what you shouldn't do. The Human Interface Guidelines (HIG) tell you how you *should* build your apps. Apple's HIG contains everything from abstract design themes, like clarity, deference and depth for iOS, to concrete advice on how to use UI controls.

In the past, Apple was more likely to reject apps for violating the HIG but, anecdotally, it's not as common anymore. Unless your app is completely unusable, you have some leeway on product design. Everyone making apps for Apple's platforms should also read the HIG at least once.

Brand and Marketing Guidelines

How you market your app is mostly up to you, except when it comes to Apple's brands and products. Apple publishes guidelines for using its brand, trademark and products in your marketing materials, such as your website and emails. There are also marketing guidelines specific to Apple Pay and Apple Wallet.

- **Marketing Resources and Identity Guidelines**: https://apple.co/3pgoDc7
- **Apple Pay Marketing Guidelines**: https://apple.co/3pewvLl
- **Add to Apple Wallet Guidelines**: https://apple.co/3p9vCnf
- **Guidelines for Using Apple Trademarks and Copyrights**: https://apple.co/3699Pof

Apple won't search through your website and emails looking for violations. However, if you deviate from Apple's marketing guidelines in your App Store Connect screenshots or inside the app itself, you run the risk of getting a rejection.

Submitting to App Review

Chapter 3, "Submitting Your First App for Review", walks you through how to submit an app for review once you have a build and app record in App Store Connect. Refer to it if you need a refresher on the basics.

This section covers more advanced options that the earlier chapter didn't have space to cover. Before moving on, make sure you're familiar with this diagram from that chapter:

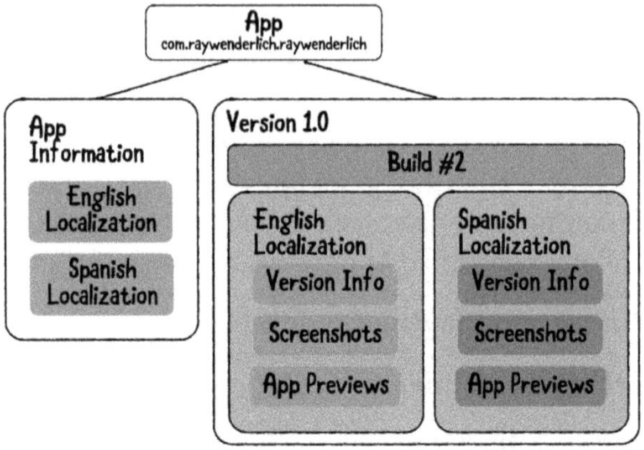

An app submission contains several parts: app-level information (left box), version-level information and a build (right box). Another way to say it is that App Review's jurisdiction includes both the actual app and all the metadata that comes with it.

Any piece of your submission can hold up the entire submission. For example, even if your app is perfectly compliant, a single screenshot in App Store Connect can be grounds for rejection.

The rest of this section is an overview of the advanced options you can set on your app submission. Apple only lets you change many of them when you submit an update for review. These are all options that affect the outcome of App Review or how you release the app afterward. As such, there's no sample project to follow along with.

Add-ons

An iOS app can be associated with a macOS app, tvOS app or watchOS app, as well as an App Clip, iMessage app and one or more In-App Purchases. Apple has guidelines for all of these add-ons, so you can only start offering them after going through App Review.

You can use the same App ID from your iOS app to publish a macOS or tvOS app. Even though apps for different platforms can share the same App ID, you must submit each platform-specific app separately.

> **Note**: Even though Apple sometimes refers to iPadOS as a separate platform from iOS, iPad apps and iOS apps are bundled into a single, universal binary that you submit to App Review. Reviewers review your iPhone app and your iPad app at the same time.

To add another platform in App Store Connect, go to your app record page. In the sidebar, click **Add macOS App** or **Add tvOS App**, depending on what you need.

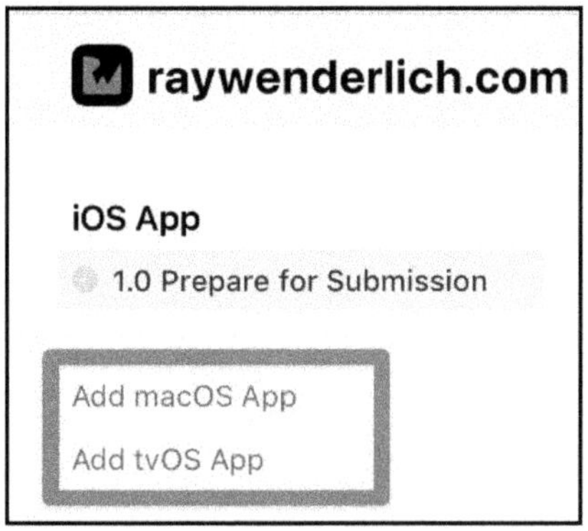

An iOS app may also contain an App Clip, an iMessage app and a watchOS app. From a code perspective, these are additional **build targets** that you ship alongside the main app's target. Unlike macOS and tvOS companion apps, you don't need separate builds to support them. These additional targets come bundled in the iOS build that you upload to App Store Connect.

If you do ship an App Clip, iMessage app or watchOS app, you must fill the corresponding sections on your app's version page in App Store Connect.

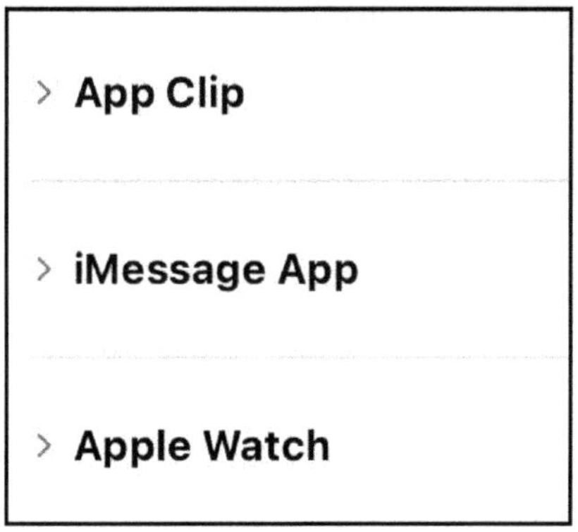

Refer to Apple's documentation for more information about submitting an App Clip, watchOS app or iMessage app with your iOS app.

- **iMessage Apps and Stickers**: https://apple.co/39EX32P
- **Distributing your App Clip**: https://apple.co/3oOzppe
- **Submit your watchOS apps to the App Store**: https://apple.co/36CRVKJ

Lastly, you can offer In-App Purchases (IAPs) in your app. IAPs allow your customers to buy additional digital content inside your app. You can use four types of IAP: consumables, non-consumables, auto-renewable subscriptions and non-renewing subscriptions.

You first have to create each IAP in App Store Connect. To do so, go to your app record page. In the sidebar, under **In-App Purchases**, click **Manage**. Click + to get started.

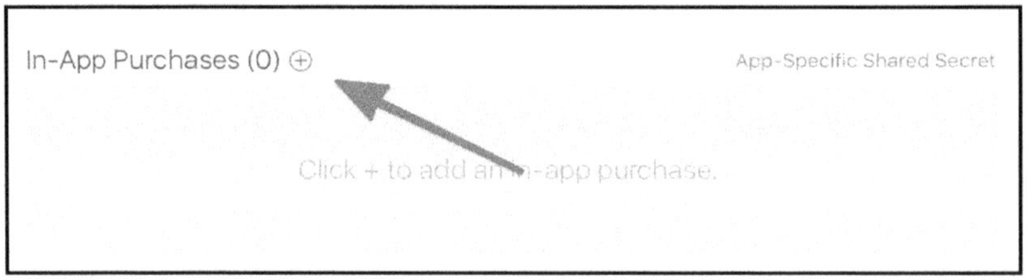

There's a review process for each IAP you offer your customers. If you're submitting your first IAP, you must submit it alongside a new version of your app. After the first one, Apple reviews IAPs separate from the full App Review process.

In-App Purchase is a large topic. Creating them in App Store Connect, integrating your app with the StoreKit framework and testing IAPs all take special consideration. Refer to Apple's documentation to learn more:

- **Offer In-App Purchases**: https://apple.co/36BRiBd
- **In-App Purchase Programming Guide**: https://apple.co/39F1ESD

App Review Information

Reviewers want to go through your app as a regular user would. If your app requires signing in, you need to create a test account in your production environment that reviewers can use.

To provide login information:

1. Open your app's version page on App Store Connect.
2. Scroll down to the **App Review Information** section.
3. Check the checkbox next to **Sign-in required**.
4. Type the login information in the **Notes** section.
5. Fill out the required **Contact Information** fields, in case someone from Apple needs to reach out with questions.

Use the Notes section to communicate any app-specific settings or anything else a reviewer might need to review your app fully. This information carries over from version to version, but you can update it at any time.

Pre-orders

Before releasing your app for the first time, you can publish it on the App Store as a pre-order. During the pre-order period, users can sign up on your App Store product page. Once you officially release the app, customers that signed up for the pre-order receive a notification and your app downloads automatically to their device. If you have a paid app, users get charged for your app at that time as well.

To submit your app to App Review as a pre-order, click **Pricing and Availability** on the sidebar. Then, check the box next to **Make available for pre-order**.

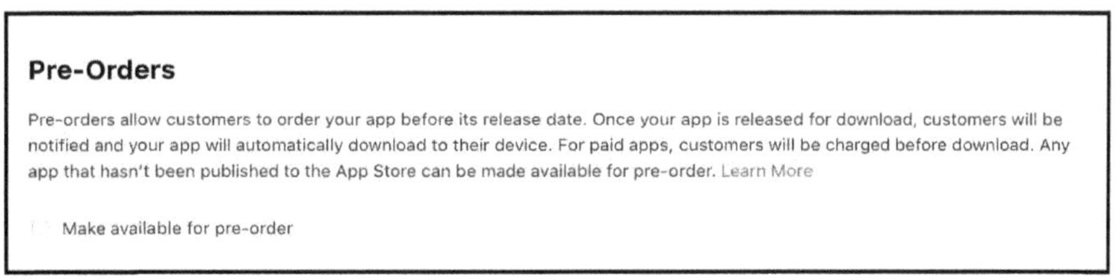

You can continue publishing new builds during the pre-order period, but new versions have to go through App Review again. Users receive the latest version of your app once you officially release it. Publishing your app as a pre-order is a good way to drum up demand and start getting the word out while you wrap up development.

Availability

One of the benefits of the App Store is reaching customers worldwide. By default, your app is available in all countries and regions, which covers 175 territories as of this writing. However, you can deselect territories where you don't want your app to be available.

Why might you want to do this? Each territory has different laws and regulations governing the entities that do business within its borders. If it's too difficult to adhere to the rules in a particular territory, companies often hold back their app.

To change your app's availability, go to your app record page in App Store Connect. On the sidebar, click **Pricing and Availability**. Click **Edit** to deselect territories.

Version Release options

When App Review approves your app, it doesn't automatically go live in the App Store. There are three release options you can choose from.

To see your options, click the version you want to set a release option for. Scroll down to the **Version Release** section.

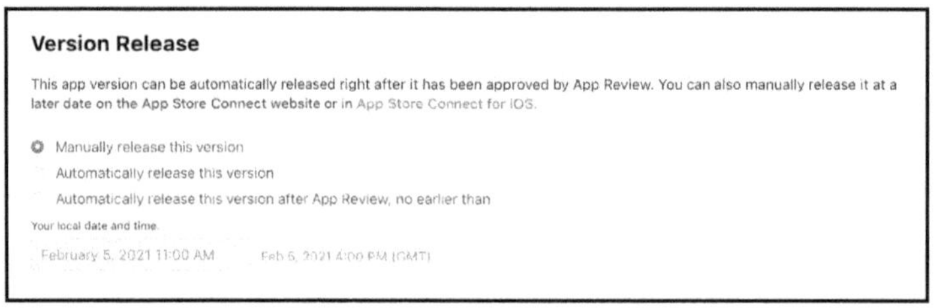

Here's what the options mean:

1. **Manually release this version**: After approval, you have to go back into App Store Connect to release your app officially. This is convenient if you need to perform last-minute sanity checks or coordinate with other team members.
2. **Automatically release this version**: You authorize Apple to release your app to the public as soon as it's approved without additional intervention from you. It takes up to 24 hours for Apple to fully distribute your app worldwide, but this is the fastest option available. This is a good option for time-sensitive updates.
3. **Automatically release this version after App Review, no earlier than**: This option is similar to automatically releasing your app, but it lets you hold back the release until a predetermined date in the future. Waiting for App Review to finish can take you past this date, which is why the option says "no earlier than".

After your initial release, you can do **phased** releases over a seven-day period to an increasing percentage of your users that have turned on **automatic downloads**. On the first day of the phased release, 1% of these users get the app's new version. This percentage grows over the span of seven days until all users that turned on automatic updates have it.

You can also pause a phased release if you find a problem. This is a good option if your update is risky in some way. Make sure to monitor your analytics and customer feedback during the seven-day period to react appropriately.

Note: Doing a phased release in App Store Connect is the only officially sanctioned way to release an update gradually.

App Store Review Guidelines, under Section 2, Performance, states:

2.3.1 Don't include any hidden, dormant, or undocumented features in your app; your app's functionality should be clear to end-users and App Review.

Many companies ship a feature "dark" and gradually turn it on after the app is on the App Store. Even though this is a common practice, it's technically against the App Store Review Guidelines. You can find some useful Q&A in Apple Developer Forum around this with comments from Apple that provide more context and tips to properly use this approach without violating App Store Review Guidelines.

Ratings and reviews

Customers have the option to rate your app on a scale from 1 to 5. They can also write reviews, which you can respond to in App Store Connect. Your App Store product page shows a summary rating as well as all customer reviews and any responses from you.

For example, here's what ratings and reviews look like for the official raywenderlich.com iOS app:

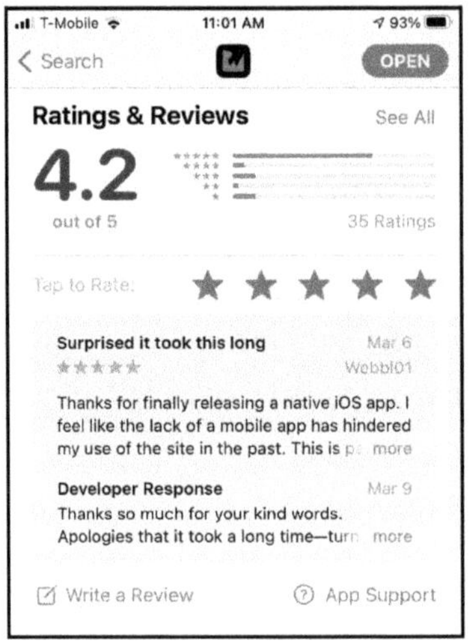

Positive ratings and reviews make new customers feel comfortable downloading your app for the first time. However, negative reviews keep people away. Fortunately, if you've worked hard to address customer feedback, there's a way to reset your app's summary rating when you release a new version.

To do so, click the version you're submitting to App Review. Under **Reset iOS Summary Rating**, select **Reset rating when this version is released**.

> **Note**: The option to reset your summary rating only shows up in App Store Connect after your initial release.

After App Review, your summary rating on your App Store product page will reset when you release the new version. Customer reviews always remain unchanged.

Expedited App Review

App Review doesn't start immediately after you click the **Submit** button. Your app submission goes into a queue. Depending on the volume of submissions and other unpublished factors, App Review can finish the same day you submit or take days or weeks.

Apple gives no guarantees about the speed of App Review, but it does publish some guidance. As of this writing, Apple states that it reviews 50% of apps within 24 hours and over 90% within 48 hours.

Although you probably wish that every review could finish in record time, sometimes you have to release a truly time-sensitive update. For example, suppose you discover a critical bug or security vulnerability that puts your entire business at risk. In that case, you'll want to distribute the bug fix to your customers as quickly as humanly possible.

In those cases, you can request an expedited app review. Apple cannot guarantee that it'll honor every request, but it's worth asking. Once you submit your app for review, log into the developer portal. In the sidebar, click **Contact Us**. Select **App Review**, then select **Expedited App Review Request**. Here's a direct link to this page: https://apple.co/2LvTD9y.

Fill out your contact information and your app's information. Select a reason for the request and provide a written explanation.

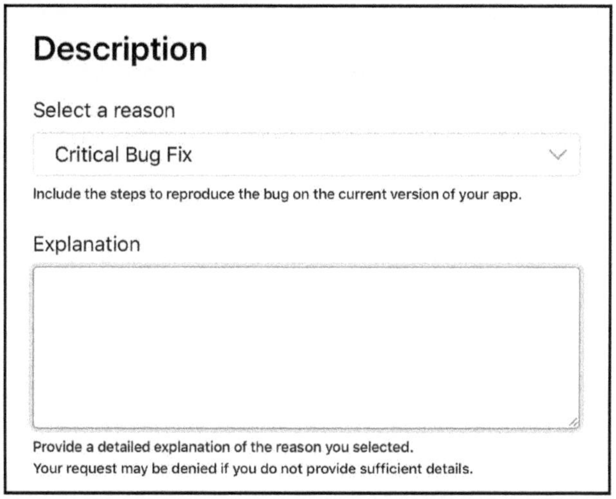

Make sure to provide enough context in your explanation, especially if the reason for the request is not a critical bug fix or a time-sensitive event. Otherwise, Apple may deny your request.

Understanding app statuses

Submitting an app to App Review is a complex, multi-step process, and knowing what to do next isn't always clear. Sometimes, Apple is waiting on you to do something. Other times, you're waiting on Apple. To help move things along, you can consult your submission's app status.

The app status is prominently displayed in several places. In App Store Connect, app status first makes an appearance on the top-level **Apps** page under your app icon. When you click your app, app status also shows up on the sidebar next to the version number.

There are 17 different app statuses in total. Here are the most important ones:

- **Prepare for Submission**: You've created a new version of your app in App Store Connect but haven't submitted it for review.
- **Waiting for Review**: You submitted your app for review. Apple received it but it's still waiting in the queue.
- **In Review**: Apple is actively reviewing your submission! Anecdotally, most of the waiting happens in **Waiting for Review**. Once you're **In Review**, you'll get an answer fast.
- **Pending Developer Release**: Hooray! Apple accepted your app, but you still need to go into App Store Connect to release it manually. You'll only see this status if you selected **Manually release this version** as your version release option.

- **Ready for Sale**: The wording of this status is a bit unintuitive. It really means "Finally on the App Store!". This status means either you or Apple released the approved app to the App Store. When you see this status, you can celebrate.
- **Rejected**: Your app didn't pass App Review. The next section deals with how to work through an app rejection. Also, look out for a related status, **Metadata Rejected**. It also means Apple rejected your submission.

> **Note**: Don't confuse "app status" with "build status". App status applies to the entire app submission, which includes the build, metadata and App Store Connect configuration. Each build you upload also has its own status — for example, **Processing**, **Invalid Binary**, etc. Read more about build statuses here: https://apple.co/2Ls0yjV.

App status is the primary way Apple communicates with you. Whenever an app submission moves from one status to the next, Apple sends an email notification to all App Store Connect users with access to the app. If they have the App Store Connect iOS app, they'll also receive a push notification. To read more about app statuses, refer to App Store Connect's documentation: https://apple.co/2YRwSQv.

Resolving app rejection issues

Even experienced developers have their apps rejected from time to time. Knowing what to expect and how to react can help you unblock yourself quickly.

You'll first hear about the rejection from an app status notification. Your new app status will be either **Rejected** or **Metadata Rejected**.

To see what the problem is, log into App Store Connect and click the version that received the rejection. The following two screenshots come from Apple's documentation. The red banner on the version page indicates there are one or more issues that need your attention. Click **1 unresolved iOS issues**.

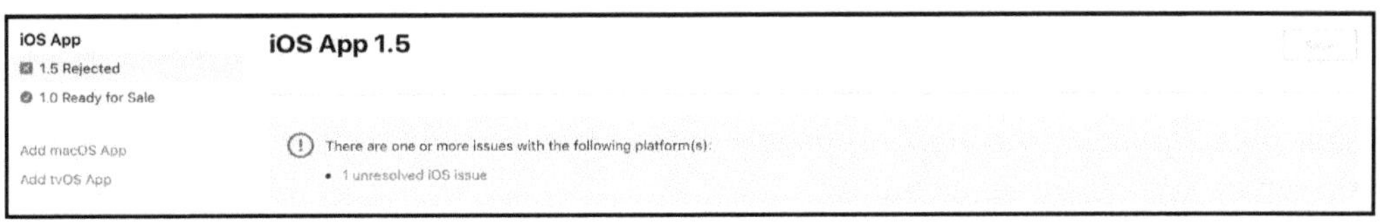

Doing so opens **Resolution Center**. Each rejection has an entry on the left, which corresponds to a thread between you and Apple on the right.

Apple starts off the conversation by telling you about the issue they found. The amount of information you get about the issue varies. Sometimes, Apple simply links to a section of the App Store Review Guidelines without additional context. In other cases, Apple uploads screenshots of what the reviewer saw and provides debugging information.

Before making any changes, make sure you understand the problem as Apple reported it. Resolution Center is a tool for you to communicate with Apple. It gives you a few options. You can:

- Request more information if you're not clear about the issue.
- Tell Apple that you disagree with the rejection and provide your rationale.
- Request to speak with someone from App Review on the phone if you're having trouble getting your point across.

Once you understand the rejection and what Apple wants to see changed, move on to fixing the problem. The app status **Rejected** means there's a problem with your app. You likely need to make code changes, generate a new build and submit it to App Review.

If, instead, your app status is **Metadata Rejected**, Apple took issue with your app's name, description, keywords or other metadata. Once you fix the faulty metadata, you can re-submit the same build.

> **Note**: Your Apple Developer Program enrollment comes with two **Technical Support Incidents (TSI)** per year. A TSI is a request for code-level support for Apple's framework, APIs and tools. If you're having trouble reproducing or fixing an issue that came up during App Review, you can use one of your TSIs to get help from Apple support engineers.
>
> For more information, refer to Apple's documentation page, **Requesting Technical Support**: http://apple.co/2ZbeNx3.

As a final piece of advice, remember that App Review is dynamic and revolves around people making decisions. Different reviewers notice different things at different times. Despite Apple's best efforts, you may encounter inconsistencies in the App Review process from app to app and over time.

Even if Apple approved your app for years, it doesn't mean a reviewer won't raise an issue with a longtime feature at some point in the future. Furthermore, for any imaginable rejection you could receive, there might be other apps currently on the App Store that suffer from the same problem but have gone unnoticed. Pointing these things out in Resolution Center won't help you. Aim to understand the problem as Apple sees it and as it applies to your individual app.

If you reach an impasse in Resolution Center, you also have the option to appeal the rejection to the App Review Board to determine if Apple should reconsider your app. As of this writing, that process is relatively new. You can start an appeal by filling out a form on the developer portal: http://apple.co/2NeRgIv.

Key points

- Apple hires and trains employees who make sure incoming app submissions adhere to the App Store Review Guidelines.
- The App Store Review Guidelines change over time, but they're based on timeless principles: provide value, ensure quality, don't cheat, respect users and assume full responsibility.
- The App Store Review Guidelines link to a number of documents that you should also abide by, including the Apple Developer Program License Agreement, the Human Interface Guidelines (HIG) and the Brand and Marketing Guidelines.
- An iOS app can be associated with a macOS app, a tvOS app and a watchOS app. It can also support App Clips, iMessage apps and In-App Purchases. App Store Connect supports all these add-ons.
- Fill out the App Review Information section in App Store Connect to provide reviewers with login information and any other notes they might need.
- Your app is available in all countries and regions by default, but you can opt-out of territories where you don't want your app to be available.
- After you pass App Review, you can choose to release your app manually or you can let Apple handle it. You can also do phased releases after your initial release.
- After your initial release, you can choose to reset your summary rating on your App Store product page when you release new versions.
- If an app update is time-sensitive, you can submit an expedited App Review request on the developer portal.
- Resolve app rejections in App Store Connect's Resolution Center. Communicate with Apple to clarify their request, make any necessary changes and submit a new build for review.

Chapter 8: App Approved! (Now What?)

By Pietro Rea

So far, the chapters in this book have followed a narrative arc. You first learned how to upload a build to App Store Connect. You then mastered the art of code signing and provisioning. You learned how to distribute your build to internal and external testers using ad hoc distribution and TestFlight. And in the previous chapter, you learned how to prepare for App Review.

This chapter deals with what to do *after* you pass App Review. You might be wondering, is there anything left after Apple blesses your app for release? Wasn't the whole point to get an app on the App Store?

Not only is there more to do, how you release and what you do after release can determine your success or failure. Think back to the app lifecycle diagram from Chapter 1, "The App Store". This chapter covers what happens during the pre-release and post-release phases. The following diagram shows the app development cycle overview:

First, between the **App Review** and **App Store** phase, imagine a thin section called **Pre-release** for those who've opted to manually release, as the previous chapter recommended. The optional **Pre-release** phase is where you do your last-minute checks before releasing your app to the public.

At a minimum, you should have a **release checklist** that helps you click the **Release** button with confidence. The next section covers the best way to perform pre-release checks and what should go on your checklist.

Second, after uploading your app to the App Store and before a new **Development** cycle, there's **Analytics**. This phase might sound like you can just kick back and wait for your numbers to come in. But in fact, Analytics might be the most challenging phase of all.

This is where your team answers the question "what should we do next?", which informs the next app development cycle. Typically, product managers use the business context, resource constraints and customer feedback to create a road map.

Even though there's no easy recipe for success, the second half of the chapter covers the different sources of feedback to monitor so you can make decisions with the best information available.

App Store Connect's built-in tools for monitoring feedback only become useful after you've had an app in the App Store for some time. Therefore, you'll look at the numbers for a real app called **Math Ninja HD**.

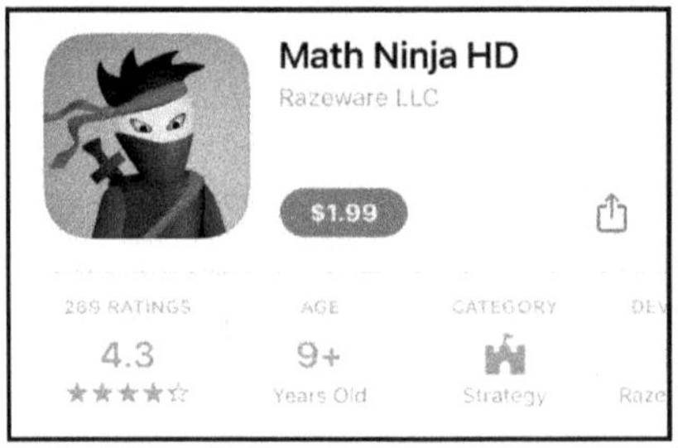

Smoke testing before release

Pre-release involves many small steps that must be done correctly. Here's a classic oversight: Many apps depend on back-end systems. Sure, testing went smoothly in the pre-release staging environment, but did anyone remember to promote the app's necessary changes to production?

If not, you suddenly have a situation where everyone who downloads your app from the App Store crashes on launch. As it turns out, you changed something so your app now expects data to come back in a new format, but is getting it in the old one. Whoops. That's something you really want to catch before release.

In the previous chapter, you learned about the three version release options in App Store Connect: manual, automatic and automatic with a target date. When you choose the manual option, you get a window of time between approval and release in which you can perform last-minute checks. These are called **smoke tests** or **sanity tests**.

Creating a checklist gives you a systematic approach to minimize many common oversights.

Creating a checklist

Before diving into the checks to perform before release, take a detour to the world of medicine. Releasing an app is a complex and high-stakes endeavor, but no one would argue it's more so than a life-or-death medical procedure. In his 2009 book, "The Checklist Manifesto: How to Get Things Right", the surgeon, writer and public health researcher, Atul Gawande, writes about the need for checklists in increasingly complex fields like medicine and engineering.

His team developed the "safe surgery checklist" and applied it around the world. The results were staggeringly positive. Many lives were saved when surgeons followed simple documents spelling out every step they needed to take. If even surgeons who've trained for decades need checklists, developers can put them to good use, too.

What goes in your release checklist largely depends on your particular situation, but it's important to have something to follow with every release.

You can go a step further and turn your release checklist into an internal-facing **release page**. In an organization with many teams and projects, a release page helps you communicate what the release included, when it was released to the public and any other internal documentation that might be relevant.

Release pages are helpful, even if your team only includes you. Whenever you have to remember what you did when, such as: "how long has this feature been on the App Store?", you can refer back to your release pages instead of digging through App Store Connect or your Git commit history.

Appendix B has a sample release page, which includes a release checklist.

Using promo codes

Back in Chapter 3, "Submitting Your First App for Review", you manually picked one build among many to send off to App Review. But what if you'd clicked the wrong radio button? App Review doesn't know one build from the next, so you could unwittingly release the wrong build.

Fortunately, before releasing your app to the public, you have the option of using a promo code to download the approved build so you can double-check that everything is correct.

To request a promo code in App Store Connect, your app's status must be **Pre-Order Ready**, **Pending Developer Release** or **Ready for Sale**. However, for a pre-release smoke test, the status will always be **Pending Developer Release**.

As a side note, Apple created promo codes to let you give free copies of your app to customers and reviewers. You're not technically using promo codes for their intended purpose, but there's no harm in redeeming one for testing.

Generating a promo code

Here are the steps to generate a promo code on App Store Connect:

1. Log in to **App Store Connect**.
2. Click **My Apps** and select your app.
3. Click the **Features** tab.
4. In the sidebar, click **Promo Codes**.

5. The promo code management page opens with the **Generate** tab selected. Under the **App Promo Codes** section, enter **1** as the number of promo codes you want to generate.
6. Click **Generate Code** in the top-right corner.

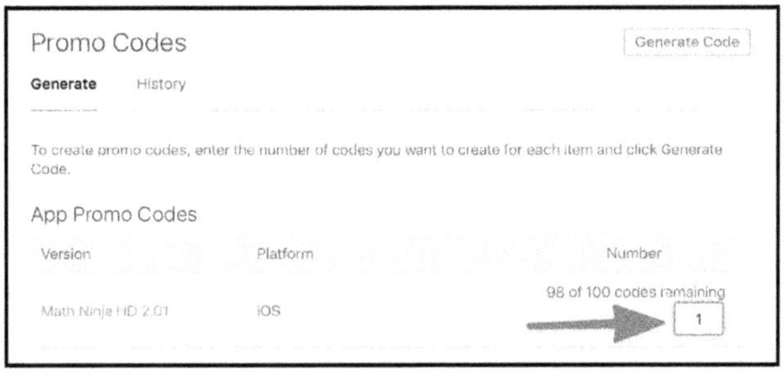

7. A modal dialog appears. Check the checkbox to agree to Apple's terms and conditions.
8. Click **Generate Code** and dismiss the modal.
9. Click **View Code.** A second dialog appears to reveal your promo code.

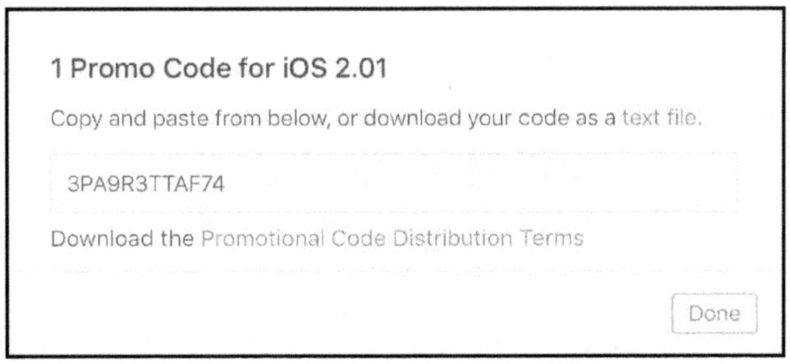

Copy your promo code and send it to yourself so you can access it on your iOS test device.

Redeeming your promo code

To redeem the promo code, open the **App Store** app on your iOS device. Sign in, if you haven't already, and tap your **profile photo** on the top right. Then, tap **Redeem Gift Card or Code**.

See the image below:

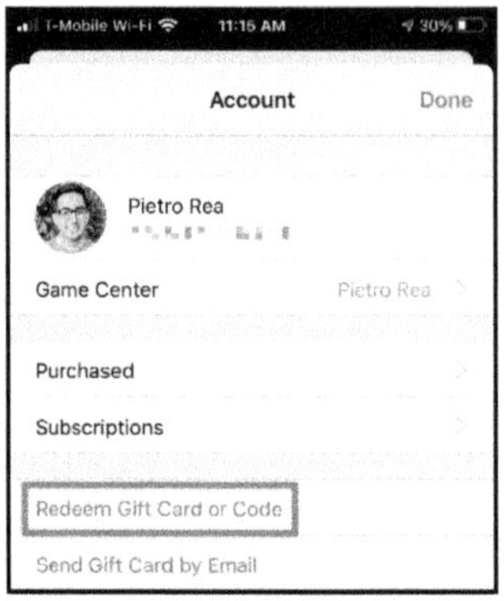

Redeeming promo codes shares the same flow as redeeming physical gift cards. The App Store prompts you to redeem your gift card using your device's camera.

Ignore this call to action. You can't use your camera to redeem promo codes. Instead, tap **Enter Code Manually**.

Paste the promo code you've generated in App Store Connect. Tap **Redeem** in the top-right corner.

Once the App Store accepts your promo code, your test device begins to download your pre-release app.

> **Note**: To prevent abuse, Apple made promo codes single-use. If you need to delete and reinstall the app to troubleshoot it, you'll have to generate and redeem a new promo code.

Using a promo code to download your pre-release app gives you the *exact* binary your users will receive when they download your app from the App Store. Use this build to go through your pre-release checklist.

If you can't get your hands on a promo code, the next best option is to run through your release checklist on the last TestFlight build for this version of your app. Of all build types, TestFlight builds are the most App Store-like. However, since you can use TestFlight to test multiple builds at once, you still run the risk of smoke testing the wrong build.

Once you're happy with your approved build, open App Store Connect and release it to the public. Congratulations!

Monitoring your app

For the post-release phase, monitoring incoming feedback is one of the primary ways to figure out how you're doing and what to do next.

Feedback can take many forms. Of course, you can receive direct customer feedback through support emails and App Store reviews. However, feedback can also be passive and less obvious. Passive feedback includes:

- Analytics about your app, like sessions and active users
- Crash reports
- Monitoring of your back-end systems

This is where you take on the role of a data scientist so you can make sense of the aggregate data.

App Analytics

Apple provides built-in analytics for all members of the Apple Developer Program. You don't need to do anything to start using the built-in tools — all you need is an app on the App Store.

Log in to **App Store Connect** to see your app's numbers. Instead of clicking **My Apps**, like you usually do, click **App Analytics**.

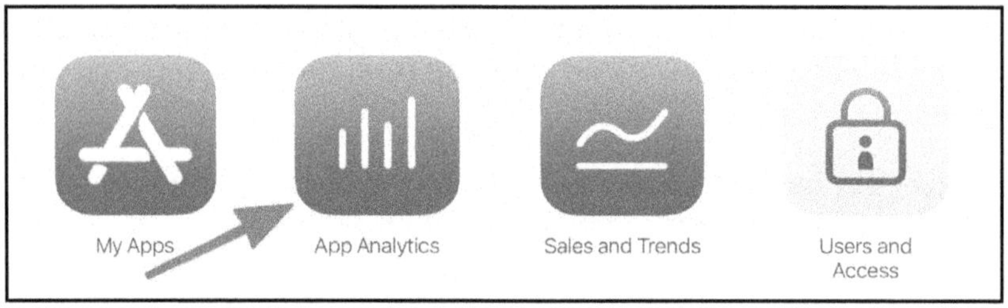

The next page shows a high-level analytics overview for every app in your account. Here's what the numbers look like for Math Ninja HD:

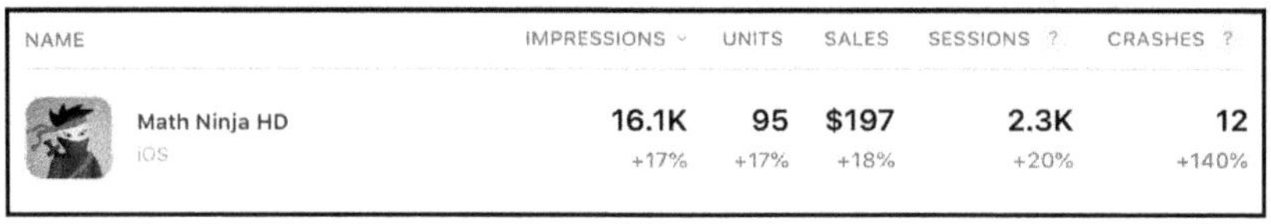

NAME	IMPRESSIONS	UNITS	SALES	SESSIONS ?	CRASHES ?
Math Ninja HD iOS	16.1K +17%	95 +17%	$197 +18%	2.3K +20%	12 +140%

The summary view defaults to the last 30 days, but you can change the date range. Here's what each metric means:

- **Impressions**: The number of times Apple surfaced your app on the Featured, Categories, Top Charts or Search sections of the App Store. This number also includes product page views.
- **Units**: The number of times someone downloaded your app.
- **Sales**: The total amount billed to your users for purchasing Math Ninja HD or any of its In-App Purchases.
- **Sessions**: The number of times someone used your app for at least two seconds. Only users who agreed to share their data with third-party developers count towards this number.
- **Crashes**: The number of times your app crashed. Only users who opted-in count towards this number.

Click the **summary** row, which brings you to a more detailed summary page with more metrics.

See the image below:

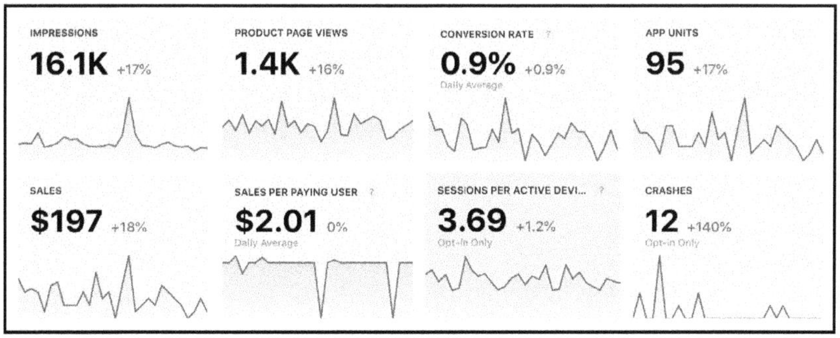

Here's what some of the new ones mean:

- **Product Page Views**: While **Impressions** gives you the number of times your app showed up anywhere in the App Store, **Product Page Views** only includes the times someone visited your App Store product page.
- **Conversion Rate**: Conversion rate represents the number of app downloads compared to the total unique impressions. Make sure to monitor your app's conversion rate if you do any work to improve your App Store product page, like adding App Previews, fleshing out the description and so on.

On this page, you also see which regions of the world your users come from, as well as how they found you and which devices they used. You can click any tile on this page to get more granular information, apply filters and more.

> **Note**: The **App Analytics** section in App Store Connect focuses on visitor and usage information. It's primarily geared toward making product improvements.
>
> If you're looking for more robust sales and financial reporting, head to the **Sales and Trends** section in App Store Connect.

Built-in versus third-party analytics

When it comes to analytics, third-party tools can only tell you what happens *after* someone downloads and opens your app. If you want to know anything before that, such as App Store impressions, the built-in tools are your only option.

Although third-party tools can't give you all the data you might be interested in, they fill gaps that Apple doesn't cover. In particular, there are two ways third-party tools can help:

1. **App-specific metrics**: If you want to know how many people reached level two in Math Ninja HD, you're out of luck without third-party tools. App Store Connect can't tell you anything specific to your app. For this, you need custom analytics.
2. **Data from all your users**: Apple only reports session and crash reports from users who agreed to share information with third-party developers. If you want data from *all* users, you need custom analytics.

If you decide to use a third-party analytics tool, make sure its data collection and data retention policies align with the App Store Review Guidelines and all applicable laws.

When you submit an app for review, you'll need to provide information about your app's privacy practices, including the practices of third-party partners whose code you use. For more information on required privacy disclosures, refer to Apple's documentation: https://apple.co/3stPWkE.

Crash reports

Crash reports are another important source of feedback. An app crashes when something unexpected occurs, usually because of a flaw in the source code.

Crashes are a fact of life — every app crashes from time to time. Each time a crash occurs, the operating system ejects the unlucky user out of your app, regardless of what they were doing at the time.

Although getting thrown out of an app is frustrating, most people won't report the crash or even complain. It's up to you to monitor crashes as they happen so you can fix the root cause promptly. Fortunately, Apple makes this easier with built-in tools in App Store Connect.

> **Note**: Chapter 6, "TestFlight", covered collecting crash reports from beta testers. The process is similar, though not identical, for App Store builds. You can skip this section if you have a good handle on TestFlight.

To see crash report information, click the **Crashes** tile on the metrics summary page. On the next page, you can filter crashes by app version, device type and OS version.

The graph only reports the number of crashes that occurred on a particular day. Do note that the crashes recorded are from users who have opted in to share analytics with developers. App Store Connect doesn't give you any other details, technical or otherwise.

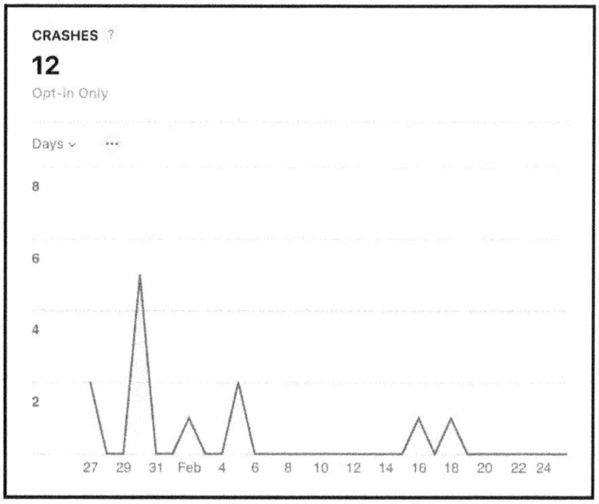

Knowing that a crash occurred is the easy part. The more challenging part is reproducing, diagnosing and fixing the crash. To do so, open **Xcode** to see a crash report's technical details. Log in to **Xcode** using an Apple ID with access to the crashing app.

Next, press **Shift-Option-Command-O** to open Xcode's Organizer. You might remember the Organizer from previous chapters, where you had to archive and upload builds. You can also use the Organizer to browse through a released app's crash reports.

On the top left, click the **drop-down** icon and select your **app**. In the sidebar, under **Reports**, click **Crashes**. Xcode then begins to download recent crash reports.

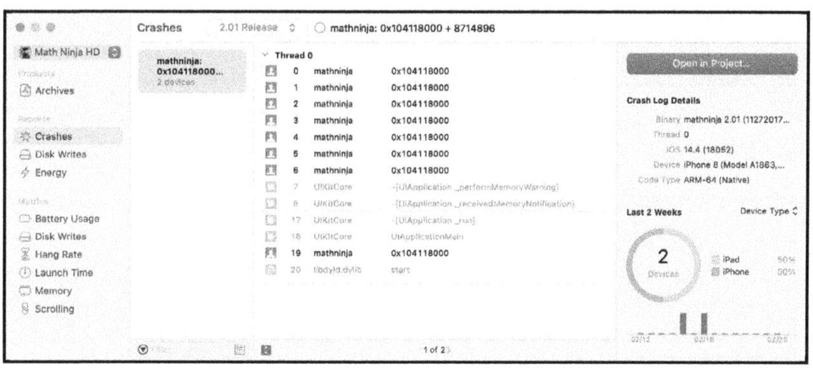

Every crash report has a **stack trace**, which is a detailed description of what your app was doing moments before it crashed. Here's part of the stack trace from the previous screenshot:

```
Thread 0 Crashed:
0  mathninja                    0x0000000104967a90 0x104118000 +
8714896
1  mathninja                    0x0000000104967a74 0x104118000 +
8714868
2  mathninja                    0x0000000104a449b0 0x104118000 +
9619888
3  mathninja                    0x0000000104a446a4 0x104118000 +
9619108
```

A stack trace is essential to the debugging process as it often has clues about why the crash occurred. This particular stack trace has memory addresses (e.g 0x0000000104967a90) instead of human-friendly pointers into the code, which a developer could more easily understand.

To make this stack trace more helpful, you'd have to **symbolicate** it. To read more about crash reports, including how to symbolicate them, refer to Apple's documentation: https://apple.co/3kpzVJE.

If you have access to the source code, you can also open the crash report inside its corresponding Xcode project. To do so, click **Open in Project...** and select the **Xcode project** that corresponds to your app. This links you directly to the line of code where your app crashed.

Like App Analytics, there's no shortage of third-party tools to help you monitor crashes. The trade-offs are similar as well. If you use a third-party tool, you'll have access to crash reports from all users instead of just those that opted-in. However, now you have to worry about implementation, privacy and data sharing.

Ratings and reviews

Ratings and reviews are another important source of post-release information. Users can rate your app on a scale from 1 to 5 stars and can also write a detailed review of your app for others to read.

Ratings and reviews both end up on your App Store product page to help potential customers decide if they want to try your app. Beyond their obvious benefits to end-users, ratings and reviews also give you useful qualitative data about your app.

> **Note**: Motivated users will find the right place on your App Store product page to leave a rating or review. However, Apple also provides an API, `SKStoreReviewController` (https://apple.co/388PW1N), which lets you programmatically request reviews from your users as they're using your app.

To see your ratings and reviews, return to App Store Connect's top-level menu. From here, click **My Apps**, then select your app.

In the sidebar, under **General**, click **Ratings and Reviews**. Here, you can see your app's aggregate star rating by territory. In this case, 4.3 out of 5 for Math Ninja HD in the United States. Not bad!

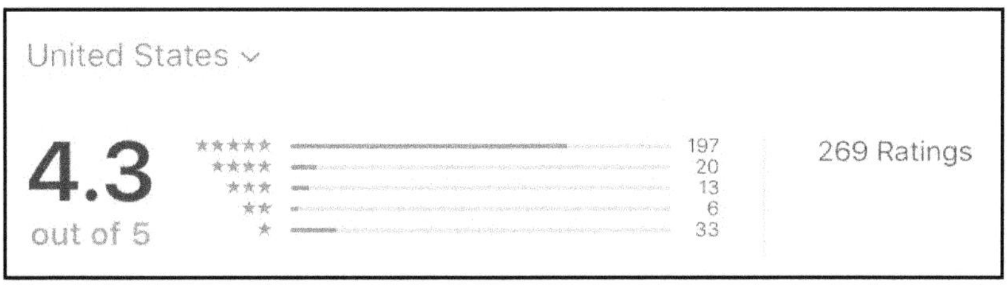

Below your app's rating information, you can also read individual reviews. You can filter them by the version or the number of stars. You can also apply filters like **Most Recent** or **Most Critical**. For example, here's a glowing review of Math Ninja HD:

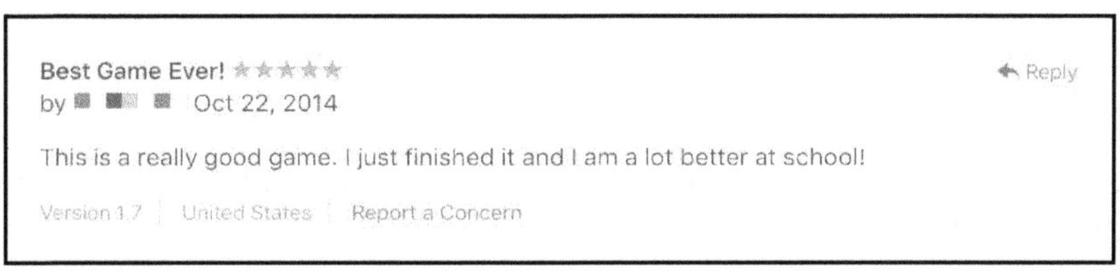

Users can only review your app once, but they're allowed to change their minds and edit their reviews at any time. For example, the user from the previous screenshot might love Math Ninja HD for the first two versions. But if they have a problem with version 3.0, they can change their previously glowing review to complain about the new release.

Apple also lets you reply to reviews. You can use this feature to provide lightweight customer service or to ask for more information. You can also edit your reply or delete it at any time.

One of the most rewarding experiences you can have as an app publisher is to see negative reviews turn into positive ones after proactively addressing their problems.

Maintaining your app

Monitoring your app after release can help you figure out what to do in the short term, such as addressing a critical bug fix, as well as in the medium term, like adding a new feature. But what about the long term?

Apple provides no fancy tools in App Store Connect to help you decide which direction to take. What you do with your app over time is entirely up to you.

As you look into the future, watch out for two forces that may prompt you to release new versions of your app. These both come from Apple, so they apply to every third-party developer.

Minimum ongoing maintenance

Don't expect your app to work for years and years without any work from you. The platform you built it on changes too quickly for that. Apple releases new hardware every year, as well as new versions of their operating systems and SDKs.

Practically speaking, this means you need to retest your app whenever Apple releases software or hardware that affects your user base. At a minimum, rebuild your app with the latest version of the SDK, test on new hardware and fix anything that doesn't work anymore.

Apple typically releases beta versions of new software in June and officially releases them in September. Most developers use the intervening time to test and update their apps. As a word of warning, be sure not to fall too far behind on maintenance. From time to time, Apple purges apps from the App Store that don't work anymore or look abandoned.

New technologies and opportunities

With every new hardware and software release, Apple brings forth new technologies and capabilities that third-party developers (that's you!) can take advantage of. Here are a few notable examples from the past decade:

- Push notifications, iOS 3
- App multitasking, iOS 4
- Touch ID, iOS 8
- Augmented Reality, iOS 11

Some of the older technologies, like push notifications, are commonplace today, but there was a time when they were brand new. It was up to app developers to adopt them.

Unlike maintenance work, adopting new platform capabilities isn't required. No one is going to remove your app from the App Store if you don't integrate with Apple's latest frameworks. It's up to you to pick the capabilities that fit your app and release app updates that take advantage of them.

If this sounds interesting, then you must pay attention to platform changes. Apple holds a yearly Worldwide Developers Conference, commonly known as **WWDC** ("dub-dub") around June, where they announce new platform capabilities and improvements to existing ones.

Attending WWDC in person is one of the most exciting things about being a developer on Apple's platforms. If you can't get a ticket to attend in person, you can always watch the videos on Apple's developer site: https://apple.co/3bIhhsv. Videos from previous years are also available.

Key points

- Use the window of time between approval and release to perform sanity checks and smoke tests. This only works if you picked the **manual** version release option.
- Create a **release checklist** that includes everything you need to do before you go live.
- Generate and redeem a promo code to download a pre-release version of your app. Use it for your sanity checks and smoke tests.
- Monitoring feedback is an excellent way to figure out how your app should evolve over time.
- App Store Connect has built-in tools to monitor analytics, crash reports, ratings and reviews. There are also third-party tools that can help.
- At a minimum, release app updates to take care of basic app maintenance.You can also release changes that take advantage of the new platform capabilities Apple ships every year.

Chapter 9: Build Customizations

By Keegan Rush

As a developer, there's only one thing you need to worry about when creating a new project in Xcode: writing the code you need to build an amazing app. Every new Xcode project comes with all the scaffolding you need to run the app on a device.

If you only need to build an app to your device, and occasionally push to the App Store, this might be good enough. With more complicated projects and apps, you'll need to go beyond what Xcode offers as the default and learn more about build customization in Xcode.

By the end of this chapter, you'll know how to:

- Build more than one app in a single project.
- Work with build settings.
- Change exactly what happens when you click **Build**.
- Understand the difference between building your device and archiving for the App Store.

Right now, Emitron has the default build setup of any iOS project. You can do a local build to your device by building and running the app as usual, or you can prepare a build destined for the App Store by using the **Product ▸ Archive** menu option. In this chapter, you'll configure another way to build the app: as an Alpha build specifically destined for internal testing.

Different build types

Any release of an iOS app goes through different stages before it's published to the App Store. How you or your team chooses to handle releases may differ, but many large-scale apps look something like this:

1. **Dev build**: A local build installed on the developer's device or simulator, with logging and debug features enabled to catch pesky bugs before they become a problem.
2. **Alpha/QA build**: Alpha builds are available internally to the members of the team or company so they can test new features and revisions right away.
3. **Beta build**: Beta builds are usually publicly available versions of your app which gives you a chance to test new features and make sure there aren't any large bugs lying around.
4. **Release build**: The version of your app that users can download on the App Store.

The different build types can go by many names — these are just some examples. For instance, you might refer to an alpha build as an **internal** or **QA** build. The terminology is less important than the ability to set it up, which you'll learn in this chapter.

If your app utilizes servers, dev and alpha builds should ideally point to a different backend server to prevent interference with production data. If you were working on a banking app, you wouldn't want to see real money change hands during testing! Using a different server when debugging or doing QA testing can prevent this issue.

Emitron's release pipeline

Every new version of Emitron goes through four stages based on the different build types.

1. **Dev**: When the team is working on new features, they'll deploy dev builds to their own devices.
2. **Alpha**: Once the dev team wraps up their work, they will create a new alpha build. The team distributes the alpha internally through either ad-hoc, enterprise or TestFlight deployment.

3. **Beta**: When the alpha build is stable and bug-free, the dev team makes a new beta build. This could be distributed internally again, or to external beta testers.

4. **Release**: The build is finally ready for the App Store!

Multiple builds at once

Multiple build types should be installable on the same device, at the same time. A developer should be able to have their latest dev build on their iPhone, the last QA build that went to the team and the latest release build from the App Store.

Bundle identifiers

Technically, you *can't* have more than one version of the same app on one device. iOS uses the **bundle identifier** to identify apps; which means no two apps can have the same bundle identifier. By using *different* bundle IDs for each build type, iOS thinks of them as different apps entirely, allowing you to have more than one build on a device. This means modifying the bundle ID is your golden ticket to having multiple types of builds running on the same device. Neat!

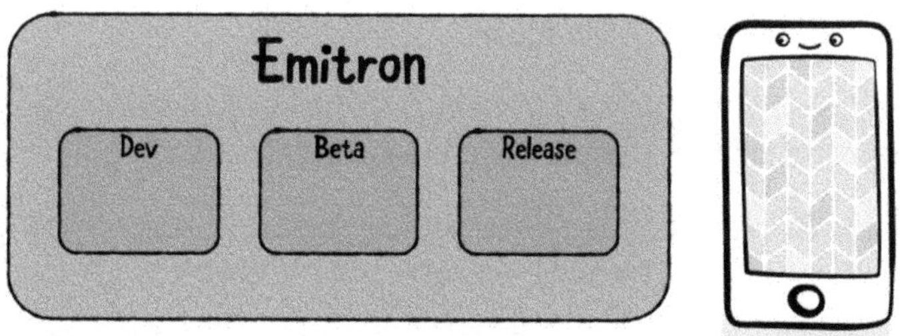

Install more than one instance of an app by using different bundle IDs.

So, how do you swap out the bundle ID based on which build you need to make? You could just change the value for the bundle ID when you're making an alpha build, but then you'd have to remember to change it back for a release build. The correct way to tackle this problem is to set up Xcode so that you can swap between build types at the click of a button.

Moving between build types

When moving between build types, be aware that unintended changes can slip through.

This is usually not a problem when going between dev, alpha and beta, because bugs are generally expected on these types of builds. Moving from beta to release can be problematic: once your app is on the App Store, it's up to your users to make sure that no unintended changes made it through!

This is why it's a good idea to *not* recompile and re-distribute your app when moving from beta to release. By recompiling and using a newly built and potentially untested version of your app as your release build, you open up the possibility that unexpected bugs could appear in your app. You should use the final **beta** build as your release build to avoid these unexpected bugs.

Because you won't be recompiling the app between beta and release, both the beta and release build types will have the same bundle identifier. That means you won't be able to have the beta build and the release build both installed on the same device. There won't be any changes in the configuration between the two.

Different build types in Emitron

In this chapter, you'll configure the build setup in Emitron to switch between three build types: **dev**, **alpha** and **release**. Each build type will vary in its bundle IDs, their app icons and the method of code signing.

Remember: You're not configuring a beta build type because there shouldn't be any configuration or code differences between beta and release.

When you're ready to send the beta build to the App Store, the binary is already waiting for you in App Store Connect. No further code changes are needed!

Emitron already has a working dev and release build type — this is the default configuration for new Xcode projects. To add the alpha build type, you'll need to get acquainted with the three cornerstones of build customization: **targets**, **build settings** and **schemes**, and learn how they work together.

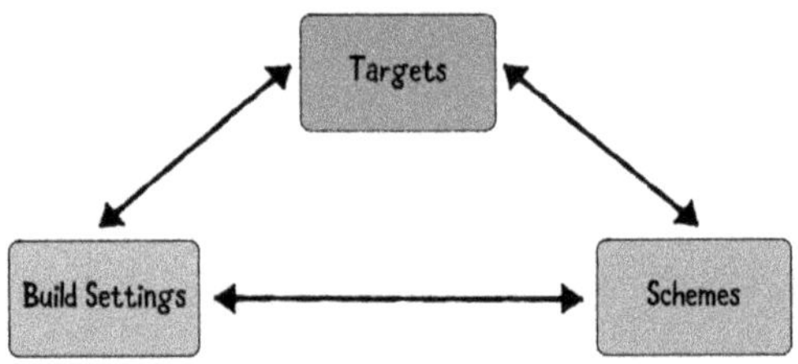

The three cornerstones of build customization.

Targets

A **target** is a list of files and instructions that tell Xcode how to build your app or app extension. When you hit Build in Xcode, the target is what you're building.

When you build and run the Emitron project, you're building an iOS App target. An Xcode project is not limited to only one target. The Emitron project has two targets: one that you use for building the app and one for unit tests.

Targets in Emitron

Open the sample project for this chapter in Xcode. In the Project Navigator, click on the **Emitron** project to reach the project screen.

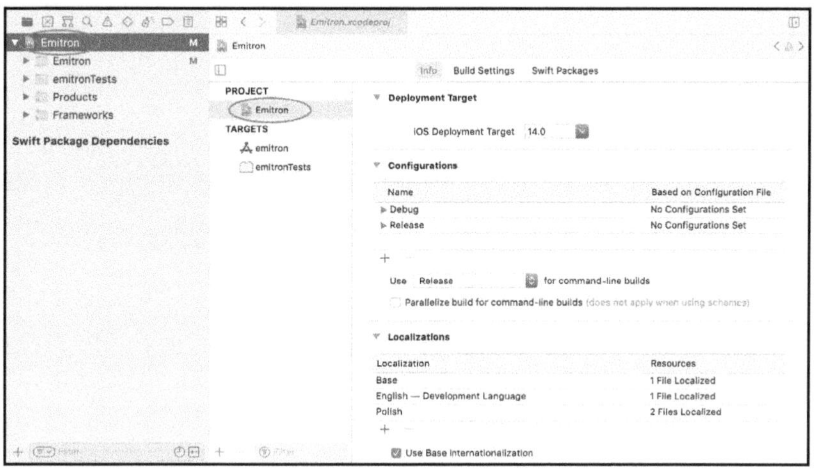

On the left, you'll see a list of projects and targets. You have two targets: **emitron** and **emitronTests**. The emitron target is an iOS App target. All of the source code for Emitron is added to this target. Xcode knows that when you build this target, the output should be an iOS app.

The second target, emitronTests, contains all of the unit testing code. When you build this target, Xcode compiles the unit testing code, which then runs on a device or simulator to test the app, which is built by the emitron target.

In the Project Navigator, expand the Emitron project. There are two folders of interest under it: **Emitron** for the main app target, and **emitronTests** for the unit test target.

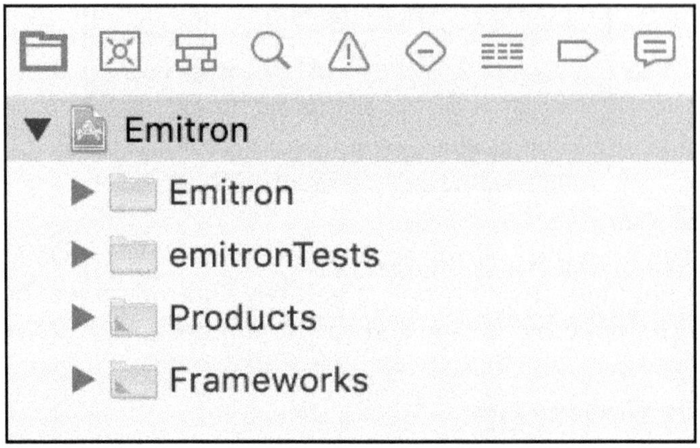

Expand the Emitron folder, and click **AppDelegate.swift**.

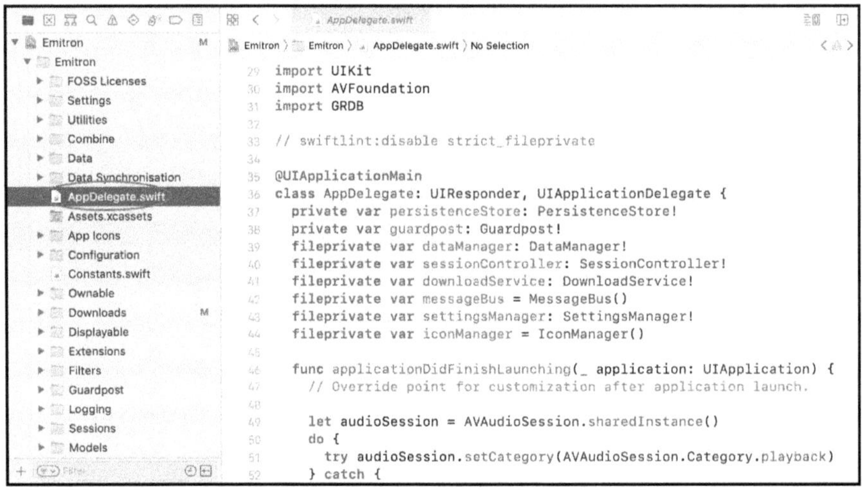

Make sure the Inspectors panel is open on the right side of the window, and click on the File inspector.

Have a look at the **Target Membership** section.

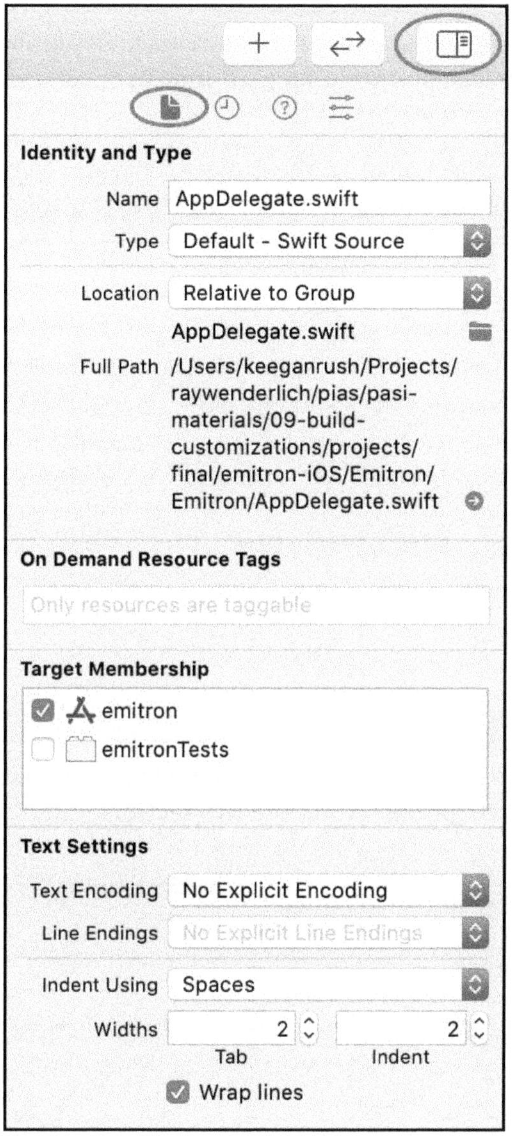

Here, you see that **AppDelegate.swift** is a member of the emitron target. When you build that target, Xcode compiles **AppDelegate.swift** along with all the other files added to the target.

Different target types

The emitron target is an iOS App target, but targets aren't limited to only producing an iOS app. You can make apps for other platforms in Xcode too, such as a watchOS, tvOS or macOS app.

Click on the Emitron project again in the Project Navigator to reach the project screen. Here, under the list of targets, click the **plus** (+) button.

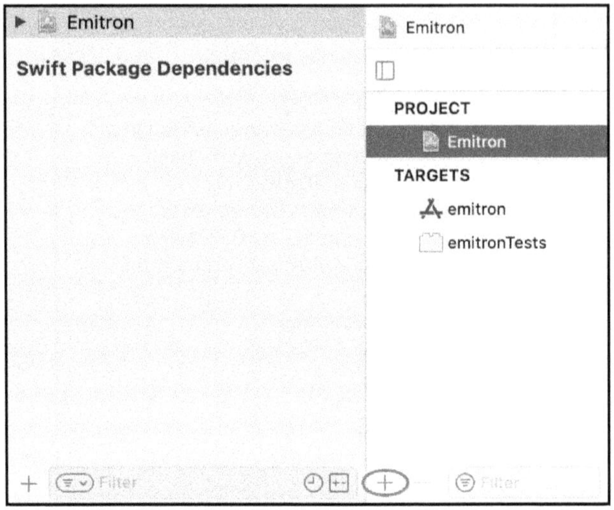

Xcode presents you with a myriad of target templates for iOS, watchOS, tvOS and macOS. There are many options within the **iOS** section — you can build almost anything!

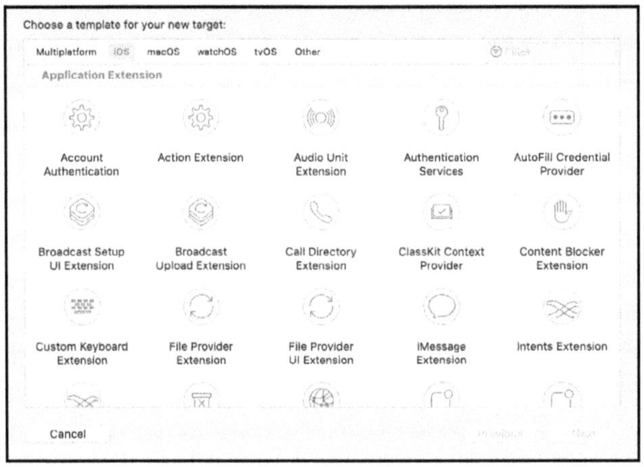

In a cross-platform app, you likely would want to share code between different platforms. To make an app for two platforms, such as iOS and macOS, you make two targets: an **iOS App** target and a **macOS App** target, both in the same project. From there, you can add the same code files to both targets. When you need to write code for macOS only, you can add that code to the only macOS target, and vice versa for iOS.

An Xcode project isn't limited to one target.

Different targets are great for different products or actions. For example, you could use multiple targets to add a watchOS app to your project, an iMessage extension to make an iMessage app, as well as a target for automated UI tests.

As mentioned at the beginning of this chapter, you'll be adding an alpha build configuration to Emitron. So, how do targets affect this?

Targets for the alpha build type

Click **Cancel** on the New Target sheet.

You don't need to make any changes to the targets in Emitron to accomplish this. The emitron target already builds the emitron iOS app, and that's all you need. To add the alpha build type, you'll still use this target, but you'll change *how* to build the target.

Next, you'll learn about build settings and how to change them for the alpha build.

Build settings

Any time you build a target, you tell Xcode how to run the build by specifying a large set of **build settings**. Navigate to the project screen in Xcode again, select the emitron target, and then click **Build Settings**.

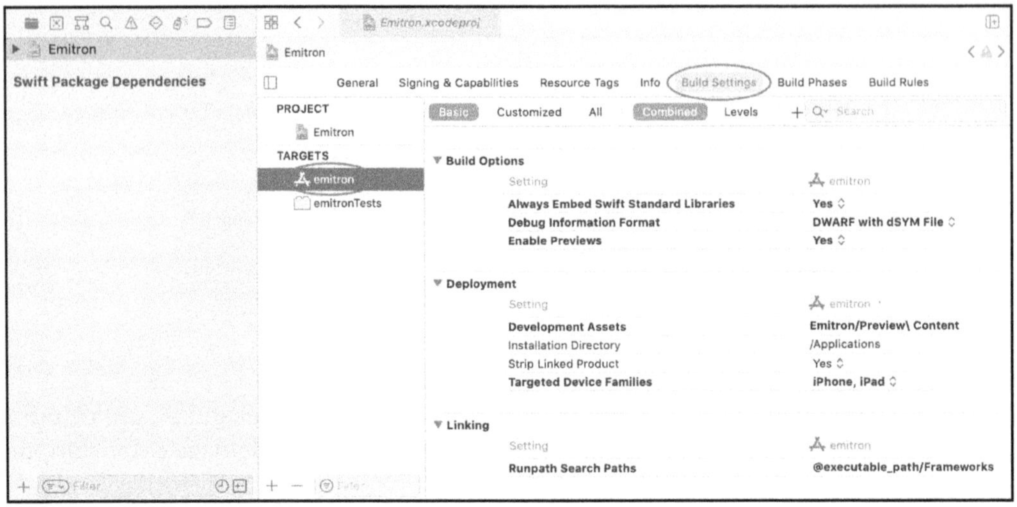

These settings are the rules that Xcode follows when building your app. Here, you change build settings on a target level: what you specify here will apply when building the emitron target, and you can have another set of build settings for a different target.

There are hundreds of settings, but you shouldn't have to worry about most of them. Feel free to scroll through the list and have a look. The settings you specify here define the Swift language version used in the app, how to package the app and its dependencies, the actual display name of the app, how to handle code signing and much more.

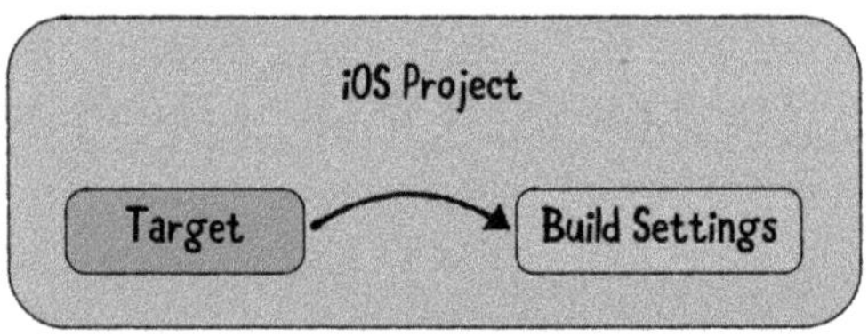

A target uses build settings to determine how to build the product.

Build settings resolution

Usually, build settings apply to the whole project. In projects with more than one target, you may want to change a build setting depending on the chosen target.

There are three different levels of specificity to take into account when configuring build settings.

1. **Target Level**: Build settings specified for an individual target.
2. **Project Level**: Settings that apply to the whole project.
3. **Platform Default**: No setting is specified, so Xcode uses a default.

When you build a target, each possible build setting gets a value determined by the build settings specified for each level. If the **Swift Language Version** build setting has a value on the target level *and* the project level, then Xcode will use the value for the target level, because it's more specific.

If you add a value for a build setting for a specific target, Xcode will use that value for the build setting. If there isn't a value on the target level, Xcode looks one level up: the project level. And, if you didn't specify a value on the project level, you'll get the iOS default value instead.

In Xcode, still on the Build Settings tab for the emitron target, you'll find a **Levels** button to the left of the build settings search bar. Click on it.

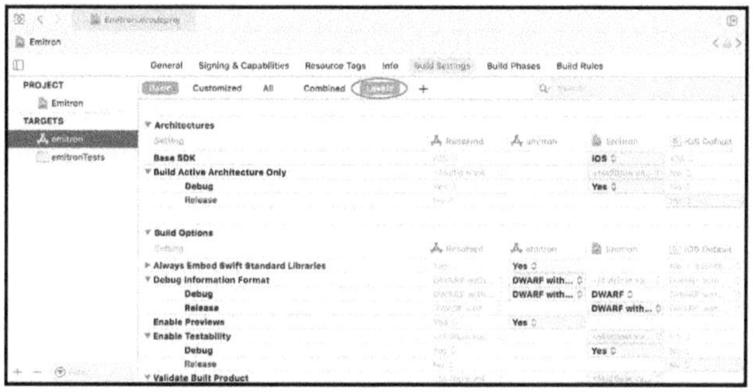

Now, you see four columns for each build setting:

1. **Resolved**: After comparing all settings levels, Xcode chooses the most specific value and shows it here. Xcode will use this value when building the chosen target.
2. **Target**: The value that you have specified for the chosen target.

3. **Project**: The value that you have chosen to be used across the whole project unless there is a value on the target level.

4. **iOS Default**: If no other value is specified, then Xcode will use the default value shown here.

In the search bar, search for **Swift Language Version**.

Here are the values for each level:

1. **Target**: Swift 5

2. **Project**: Unspecified

3. **iOS Default**: Unspecified

Under the **Resolved** column, you can see that the value will be **Swift 5** when you build the project, which is taken from the target level.

Xcode resolves build settings by choosing the most specific level that has a value.

To the left of the **Swift Language Version** build setting, click the ▸ icon. Here, you see another way to customize a build setting: by **build configuration**.

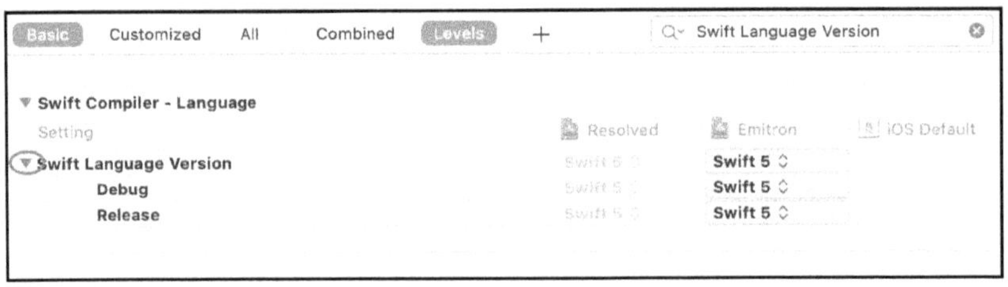

Build configurations

Build configurations are a template for build settings. There are two default configurations in every iOS project: **Debug** and **Release**. Using these configurations, you can specify a value for a build setting when performing a Debug build, and a different value for a Release build. This comes in handy because you need a different provisioning profile and code signing certificate when doing a release build as opposed to a dev build.

Release builds also have heavier optimization to keep them running smoothly. Can you guess how Xcode knows that it should enable optimizations for a release build, but not for a dev build? That's right, by using build configurations!

Targets use build configurations to resolve build settings.

You aren't limited to Debug and Release configurations. You can create your own, such as an alpha or a beta configuration. You'll do that now so that you can use the alpha configuration to do an alpha build of Emitron.

Creating your own build configuration

Build and run the sample project. Once it's running on your device, minimize the app to reach the home screen.

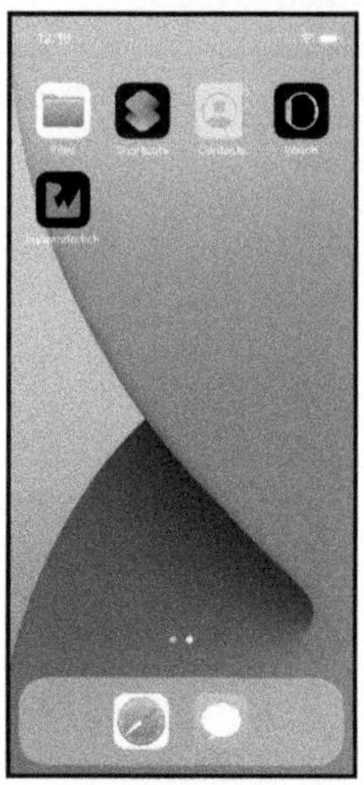

Here, you see the Emitron app installed on your device. When you're done configuring the alpha version, you will be able to have a different copy of Emitron installed on your device for each different build type: dev, alpha and release.

> **Note**: You won't have a beta and release build on the same device, because you shouldn't be recompiling the code between beta and release.

You'll accomplish this by swapping out the bundle identifier for different build configurations. Right now, Emitron has the default Debug and Release configurations. You'll need to create the Alpha configuration yourself.

In Xcode, make sure you're still on the project screen by clicking on the Emitron project in the Project Navigator. Then, click **Emitron** under the **Project** section of the sidebar. Click on the **Info** tab. Here, you'll find a **Configuration** section.

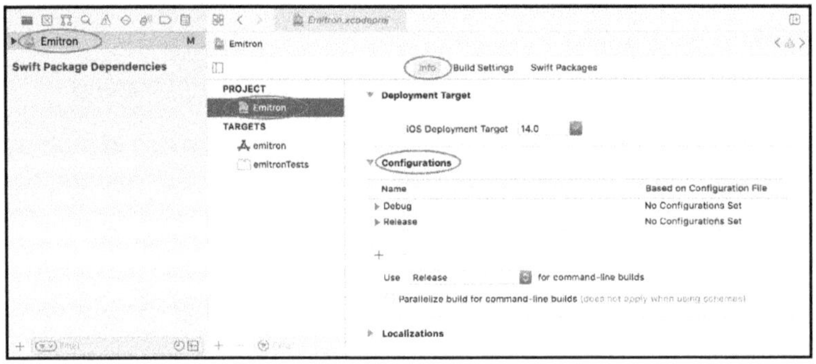

Click the **plus** (+) button near the bottom left of the Configurations section, and choose **Duplicate "Release" Configuration**.

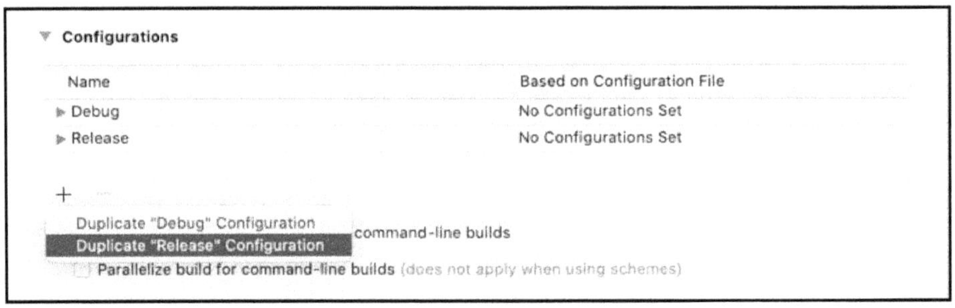

Change the name to **Alpha** and press **Enter** to save your changes.

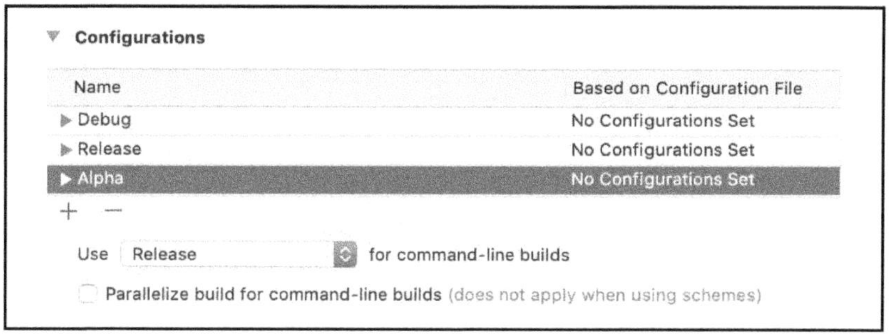

Now, you have three configurations: the default Debug and Release configurations and a brand new Alpha configuration that is an exact copy of the Release configuration.

Having a separate build configuration for alpha builds means that you can change build settings for the Alpha configuration but leave the settings unchanged for all other build types. Next, you'll add more distinction to the Alpha configuration by changing its build settings.

Swapping settings by build configurations

Still in the project screen in Xcode, click on the emitron target in the sidebar to the left, and click on the Build Settings tab. Change the view from **Levels** to **Combined** to simplify the settings view:

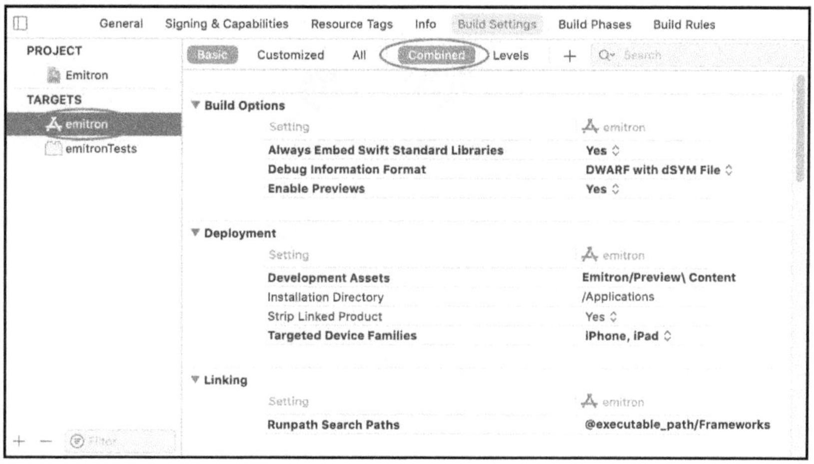

In the search bar, search for **bundle identifier**. Next to the **Project Bundle Identifier** build setting, click the ▸ icon to expand the setting.

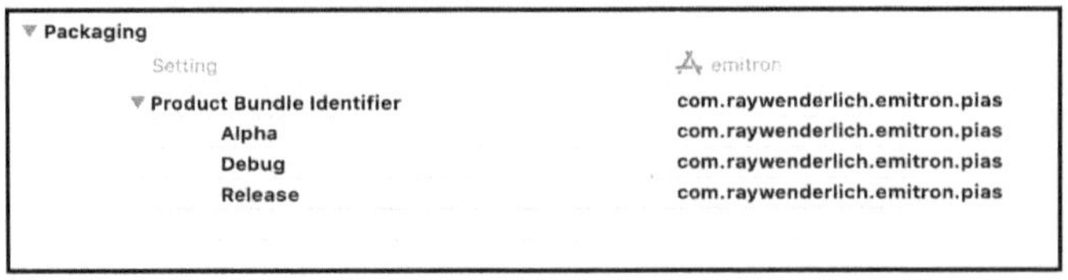

Here, you can see that the build setting can have three possible different values for each build configuration. Change the value for the Alpha configuration to `com.raywenderlich.emitron.pias.alpha`. Then, change the value for the Debug configuration to `com.raywenderlich.emitron.pias.dev`.

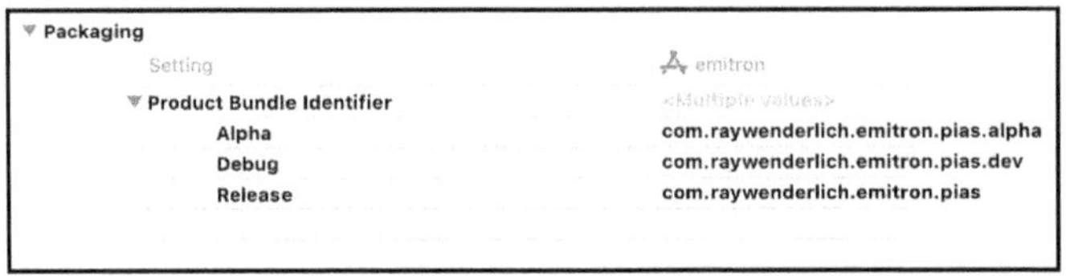

Now, you can have three different versions of the app running on your device, thanks to the three different build configurations and their 5varying bundle identifiers!

When you run the app on your device for development purposes, you build it using the Debug configuration. So, the next time you run the app, it will install using the new `com.raywenderlich.emitron.pias.dev` bundle identifier.

Build and run. Once the app is running on your device, minimize it.

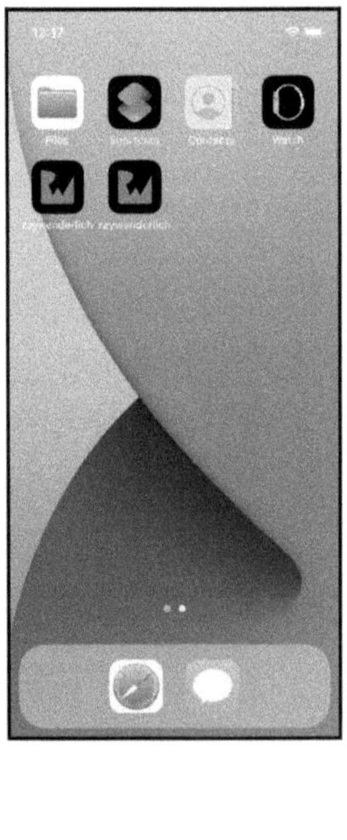

You should now see two different copies of Emitron on your device.

Earlier, when you ran Emitron, Xcode built it with the default `com.raywenderlich.emitron.pias` bundle identifier. That version is still there on your device, but now you've deployed the app again using the `com.raywenderlich.emitron.pias.dev` bundle identifier.

Changing the app icon

You can also change the app icon based on the build configuration. Head back to Xcode. Still in the build settings, in the search bar, search for **icon**. Next to the **App Catalog App Icon Set Name** build setting, click the ▸ icon to expand the setting.

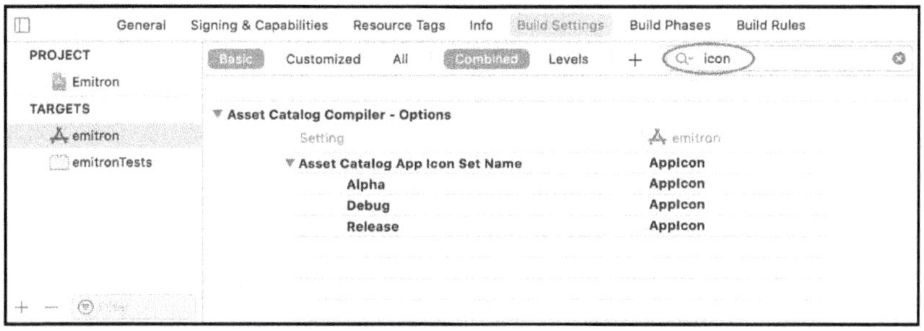

Now, change the value for the Alpha configuration to `AppIcon.alpha` and the value for the Debug configuration to `AppIcon.dev` Your settings should look like this when you're done:

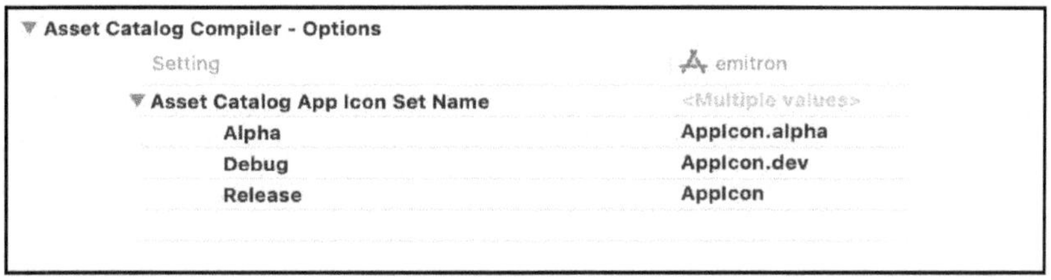

The sample project files contain three different app icons: **AppIcon**, **AppIcon.alpha** and **AppIcon.dev**. The dev and alpha icons were previously unused, but now you're swapping them in based on the build configuration.

Build and run. Once the app is running, minimize it again. Now, your dev build has the right app icon, so there's much less chance of mistaking the two!

See the image below:

So far, you've made changes to the Debug configuration so that they differ from Release, and you've seen the results on your device. You can't see any changes that you've made to your Alpha configuration yet. To do that, you'll need to add the Alpha configuration to a **scheme**.

Schemes

A scheme is a collection of targets and a build configuration that Xcode uses when building. Schemes are the amalgamation of everything you've learned so far in this chapter. You can think of them as a blueprint that tells Xcode exactly what to do when you click the build button. It specifies the actual targets to build and what build configuration to use.

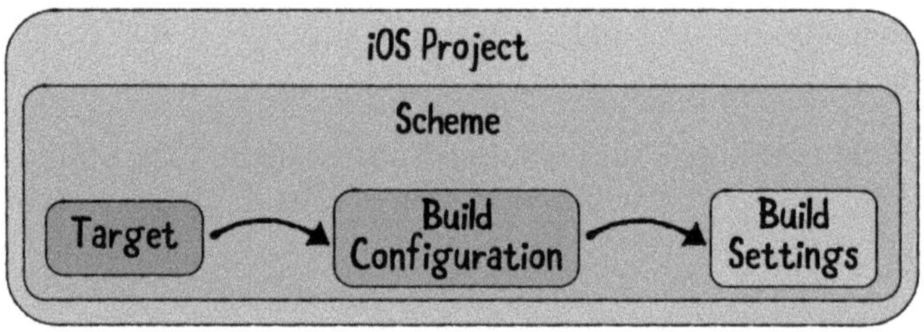

A scheme sets the targets to be built and the configuration to use.

When you build in Xcode or run the app on a device, Xcode is building a scheme that specifies what target is to be built. You can see the active scheme in the Xcode toolbar:

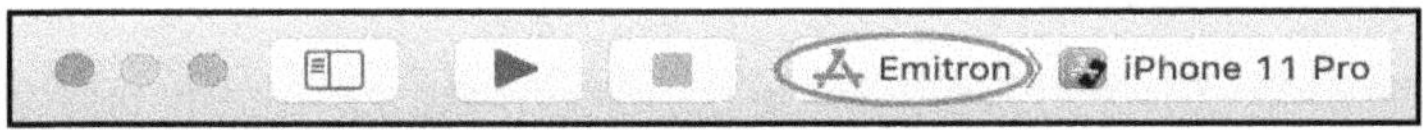

Building the project will use the active scheme, Emitron, as the blueprint. Xcode will resolve build settings based on the build configuration that the scheme specifies. Then, it uses those settings to build the scheme's target.

Scheme actions

Schemes come with a set of different **scheme actions**. When you build, archive or run tests on a project, you're telling the active scheme to execute a particular scheme action.

Click on the active scheme, Emitron, and then click **Edit Scheme...** in the dropdown.

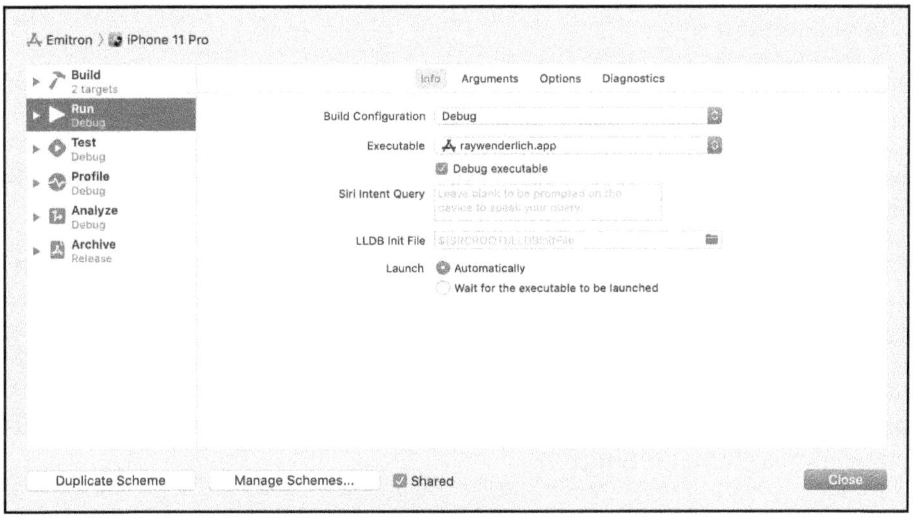

On the left, you see six different **scheme actions**:

1. **Build**: The most basic action, Build compiles a target.
2. **Run**: First builds a target, then deploys it to your device.
3. **Test**: Builds a target along with a Test target before running the tests on your device.

4. **Profile**: Starts the same as the Run action, but also attaches the running app to Instruments.
5. **Analyze**: Builds a target and then runs a static analyzer on the result.
6. **Archive**: Usually done with a Release build configuration, this builds a target and then opens a window to let you submit it to the App Store.

Each build action further customizes how to configure your build using the tabs at the top of the sheet.

Depending on what action you have selected, you'll see some of these tabs:

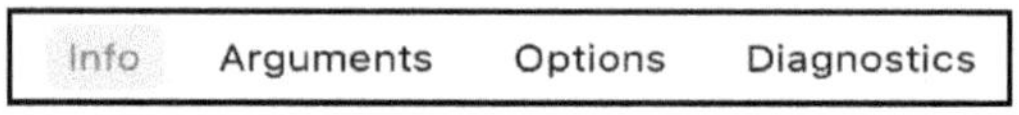

1. **Info**: Lets you choose the target and build configuration to apply.
2. **Arguments**: Allows you to pass arguments and set environment variables.
3. **Options**: Provides various options that you can enable to help test and debug different scenarios.
4. **Diagnostics**: Enables diagnostic tools to help you catch and prevent many of the trickier bugs.

At the bottom of the scheme editor, the **Shared** checkbox lets you make a scheme public and add it to Git.

Right now, the Emitron scheme is set up to build a dev build for your device, run the emitronTests target to execute unit tests, or archive a release build depending on the build action you choose.

You don't need to make any changes to the Emitron scheme for the alpha build that you're adding to the project. Instead, you'll duplicate the Emitron scheme and use it to change the way it builds Emitron.

Creating and modifying a scheme

The version of Emitron in your sample project files has been localized and translated into Polish, but there isn't an easy way to test the localization. You could change the language of your device, but it might not be so easy to get it back to English again! :]

As part of the options on the Run action, you can change the language of the app once it's deployed to your device. Changing this for the Emitron scheme means that every time you run the app, it'll be in a foreign language. So, rather than changing the Emitron scheme, you'll duplicate it and use that scheme for testing localization.

Still in the scheme editor, click **Duplicate Scheme** near the bottom of the sheet.

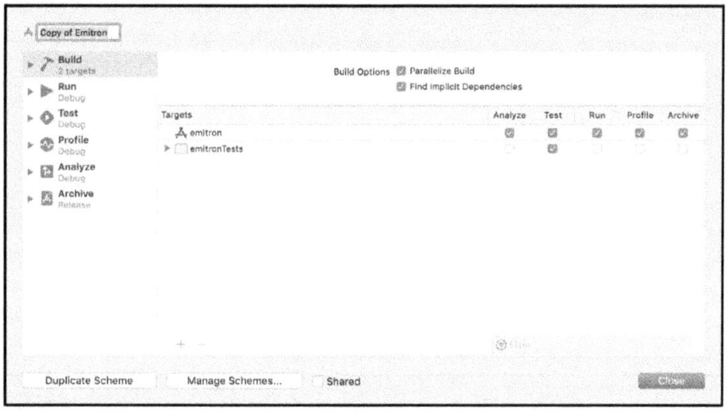

You're now editing the text box with the scheme name. Change the name to `Emitron (PL)`, but **don't press Enter** yet, as it'll close the scheme editor.

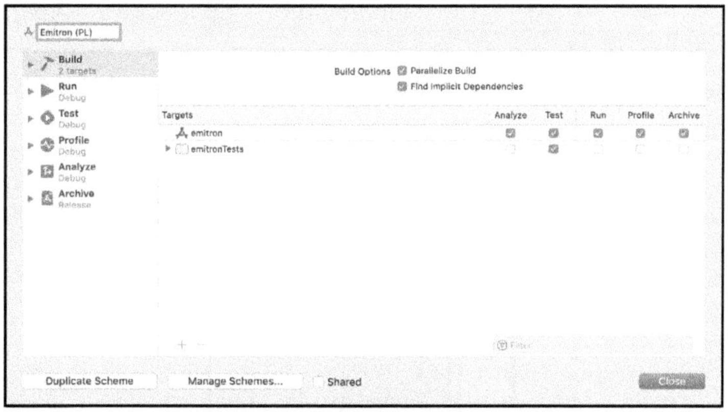

Next, click on the Run action, and then **Options**.

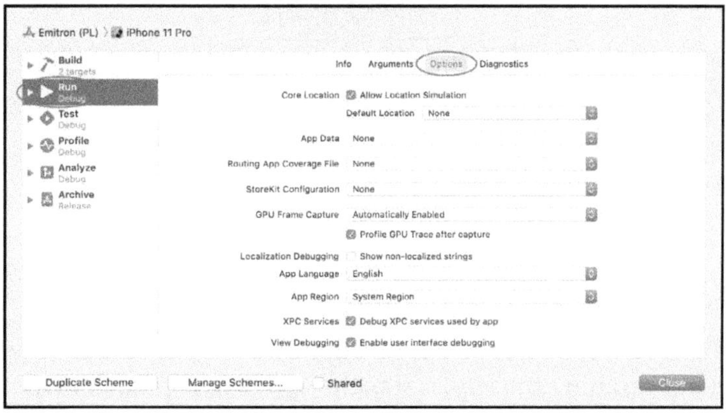

The **Application Language** is set to **English**. Change it to **Polish**.

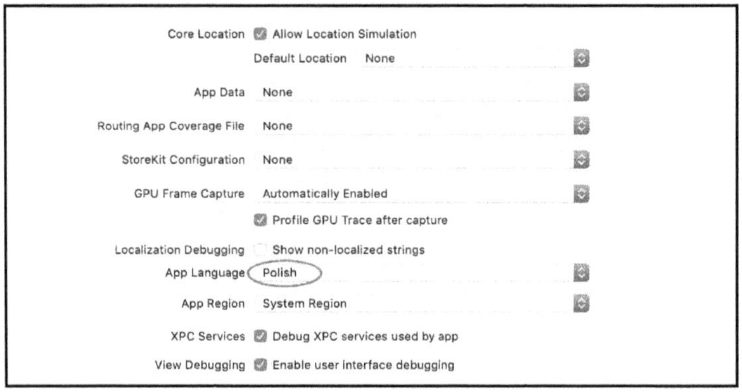

Finally, click **Close**. Xcode changes the active scheme to your new scheme, **Emitron (PL)**.

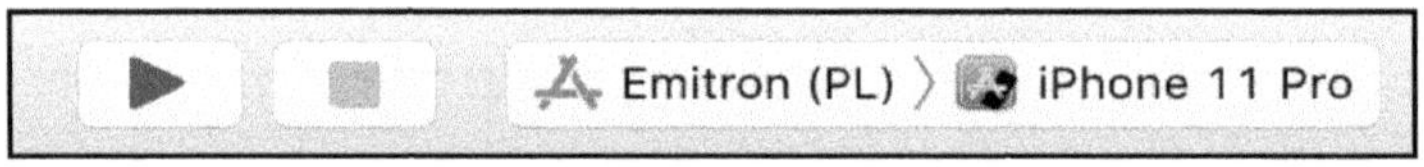

Build and run, and take a look at the text in the app.

Your new Emitron (PL) scheme is an exact duplicate of the familiar Emitron scheme, except that when installing the app, it sets the app language to Polish.

Lucky you, now you can learn both Polish and iOS programming at once! :]

Now that you've seen how to create additional schemes, you can use what you've learned to create a scheme for the alpha build.

Preparing your alpha build

Earlier, you created an Alpha build configuration and used it to change the bundle identifier and app icon, but you can't make an alpha build until there's a scheme using the Alpha build configuration.

In Xcode, click on the active scheme and choose **Manage Schemes...** to bring up the scheme manager.

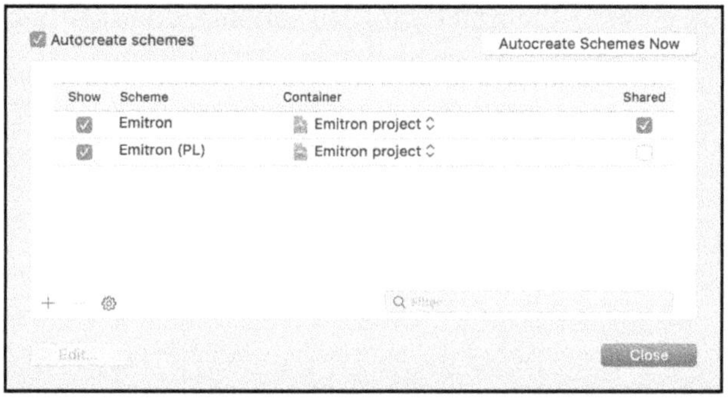

From here, you can see a list of all your schemes, not just the active one.

You can also see that your new scheme, **Emitron (PL)**, isn't marked as **Shared**. New schemes aren't shared by default. This is fine for a scheme that you're using for some localization testing, but remember to share your schemes if you want other developers to get them, too.

Select the Emitron scheme and then click **Edit...** at the bottom of the scheme manager.

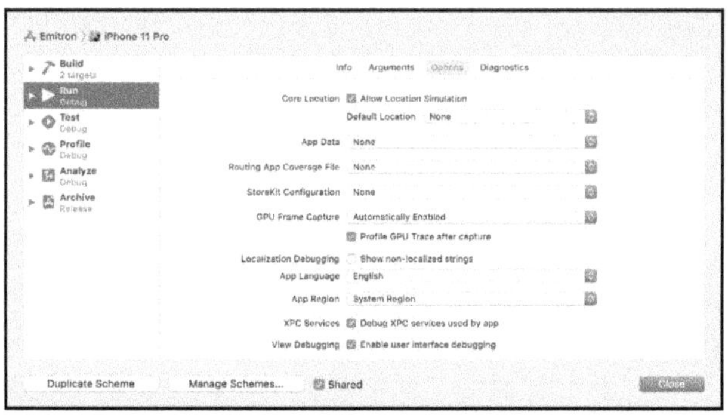

Now, click **Duplicate Scheme**.

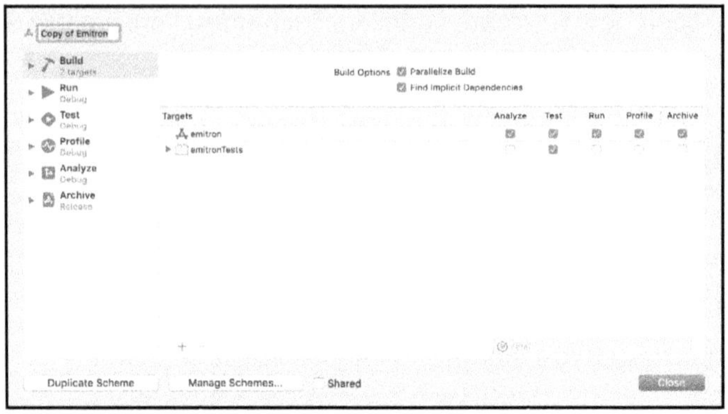

Similar to when you created the **Emitron (PL)** scheme, change the name to `Emitron Alpha` but **don't** press Enter.

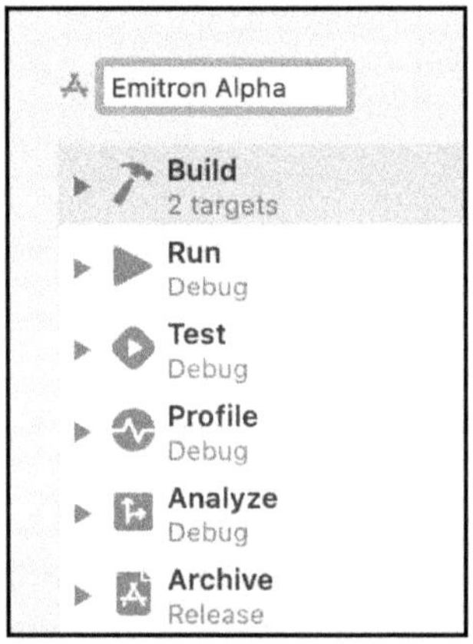

Next, click on the **Run** action, and switch to the **Info** tab.

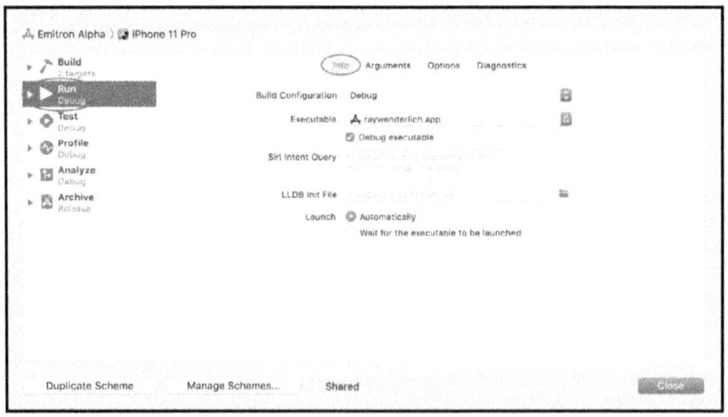

Change the **Build Configuration** to **Alpha**:

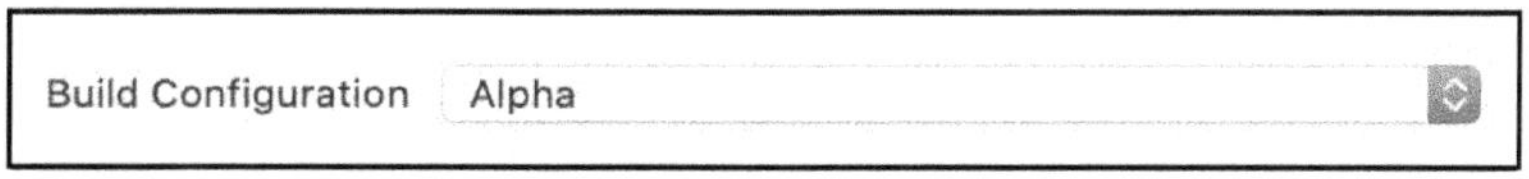

Now, when you run the **Emitron Alpha** scheme, Xcode will use the Alpha configuration to resolve build settings.

When you prepare an alpha release, you also want to use the Alpha configuration. Click the **Archive** action in the scheme editor.

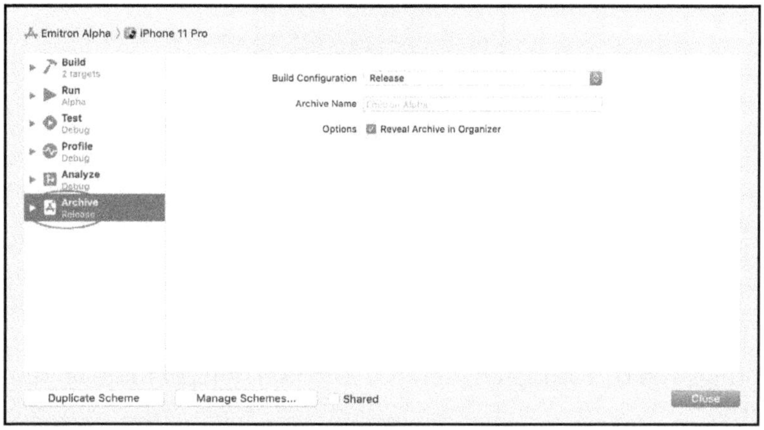

Once again, change the Build Configuration to **Alpha**.

Finally, click the **Close** button at the bottom of the scheme editor.

Emitron Alpha is now your active scheme:

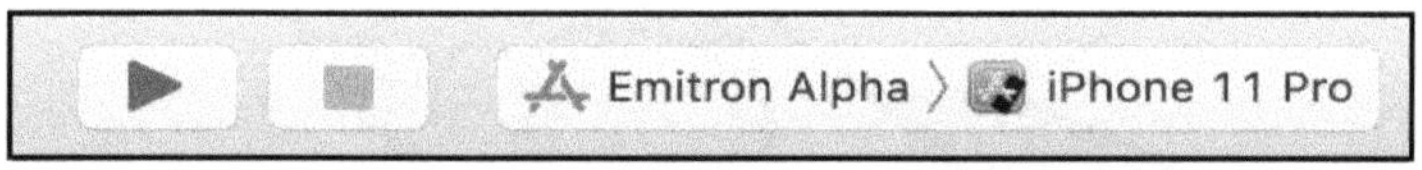

Build and run to test your changes. Once the app is running, minimize it to have a look at your home screen.

Xcode installed Emitron on your device with a different bundle identifier and app icon. That brings you to a whopping total of three versions of Emitron running on your device!

So far, you've managed to get an alpha build running on your phone, but it's not ready for TestFlight yet. In the next chapter, you'll set up code signing and everything else you need to start sharing your alpha with other users.

Key points

- Not every build is destined for the App Store. Builds can be separated by purpose into different build types such as Dev, QA or Release.
- Targets represent a product to be built. Xcode offers a large variety of target types including different platforms and extensions.
- Build settings tell Xcode how to build your target.
- Build configurations swap out build settings for different build types.
- Schemes are blueprints instructing Xcode how to compile a target using a chosen build configuration. When you build and run an app in Xcode, you're executing the Run action for the currently active scheme.
- Different schemes can build the same target with different scheme options. You could simulate a different location for Core Location, change the app language, enable a variety of debugging tools and more.

Chapter 10: Advanced Build Configurations

By Keegan Rush

When you think about changing an app's behavior, the first question that comes to mind is, "What code changes should I make?" As you've learned, changing code isn't the only way to change what your app does.

By the careful composition of your project's schemes, settings and configurations, you can change how Xcode builds your app.

In this chapter, you'll take build customizations to the next level by learning how to:

- Change build settings in a maintainable manner with **build configuration files**.
- Sign your app differently depending on the build configuration.

It's time to take your first steps out of Xcode's comfy UI when it comes to preparing your build pipeline. Xcode will still do the compilation for now, but you'll prepare your build settings with configuration files instead of Xcode's build settings editor.

Build configuration files

In the previous chapter, you customized Emitron by adding your own build configuration and changing build settings depending on the current configuration.

The app's bundle identifier and icon change based on build configurations. However, are there any other settings that change between dev, alpha and release build? To find out, you'd need to scroll through over a hundred different build settings. And, check to see if they change based on configuration.

Scrolling through build settings is tedious work. Wouldn't it be easier if you could store all the customized build settings together in one place? That way, you'd know exactly where to go to modify build settings for a particular release type.

This is where **configuration files** come in. A configuration file is a simple text file where you can keep build settings and their values. The contents of a configuration file look something like this:

```
PRODUCT_BUNDLE_IDENTIFIER = com.raywenderlich.emitron.pias

SWIFT_VERSION = 5.3
```

On the left of the =, you write the name of the build setting. On the right, you set the value. And that's it! Configuration files are easy to read and easy to change.

By using different configuration files for different build configurations, you can keep all the changes to settings in one place. If you tend to forget about the changes you made six months ago, your future self will thank you. :]

Benefits of configuration files

An Xcode project keeps all its build settings in the **project file**, known by the name **project.pbxproj**. This file holds everything unique about the project, including every target, configuration and scheme.

When you edit your project data, Xcode reads from and writes to the project file. While Xcode does a great job of letting you read and edit the project data, the actual project file isn't very readable to human eyes.

Emitron's project file is over 2,000 lines long. When opened in a text editor, you can see that it's mostly confusing identifiers meant for Xcode that looks like this:

```
/* Begin PBXVariantGroup section */
		955CED3724E1AAED00276B85 /* Localizable.strings */ = {
			isa = PBXVariantGroup;
			children = (
				955CED3624E1AAED00276B85 /* en */,
				955CED3824E1AAEF00276B85 /* pl */,
			);
			name = Localizable.strings;
			sourceTree = "<group>";
		};
		B6D7DC3922C79745006DD325 /* LaunchScreen.storyboard */ = {
			isa = PBXVariantGroup;
			children = (
				B6D7DC3A22C79745006DD325 /* Base */,
				955CED3224E1A9FC00276B85 /* pl */,
			);
			name = LaunchScreen.storyboard;
			sourceTree = "<group>";
		};
/* End PBXVariantGroup section */

/* Begin XCBuildConfiguration section */
		22D176C423460A060038333D /* Debug */ = {
			isa = XCBuildConfiguration;
			buildSettings = {
				BUNDLE_LOADER = "$(TEST_HOST)";
				CODE_SIGN_STYLE = Automatic;
				DEVELOPMENT_TEAM = MC7X4Q9BS6;
				INFOPLIST_FILE = emitronTests/Info.plist;
				LD RUNPATH SEARCH PATHS = (
```

You can't easily open **project.pbxproj** in your favorite text editor to change build settings. An **.xcconfig** file, on the other hand, is human-readable because it's a regular text file.

Because **project.pbxproj** isn't human-readable, it's also subject to nasty merge conflicts. Whether changing one of many build settings, editing your targets, or adding new project files, two different developers changing the project file at once can lead to conflicts. Moving your customized build settings to a configuration file makes the project file's job a little easier.

Another problem with Xcode's build settings editor is its lack of undo/redo functionality. **Command-Z** does nothing for build settings. Instead, you need a good memory. Or preferably, you need a configuration file! :]

Refactoring build settings to configuration files

To learn how to set up build configuration files, you'll refactor some build settings in Emitron and create a configuration file for each build configuration.

To start, open this chapter's **starter project**.

Emitron has three build configurations: **Debug**, **Alpha** and **Release**. You'll create a configuration file for each build configuration with specific build settings.

In Xcode's menu bar, click **File ▸ New ▸ File...** and select the **Configuration Settings File** template.

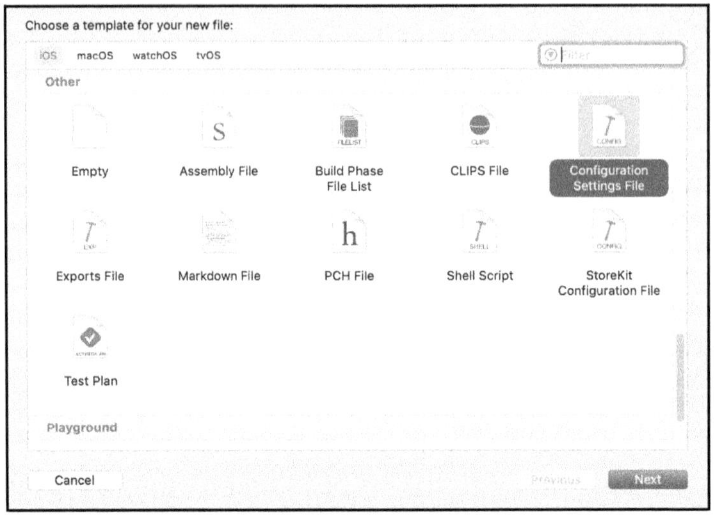

Click **Next**. Set the file name to **Dev**. Change the group to **Configuration** located at **Emitron ▸ Emitron ▸ Configuration**. Leave the **Targets** selections unselected.

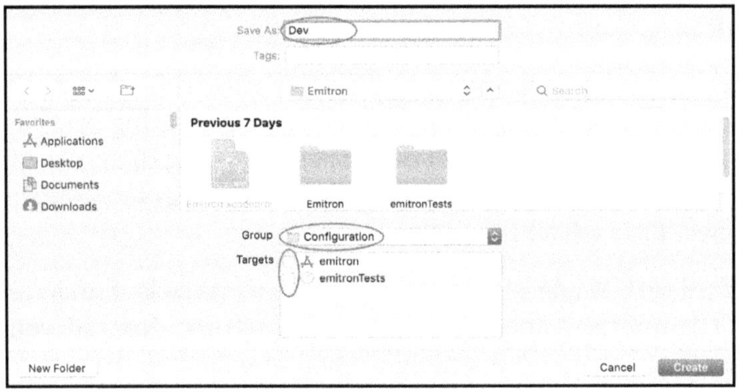

Click **Create**, and you'll see your first blank build configuration file! **Dev.xcconfig** is the file you'll use to store the build setting values that are specific to the Debug build configuration, but you'll need to populate it first.

Adding build settings

Currently, both the bundle identifier and app icon change depend on the build configuration. They're buried within the **project.pbxproj** file, and now you'll move them to your new configuration file.

Add the following to **Dev.xcconfig**:

```
PRODUCT_BUNDLE_IDENTIFIER = $(inherited).dev

ASSETCATALOG_COMPILER_APPICON_NAME = $(inherited).dev

PRODUCT_NAME = rwenderlich Dev
```

Those screaming uppercase variables may look odd. However, they're familiar conventions found in Xcode build settings.

`PRODUCT_BUNDLE_IDENTIFIER` is the actual name for the **Product Bundle Identifier** setting that you see in the Build Settings editor.

`ASSETCATALOG_COMPILER_APPICON_NAME` is the name for the **Asset Catalog App Icon Set Name** that you use to set the app icon.

The last build setting in the file, `PRODUCT_NAME`, is a new one: it refers to the **Product Name** build setting, which is the app name you see on your device.

For a complete list of build settings, look at the Build Settings Reference on the Xcode Help site at https://apple.co/3j2F9JL.

Now, look at the `PRODUCT_BUNDLE_IDENTIFIER` setting in the **emitron** target's bulid settings, without taking values from **Dev.xcconfig**:

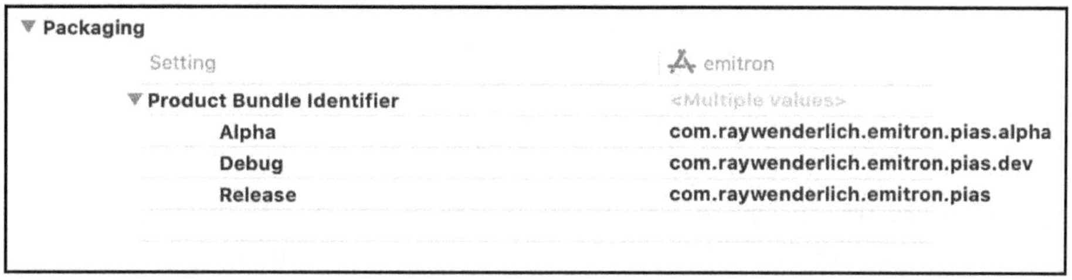

The default bundle identifier is `com.raywenderlich.emitron.pias`. The Debug configuration appends `.dev` to the default bundle identifier.

The configuration file does the same by using a special `inherited` variable. By using `$(inherited)`, a build setting can dynamically refer to a default value, one further up the chain of resolution. That way, if the bundle identifier is declared at the project level changes, you don't need to update configurations that use `$(inherited)` to reference the project level bundle identifier.

Build settings aren't limited to referencing themselves with `$(inherited)`. You can reference any other build setting as a variable in a similar fashion: `$(SWIFT_VERSION)` references the Swift Version build setting.

The `ASSETCATALOG_COMPILER_APPICON_NAME` setting follows the same strategy as `PRODUCT_BUNDLE_IDENTIFIER` to set the icon name. It uses `$(inherited)` to reference a default value, `AppIcon` in this case, and appends `.dev` to get the app icon specific to the dev build.

`PRODUCT_NAME` works differently. If you use `$(inherited) Dev`, the app name becomes **raywenderlich (Dev)**. That's a bit wordy for an iPhone's home screen, and the name would appear as **raywenderlich...**. To keep it short and readable, you abbreviate the name to `rwenderlich (Dev)`.

Build and run. Once the app runs, go to the Home Screen. Take a look:

The app name for the dev build is still **raywenderlich**. That's because you've created a configuration file, but it isn't applied to any build configurations. You'll do that next.

Applying configuration files

In the Project navigator, click on the Emitron project to reach the project screen. Make sure you're on the project's **Info** tab.

See the image below:

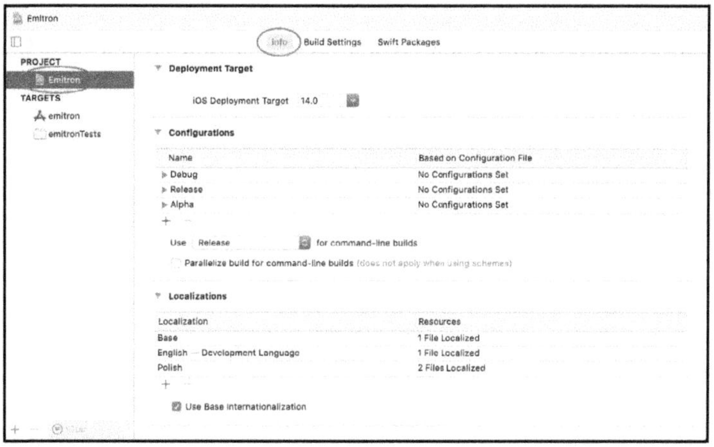

In the **Configurations** section and next to the **Debug** configuration, click the ▸ icon to expand it.

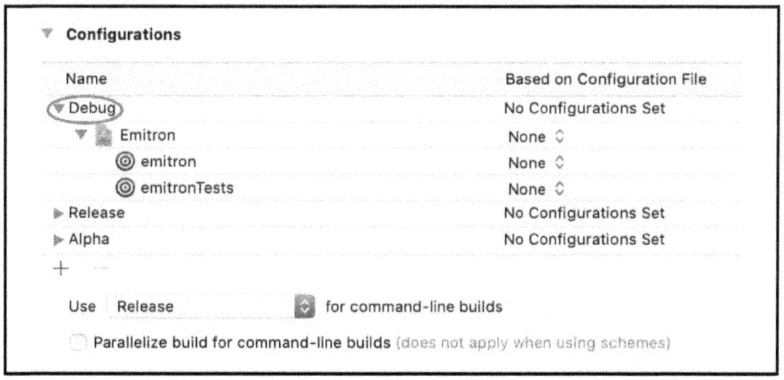

Click on the dropdown to the right of the **emitron** target, *not* the **Emitron** project, and change its value to **Dev**.

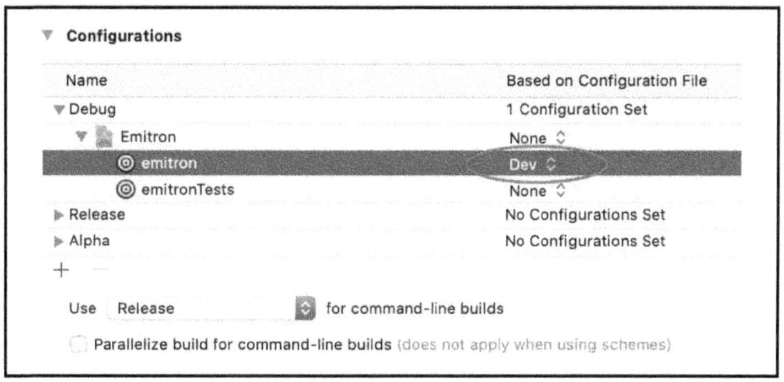

Now, Xcode accounts for **Dev.xcconfig** when resolving build settings.

Resolving build settings

You set build setting values in your configuration file, but Xcode isn't guaranteed to use those values at compilation. When Xcode needs to resolve the build setting, it chooses the most specific value it can find between the three different levels:

1. Target level
2. Project level
3. Platform default

Now that you've applied a configuration file at the target level, Xcode needs to look for values at the target level. When you add configuration files at either the project or target level, Xcode resolves build settings in the following order:

1. Target level
2. Target configuration cile
3. Project level
4. Project configuration file
5. Platform default

Only a build setting declared at the target level in Xcode's build settings editor can override a build setting declared in **Dev.xcconfig**.

Because of this, you need to make sure that no build settings at the target level are overriding your configuration file.

Still on the project screen, do the following to reach the **Product Name** build setting:

1. Select the **emitron** target.
2. Click the **Build Settings** tab.
3. Change the scope to **Levels**.
4. Search for **Product Name**.

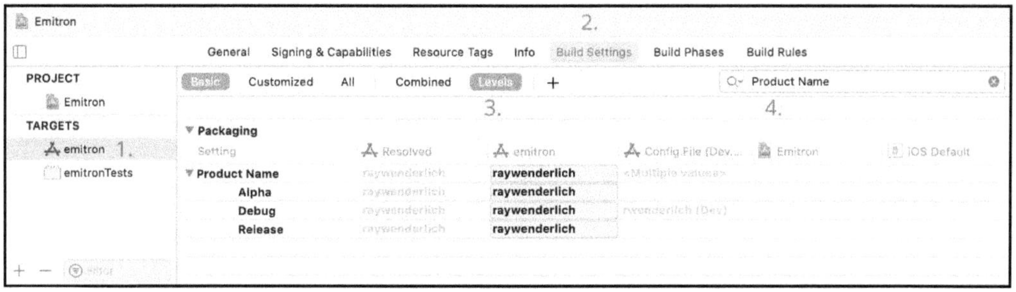

Here, you can see that the setting has a value at the target level. This means that your value in **Dev.xcconfig** will never shine through; the Debug configuration's resolved value is **raywenderlich** instead of **rwenderlich (Dev)**.

To the right of the **Product Name** build setting title and above the three configurations, change the value to **$(inherited)**.

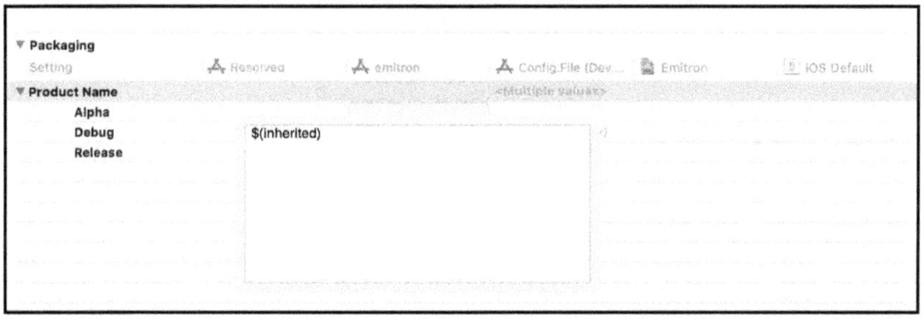

Remember how using `$(inherited)` in a build setting lets that setting use a default value? In this case, setting the target level to `$(inherited)` uses the next value Xcode finds up the resolution chain. Now, the Debug configuration will inherit the value from **Dev.xcconfig**, which you set to `rwenderlich (Dev)`.

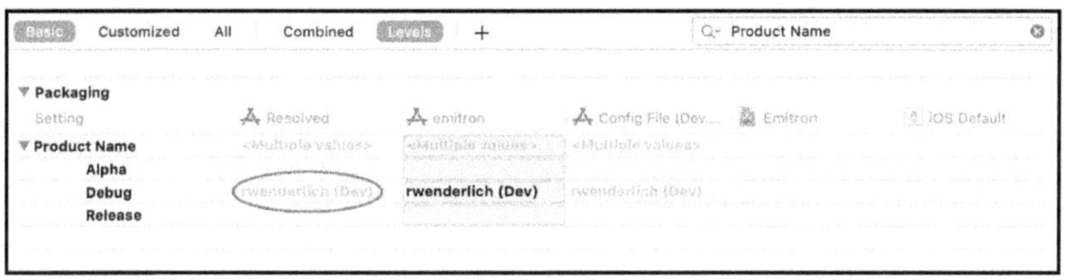

Finally, build and run to see the results of your effort! Go to the Home Screen.

You'll see **Dev.xcconfig** sets the Product Name.

Resolving bundle identifier and app icon settings

The Product Name gets its value from **Dev.xcconfig**, but the app icon and bundle identifier don't do the same.

Back to the emitron target's build settings editor, search **Bundle Identifier**.

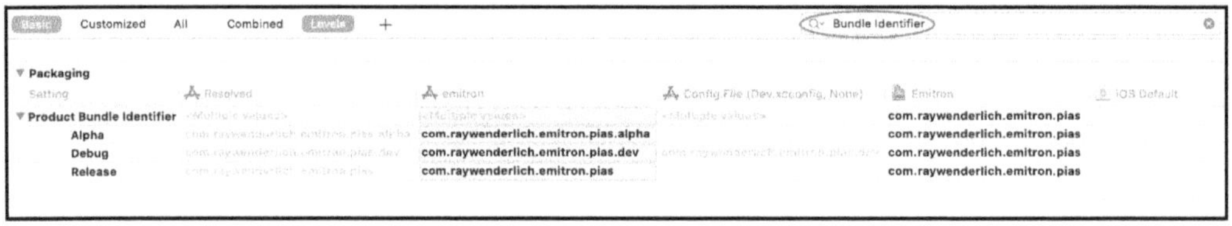

Expand **Product Bundle Identifier**. Set the configurations' values at the target level to **$(inherited)**.

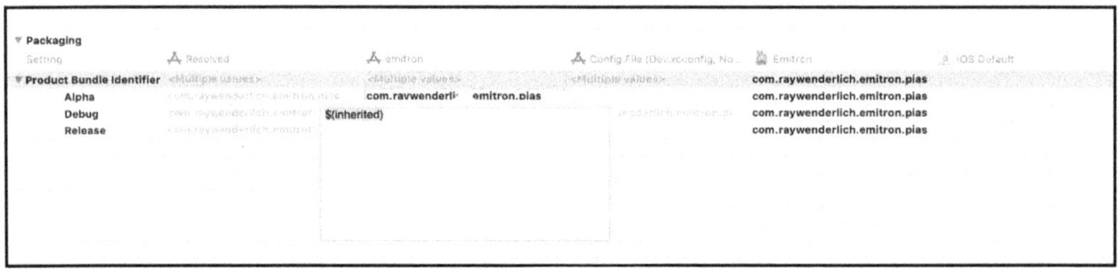

Next, search **App Icon**.

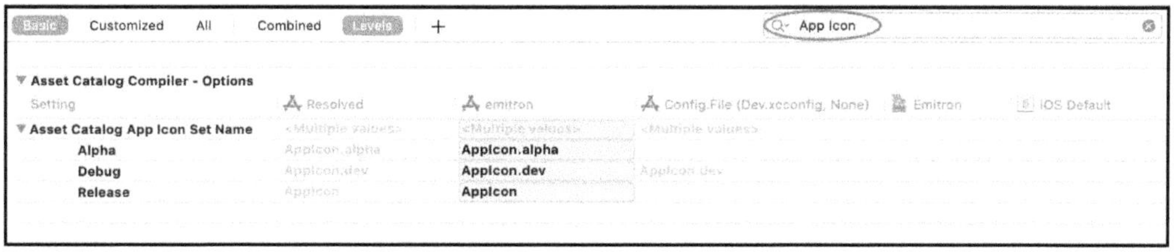

Set **Asset Catalog App Icon Set Name** at the target level to **$(inherited)**.

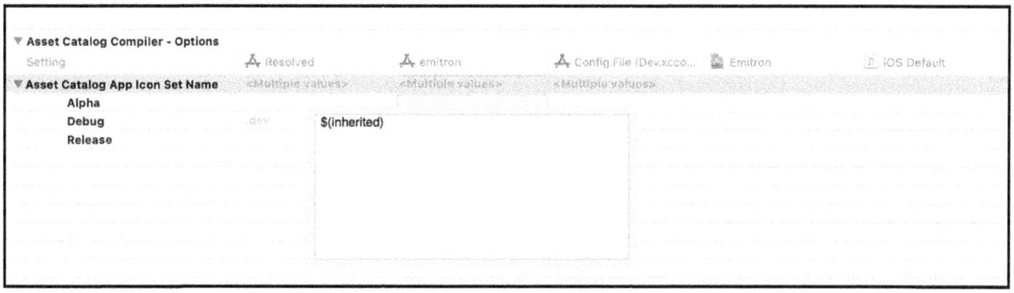

Build and run.

Great job! Now, you're correctly applying the build settings from **Dev.xcconfig**. You won't notice any changes because **Dev.xcconfig** values are the same as previously set for the target level.

The dev build type is set up to use a configuration file, but the alpha build type is still configuring its settings in the Xcode UI. Next, you'll use what you learned to make a configuration file for the Alpha build type.

Creating an Alpha configuration file

Now that you've set up the Product Name, Bundle Identifier and App Icon build settings to inherit values from configuration files, setting up a configuration file for the alpha build type becomes a lot quicker.

Follow the same steps you took to create Dev.xcconfig.

This time, create a **Configuration Settings File** named **Alpha**. Set the file's group to **Configuration**. Leave the **Targets** selection unselected.

Next, replace the contents of **Alpha.xcconfig** with this:

```
PRODUCT_BUNDLE_IDENTIFIER = $(inherited).alpha
ASSETCATALOG_COMPILER_APPICON_NAME = $(inherited).alpha
PRODUCT_NAME = rwenderlich (α)
```

In the Project navigator, click on the **Emitron** project. Make sure you're on the project's Info tab.

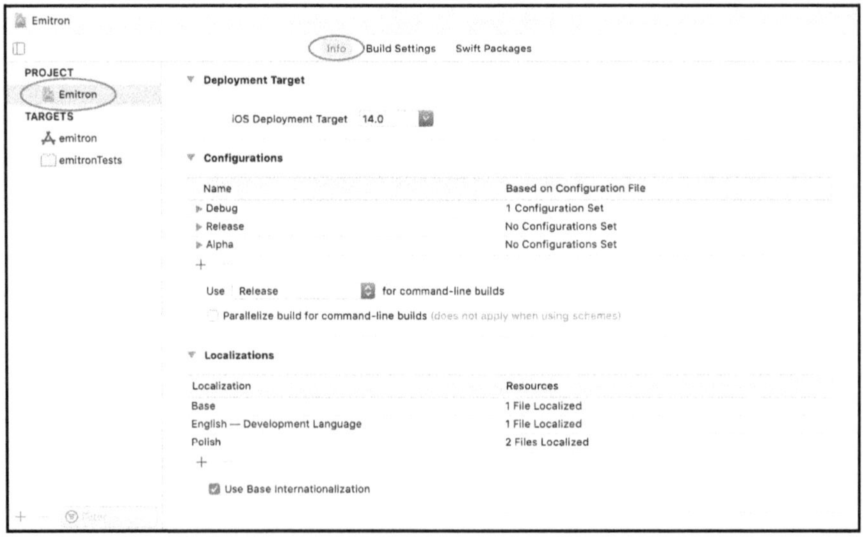

Expand the **Configurations** section.

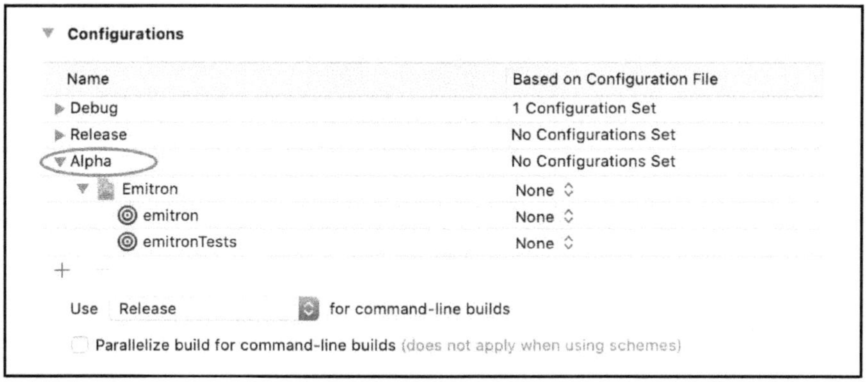

Click on the dropdown to the right of the **emitron** target, and change its value to **Alpha**.

Under the **Alpha** configuration and to the right of the **emitron** target, click the **dropdown menu**. Then, select **Alpha** as the configuration file.

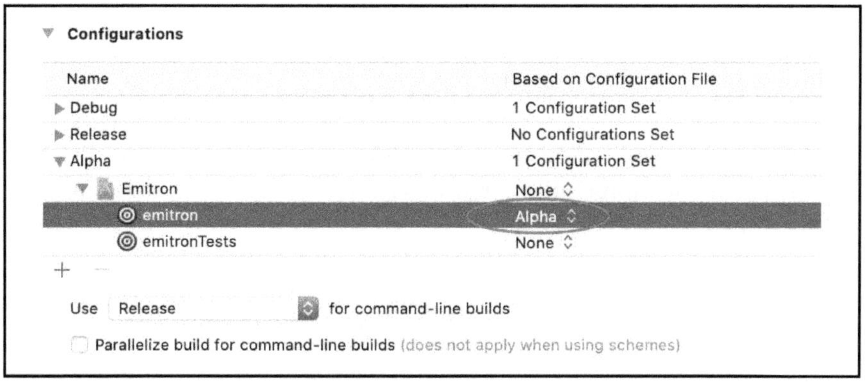

Since you've already configured the target-level build settings to inherit from the configuration files, that's all you need to do!

You're ready to test your changes. Change the active scheme to **Emitron Alpha**:

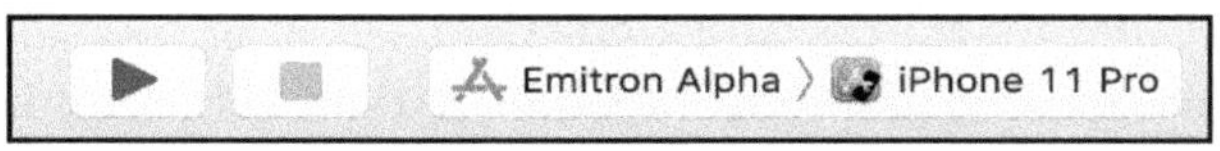

Build and run. Go to the Home Screen.

The alpha build gets its name from **Alpha.xcconfig**.

Configuration file for the release build

So far, you've created two configuration files: **Dev.xcconfig** for the dev build and **Alpha.xcconfig** for the alpha build. That leaves the release build without a configuration file:

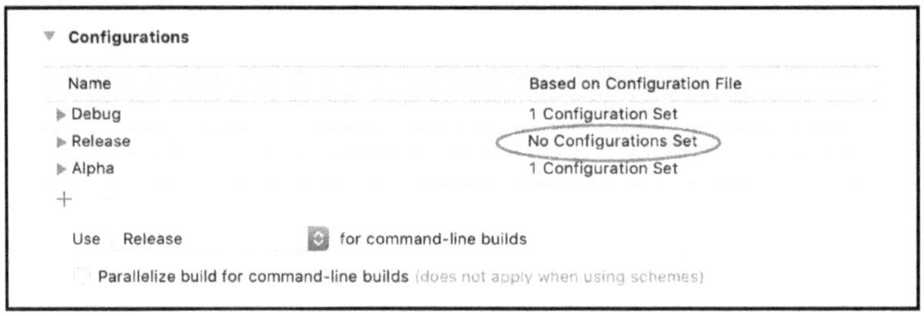

Your configuration files for the dev and alpha builds exist to override default build settings. The release build is different. All of the default values for the build settings are set up for the release build:

- **Product Name**: `raywenderlich`
- **Product Bundle Identifier**: `com.raywenderlich.emitron.pias`
- **Asset Catalog App Icon Set Name**: `AppIcon`

Since these default values don't need to change for the release build, there's no need to create another xcconfig file for release configurations here.

With your configuration files set up correctly to change bundle identifiers, product names and app icons based on the different build types, you're almost ready to upload an alpha build to TestFlight to share with your time.

Before you hit **Archive** in Xcode and upload Emitron Alpha to App Store Connect, however, you'll need to differentiate your code signing between alpha and release.

Code signing for different build types

Now that you have a shiny new alpha build, you also need a new **provisioning profile** for it. You need to do this because Emitron Alpha is a different app compared to the Emitron release build. In order to upload builds to App Store Connect, you can't use the same provisioning profile for two different apps.

The Alpha build configuration is a duplicate of the Release configuration, with a few important changes: the most important of which is the **bundle identifier**.

By changing the bundle identifier, the alpha build type is essentially a completely different app from Apple's point of view. That's why you can install it on a device alongside the dev and release builds; they're not the same app!

When you first created an app record for Emitron in App Store Connect, you also created a provisioning profile. With your provisioning profile in hand, you have what you need to take Emitron to the App Store. Now, you need to do something similar for Emitron Alpha. Don't worry, though, you'll be doing less clicking around in App Store Connect this time around!

First, look around Emitron's code signing setup to understand how it's done for dev, alpha and release builds.

In Xcode's Project navigator, click the **Emitron** project to reach the project screen. Select the **emitron** target. Then, select the **Signing & Capabilities** tab.

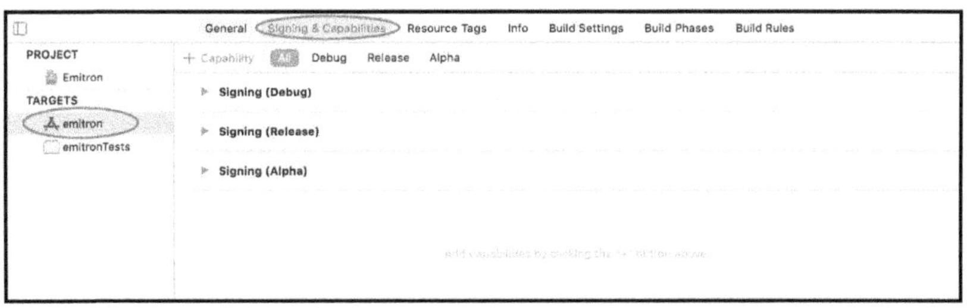

The three sections correspond to your three different build configurations. Expand them and compare the differences.

In the **Debug** section, you'll see that **Automatically manage signing** is enabled. This lets Xcode handle the work for you of creating your app ID, certificates and provisioning profiles. The bundle identifier is different from that of the release build, so having Xcode manage all of this is a nice convenience.

In the **Release** section, Xcode leaves you to manage your code signing.

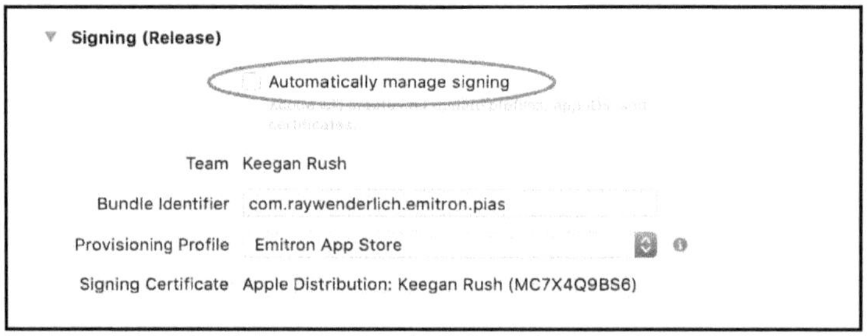

Your release build is the most important of them all. Since you're a code signing pro thanks to this book, you have all the knowledge you need to manage code signing yourself.

Putting in the extra effort for a release build can be worth it when you know what you're doing. You're in full control of code signing, so you can make sure that everything is set up exactly as you need it in App Store Connect and the Apple Developer Portal.

Signing the alpha build

Finally, take a look at the **Alpha** section.

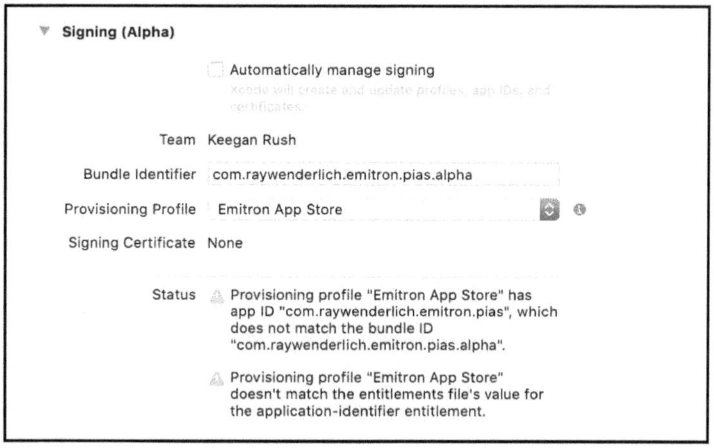

Because it's a clone of the Release configuration, code signing is an exact duplicate as well. Xcode configured the Alpha configuration with the Release configuration's provisioning profile.

There are a couple of warnings at the bottom because the release build's provisioning profile doesn't match the alpha build's bundle identifier. You'll have to fix that before you can upload Emitron Alpha to TestFlight.

To fix the code signing for the alpha build, you need to do one of the following:

1. Create your app ID and provisioning profile in the Apple Developer Center.
2. Let Xcode automatically manage the signing of the alpha build.

Since it's not as critical as the release build, it makes sense to let Xcode handle the dirty work for you. Click the **checkbox** next to **Automatically manage signing**.

You'll see a pop-up asking to reset the **Code Sign Identity** and **Provisioning Profile** build settings.

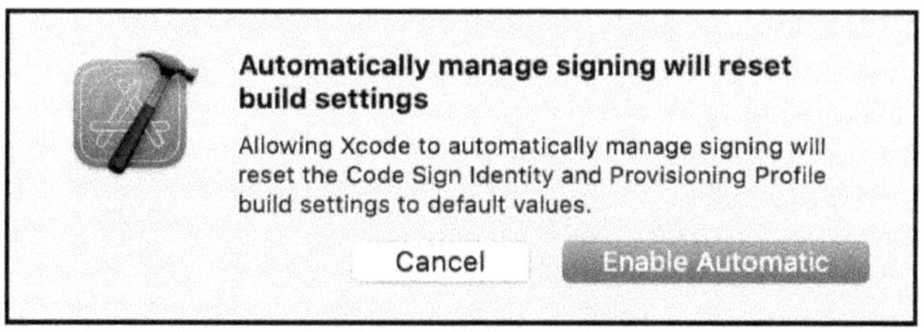

Click **Enable Automatic**.

If your **Team** is set to **None**, you'll get a warning:

Set your development team and let Xcode spin up your code signing setup for you.

And that's it! With code signing in place, and all your build setting customizations coming from build configuration files, you've successfully set up an alpha build type from compilation to code signing. You're ready to hit **Archive** and start distributing an alpha build to testers. Great job! :]

Key points

- Build configuration files are a maintainable way to handle changes between builds.
- A setting in a configuration file can reference itself, with `$(inherited)`, or any other build setting.
- The chain of resolution determines the resolved value of a build setting, so always check to make sure that the values in a configuration file will resolve as expected.
- Code signing can change by your chosen build configuration.

Chapter 11: Managing Secrets

By Keegan Rush

You may not have known, but Emitron has a secret — something that Emitron's developers want to keep hidden from prying eyes. In fact, many apps work with one or more secrets: a special token that some APIs require, known as an **API secret**!

A **secret** is private data that your app needs to function. It could be an API secret, also known as an **API key**, or a password to a particular service or tool, like database credentials.

Many web services require that you use a secret when accessing their API. An API key is a private token that's unique to you. By providing your secret when making API calls, the owner of the API you're using can verify your identity.

There could be one API key per app, or keys could be unique for each developer. They let the creators of an API know who is using (and possibly abusing) their service. For paid services, it lets the service provider charge based on your usage.

To use an API that works with secrets, you need to add code to your app to send the secret on every API call. That's the easy part. Choosing where to store your secrets is a little trickier.

In this chapter, you'll learn of some choices you can make when managing your secrets. You'll use a special build configuration file to store Emitron's secret, and learn about the tradeoffs between different approaches of secret management.

Along the way, you'll pick up some new skills to use with build configuration files. Time to get started!

Why secrets are secret

A secret is a sensitive piece of data, like a password, that you need to protect from prying eyes. Revealing an API key isn't as bad as revealing your database credentials, but if someone has your API secret, they can use it to authenticate with that API as if they were you.

For something like an analytics API, having someone else authenticating as you can muddy up your data. For paid services like Amazon's AWS, it means someone else is using the service you paid for.

Even if exposing an API secret won't hurt you directly, it likely hurts the API provider that gave you the API key. So, it's important that you keep it secure, because one day, *you* might be the one creating the API! :]

How secrets get exposed

Your API secrets could be exposed to three groups of people:

1. Anyone that downloads your app.
2. Anyone with access to your Git repository.
3. Other developers you work with.

When you make an API call in your app, you need to provide the secret as well. If the secret is coded into the app, that means your secret is tucked away on every iPhone that has your app installed. A user with enough know-how could potentially reverse-engineer your app to get to your secrets.

On top of that, you're probably storing your code in some form of source control. Anyone with access to your app's source control repository has access to the secrets stored within. If your repository is public, *everyone* has access! In fact, as a research team from North Carolina State University revealed, every day *thousands* of new public GitHub repositories expose new secrets.

Even if you make your repository private, you still run the risk of other developers on your team gaining access to secrets that weren't meant for them. Sure, your fellow developer sitting beside you probably won't use your API key for evil, but the fewer people that have access to important secrets, the better. If everyone on a team has access to credentials for a production database, for instance, the possibility of making mistakes with client data skyrockets.

Next, you'll take a look at Emitron's secret, and learn how you can prevent it from becoming exposed to other developers or the general public.

Secrets in Emitron

In Xcode, open **AppDelegate.swift**. In `applicationDidFinishLaunching(_:)`, find the line that initializes `guardpost`:

```
guardpost = Guardpost(
  baseUrl: "https://accounts.raywenderlich.com",
  urlScheme: "com.razeware.emitron://",
  ssoSecret: "155bdf4d4f847e77aec11624ab9c17b4",
  persistenceStore: persistenceStore)
```

Guardpost is the raywenderlich.com API's authentication service. The `ssoSecret` parameter ensures secure communication with the service. A consumer of the API should generate their own SSO secret, but the open-source Emitron app comes with a sample secret that you can use.

The sample secret is already hard-coded into the initializer for `Guardpost`:

```
ssoSecret: "155bdf4d4f847e77aec11624ab9c17b4"
```

The problem with hard-coded secrets

Secrets are subject to change. The SSO Secret that's hard-coded in **AppDelegate.swift** is only a sample. If you were building your own app with the raywenderlich.com API, you'd need your own secret.

For larger apps, different build types use different secrets. The SSO Secret that the app uses for a release build might not be the same as the one used for an alpha build. What's more, the secret can change between developers on the team.

When you're swapping out a secret for one that's specific to you, or specific to a particular build type, you need to edit the code that stores the secret.

If you leave your secret in code, its days as a concealed bit of information are numbered. Your secret is there to see for anyone looking at **AppDelegate.swift**. If you use Git or a different kind of version control, your secret is public to anyone that has access to the repository!

Swapping out secrets by build type can also lead to mistakes. You have to be careful to use the correct secret for the correct build type.

Instead, when using secrets, you want to store them somewhere that:

1. Allows you to "set it and forget it" so you don't have to change the secret when you change build types.
2. Prevents other developers from changing the code to match their own secrets.
3. Protects your secret from prying eyes looking at the code in a public repository.

As it turns out, build configuration files work for more than overriding build settings. They're a solution for secrets management, too.

Secrets in configuration files

By putting your secrets into a build configuration file, it becomes easier to change them based on build types.

Storing secrets meant for alpha builds in **Alpha.xcconfig** and those for release builds in a **Release.xcconfig** will automatically swap out your secrets when you change build types.

So, using your existing build configuration files solves the first problem of storing secrets in code, if your secrets change depending on the build type. But, if different developers use different secrets, you still have to edit the configuration files to update them for your own secrets. For configuration files checked into Git, version control and sharing code are just as messy as they are when storing the secrets in code.

The solution is to create a *new* configuration file — one that *isn't* shared or added to version control. Here's the recommendation for how to handle secrets in your projects:

1. Create **Secrets.xcconfig** to store your secrets.
2. Keep the configuration file *out* of version control. Add it to **.gitignore** if you're using Git.
3. Reference your secrets in code.

Next, you'll create and use **Secrets.xcconfig** to store Emitron's SSO Secret.

Step 2 is important because, if your secret is version controlled, it's available for anyone with access to the repository to see. The open-source Emitron app uses Git, but your sample project version of Emitron does not. You won't have to change any **.gitignore** files this time.

Secrets and security

Keeping your secrets in a configuration file solves the problems mentioned above, but that still isn't the most secure option.

If someone tries hard enough, there's always a way to get to a secret that's compiled into your app. Think of it like keeping a secret diary. You could hide the diary and put a lock on it, but someone determined enough can still find a way in.

The only true way to keep secrets from prying eyes is not to compile them with the app at all. Instead, think about fetching your secrets from a secure and trusted server.

So, without further ado, it's time to learn how to store your deepest, darkest API secrets in a configuration file. :]

Storing the SSO secret

For the secrets configuration file, you'll do something similar to **Dev.xcconfig** and **Alpha.xcconfig**.

In Xcode's menu bar, click **File ▸ New ▸ File...** and choose the **Configuration Settings File** template.

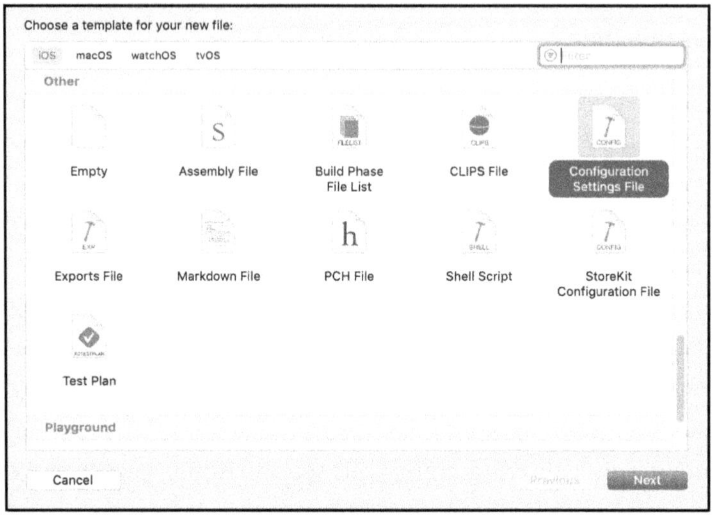

Click **Next**. Change the name to **Secrets** and change the group to **Configuration.** Leave **Targets** unselected.

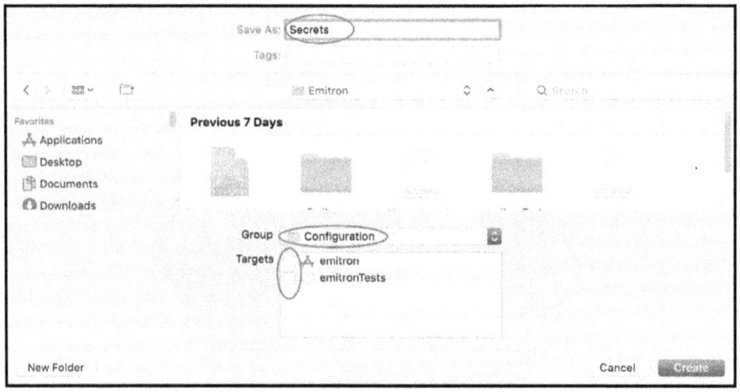

Next, replace the contents of **Secrets.xcconfig** with this:

```
SSO_SECRET = 155bdf4d4f847e77aec11624ab9c17b4
```

By doing this, you've created a *brand new* build setting named SSO_SECRET.

Whether in build configuration files or directly in Xcode's UI, you aren't limited to the many build settings that Xcode provides. You can create your own, too.

Applying the secrets configuration file

In the Project navigator, click on the Emitron project to reach the project screen. Make sure you're on the project's Info tab.

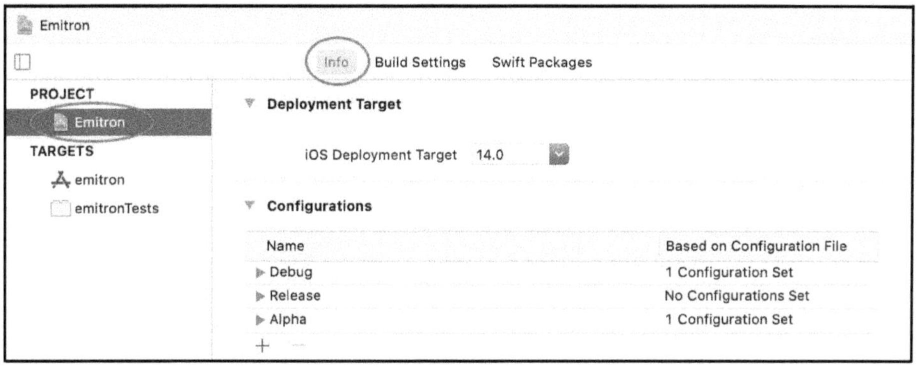

Now, in the **Configurations** section, click the ▸ icon next to the **Debug** configuration to expand it. Then, do the same for the **Release** and **Alpha** configurations.

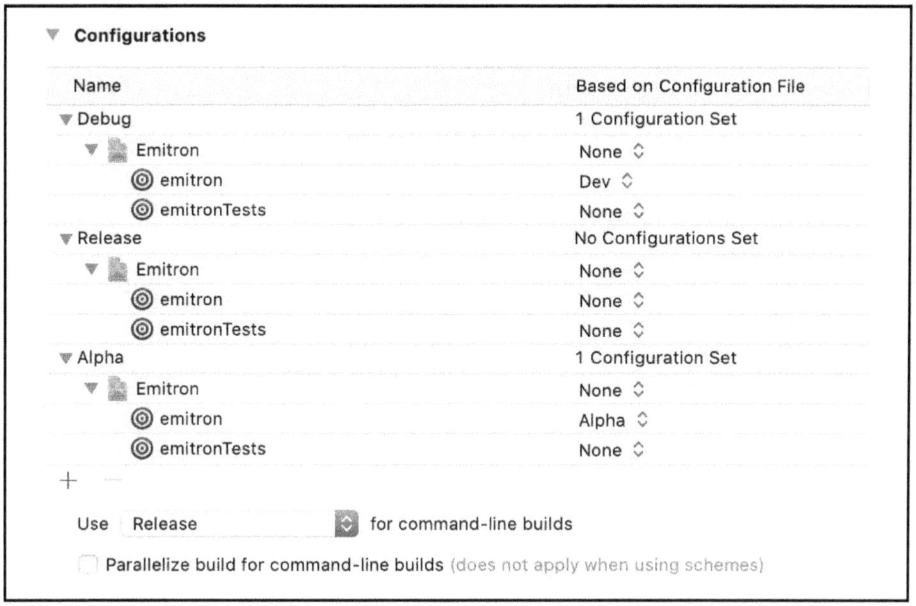

Here, you'll see that under the Debug configuration, the Emitron target's configuration file is set to **Dev**. Above it, the Emitron **project** configuration file is set to **None**.

Click on the drop-down to the right of the Emitron project and change its value to **Secrets**.

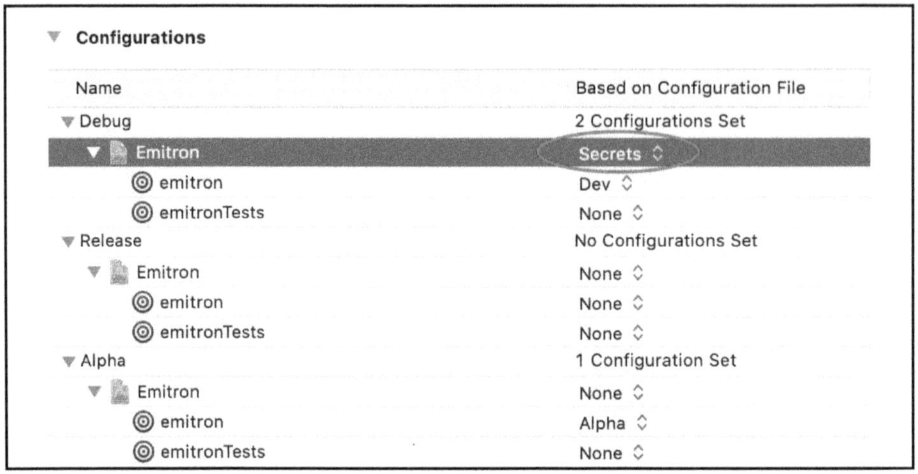

If you wanted to set a different secrets configuration file for each build configuration, you'd do that here. But because you only have one secret, and that secret is the same for each build type, you can set **Secrets.xcconfig** for every build configuration.

So under the Release configuration, click the drop-down to the right of the Emitron project and change its value to **Secrets** as well. Then, do the same for the Alpha configuration.

Here's how your configurations should look when you're done:

No matter which build configuration you use, you'll have a `SSO_SECRET` build setting that's set to the sample value.

To prove this, change from the Info tab to the **Build Settings** tab. In the search bar, search for `SSO_SECRET`:

Your secret is set and ready to go.

Configuration file imports

While setting the project's configuration file to **Secrets.xcconfig**, you may have noticed that you can't have multiple configuration files at the same level.

You've set the secrets configuration file at the project level for each build configuration; that means you can't use another configuration file at the project level. You also can't apply **Secrets.xcconfig** at the target level because that level is already taken by the Dev and Alpha configuration files, respectively.

What if you already filled the slots for both the project level and target level? There would be nowhere to apply **Secrets.xcconfig**. Luckily, you can still **import** one build configuration file into another.

If you wanted to import **Secrets.xcconfig** into **Alpha.xcconfig**, you'd do so like this:

```
#include "./Secrets.xcconfig"
```

By adding the `include` statement in a configuration file, such as **Alpha.xcconfig**, you can use the build settings available there without applying **Secrets.xcconfig** in the project's **Configurations** section like you did earlier.

Note that the `include` statement takes a path to the configuration file. `"./Secrets.xcconfig"` assumes that **Secrets.xcconfig** is in the same folder as the file that's importing it.

Next, it's time to use the secret in place of the hardcoded value in **AppDelegate.swift**.

Referencing build settings in code

Unfortunately, your Swift code can't directly access any build settings. But, your code *can* read values from your app's **Info.plist**, which is a file containing special metadata for your app.

In Xcode, open **Info.plist**. Here, you see some important metadata such as the bundle identifier, product name and app version.

See the image below:

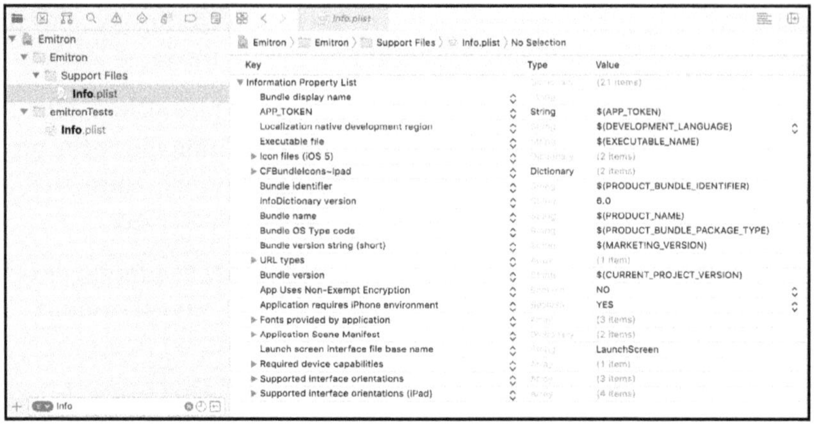

But wait, isn't the bundle identifier actually a build setting that you've been manipulating in your configuration files? It is, and the **Bundle identifier** key that you find in **Info.plist** is a reference to the `PRODUCT_BUNDLE_IDENTIFIER` build setting you worked with earlier.

See, an entry in **Info.plist** can reference a build setting. By adding the bundle identifier, product name and app version to **Info.plist**, you can indirectly reference the underlying build settings in code:

Your code can read Info.plist, which can then read the build settings.

Adding the SSO secret to Info.plist

You need to put the SSO secret in **Info.plist** for it to be accessible in code.

At the top of the file and to the right of **Information Property List**, click the + button.

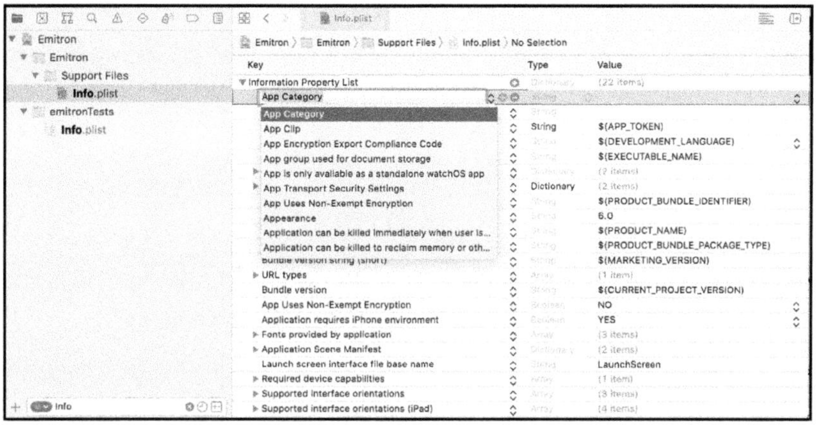

Change the **Key** to **SSO_SECRET**, leave the **Type** as **String**. Change the **Value** to **$ (SSO_SECRET)**.

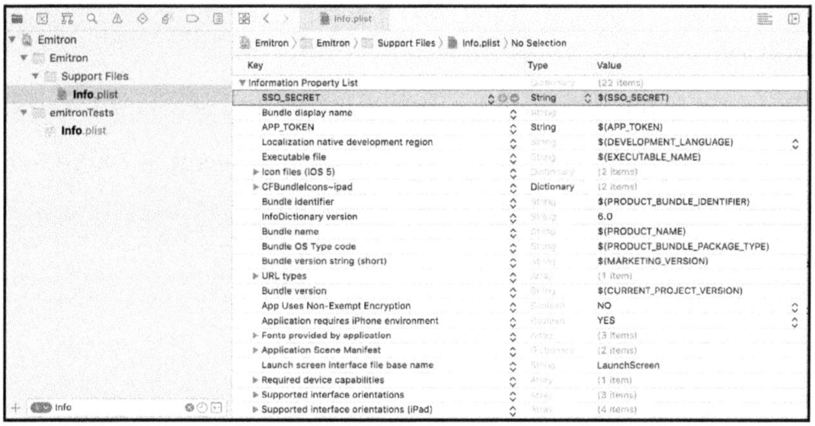

Now, you have a value in your **Info.plist** that'll work in code. The **SSO_SECRET** key references the **SSO_SECRET** build setting, so you can use whatever secret you've stored in your secrets configuration file.

Getting the value of the SSO secret in code

Open **AppDelegate.swift**. In `applicationDidFinishLaunching(_:)`, replace initialization of `guardpost`:

```
guardpost = Guardpost(
  baseUrl: "https://accounts.raywenderlich.com",
  urlScheme: "com.razeware.emitron://",
  ssoSecret: "155bdf4d4f847e77aec11624ab9c17b4",
  persistenceStore: persistenceStore)
```

With this:

```
// 1.
let ssoSecret = Bundle.main.object(
  forInfoDictionaryKey: "SSO_SECRET") as? String
guardpost = Guardpost(
  baseUrl: "https://accounts.raywenderlich.com",
  urlScheme: "com.razeware.emitron://",
  // 2.
  ssoSecret: ssoSecret ?? "",
  persistenceStore: persistenceStore)
```

Here's what's happening:

1. Get the SSO secret from **Info.plist**, which in turn references the `SSO_SECRET` build setting.
2. Pass the secret to the initializer for `guardpost` instead of a hard-coded string.

Build and run. You need to be signed out to test the SSO secret. If you're signed in, then either sign out or use a different simulator.

On Emitron's login screen, tap **Sign In**. Without an SSO secret, you won't be able to get to this screen:

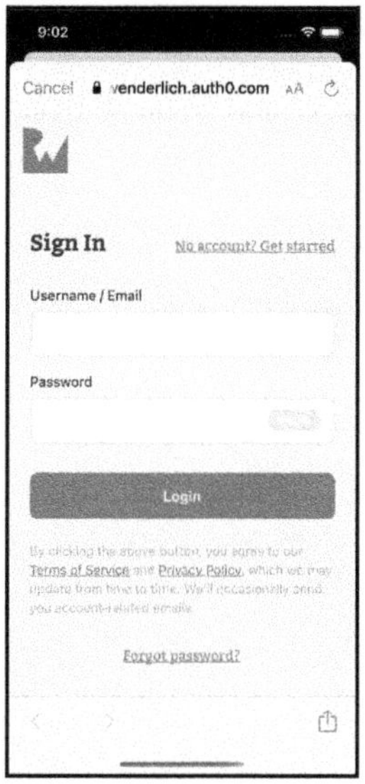

So, if you get that far, your SSO secret is loading correctly from **Secrets.xcconfig**!

By referencing your secret in **AppDelegate.swift**, you've delved into the world of bringing your configurations into code via your app's **Info.plist**.

Storing secrets in a build configuration file and keeping it out of source control lets different developers use different configuration files. Everyone on the team can have their own version of **Secrets.xcconfig**.

Because **Secrets.xcconfig** isn't stored in version control, each developer's copy of the file stays on their local machine, removing the danger of an embarrassing exposé of your secrets in a public GitHub repository.

Key points

- Secrets don't belong in code, but they can be stored in configuration files.
- Leaking an API key isn't as bad as leaking a database password, but you should take care with any secret.
- You can create your own build settings and use them how you choose.
- Build configuration files can import one another.
- You can't access build settings in Swift code directly, but you can access entries in your **Info.plist**.

Chapter 12: Build Automation

By Keegan Rush

The world of computing has come a long way in the last century.

The ancient predecessor to a modern computer is an abacus, used to add numbers. This became the inspiration for more sophisticated adding machines, and then calculating machines that could add, subtract, multiply and divide. But, until the twentieth century, computer programming was a non-existent profession.

In 1936, the first programmable computer was invented, and soon the modern age of computing was underway. In the early days, programmers had to work directly with machine code that was unique to each type of computer. It wasn't until the invention of assembly language that programmers could worry less about the intricacies of ones and zeros and focus more on the software they were writing.

Eventually, in the 1950s, the industry took another leap forward with the invention of the first high-level programming language: FORTRAN. With each step to higher level, more abstract programming languages, a programmer has to worry less about how to write the code and more about the problems they're trying to solve. The journey towards higher-level programming languages continues even today, with you writing Swift in Xcode's cushy interface.

Before the adoption of integrated development environments (IDEs) like Xcode, programming was done in text editors, and before that, on the command line. Without an IDE, you have to invoke compilers from the command line to build apps.

Using Xcode means you get to worry less about the technical details and more about making an app that people will love. But, sometimes, you have to take a step back to take another gigantic leap forward.

In this chapter, you'll step outside of Xcode and learn how to leverage the command line to build your apps. You'll automate Emitron by creating a simple build script that does the following:

1. Builds and archives Emitron.
2. Exports the archive into an **.ipa**.
3. Uploads the exported archive to App Store Connect.

In doing so, you'll learn how you can automate the distribution process.

With automation, you can let your Mac do the work for you while you brew yourself some coffee and catch up on the latest news. :]

> **Note**: This chapter requires some basic knowledge of the command line.
>
> Also, if you're already sold on the benefits of automation, feel free to skip to the next chapter. There, you'll learn how to use **fastlane**, a powerful tool for automating builds and more.

Why automation?

Imagine the following manual release process:

You need to release a new build of your app to the App Store. The code is ready, but you need to build the app for distribution using Xcode's **Product ▸ Archive** menu option. Then, you sign the archive for App Store distribution and upload it to App Store Connect.

On App Store Connect, you have to add in all the metadata for your release: your app categories, copyright info, marketing copy, review information and more.

Next up is one of the most tedious parts of releasing an app: the screenshots. You'll need to go back to Xcode, run your app in a handful of different simulators to take a handful of different screenshots. If your app is localized into other languages, don't forget to take screenshots for those languages, too.

Once you've added your metadata and screenshots, you're ready to submit your app for review.

From build to App Store

Now, consider the alternative automatic release process.

The code is ready, so you run your automation script. While that's running, go catch up with a friend or take your dog for a walk, because your Mac is about to handle everything for you.

First, script builds your app for the App Store and signs it.

Next, your automation script uploads the archive to App Store Connect. Then, the script takes the screenshots for you. It spins up five different device simulators to take screenshots across all the languages you support. Afterward, it updates your build on App Store Connect with your screenshots and app metadata.

Once everything is ready, the automation script submits the build for review automatically. All you have to do is sit back and wait for that glorious email from Apple telling you that your app is ready for sale.

Other benefits of automation

Besides the automation script handling all the steps from build to App Store, there's a myriad of other benefits to automating your build. This includes:

- Validation by testing
- Consistency
- Shared knowledge
- Frequent builds
- Continuous integration

Validation by testing

The benefits of automated testing are well known, but that doesn't mean developers remember to run tests before every release build. By including tests in an automated build, you have the assurance that everything works as expected. Any failing tests will stop the build to let you catch bugs before they hit the App Store.

You can take your testing even further by incorporating **static analysis** in your build script. Before even compiling your code, static analysis tools inspect your app for code smells and bad patterns and let you know where you can improve. It's like an automated code review to catch issues before they become a problem.

Consistency

Leaving release builds as a manual process opens it up to human errors if you don't pay enough attention. You could forget to run your automated tests, or compile the app with the wrong build configuration or provisioning profile. Or even worse, you might end up mistakenly releasing a feature that you haven't finished yet!

Automating your build is sort of like following a recipe. You're the chef writing the recipe, and the computer doing the build is a line cook that executes the recipe perfectly every time. With automation, the steps you follow for a new release build is the same as the steps for the last one.

By writing a script to automate all the steps needed to go from building the app to putting it on the App Store, you know that every step will be followed exactly as intended. You only have to build that perfect recipe once, and your computer will always follow it line by line without mistakes.

Shared knowledge

Have you ever taken over development of an old app that someone else built?

For a complex legacy app, the setup process can be more involved than just downloading the code from GitHub. You might need to have certain tools installed on your laptop, or maybe you need to edit some configuration. You might be subjected to a lot of back and forth trying to build the app with the correct dependencies and linked frameworks.

This isn't a problem for the developers that built the app originally. For new developers on the team, however, it can be tiring. For these old apps, there's a good chance that the knowledge you'd need to get up and running is **implicit**. The knowledge is in the heads of the developers that came before, but it's not written down anywhere.

By writing down all the steps to build an app in a recipe like a build script, that knowledge becomes **explicit**. The knowledge leaps out of the heads of developers and into the world, where a new developer can follow the steps with ease.

The idea of an automated build means that any authorized team member on any Mac can get your app's code and build it at the click of a button. The build script acts as a living document of everything that's needed to get an app up and running on devices.

Frequent builds

Because it's so easy to release new builds when you've automated the process, builds can come more frequently. The lower barrier to building means getting your latest work into the hands of testers and the general public much sooner.

One benefit of frequent builds is how easy it becomes to identify and fix issues. If you're only making new alpha builds every three months, it can be difficult to know the cause of a problem when something goes wrong. Was it a change you made a week ago, or a month ago? When your alpha builds come regularly and in small chunks, testing becomes more manageable.

Your users will thank you, too. The quicker you can release a new version of your app, the sooner everyone gets a chance to play with your shiny new features. :]

Continuous integration

The pinnacle of frequent builds, **continuous integration** lets you build and deploy your app as soon as you push your changes to GitHub. You don't even have to run the automation script yourself.

Rather than deploying directly from your development machine, continuous integration services connect to your Git repository in the cloud.

To find out more, have a look at Chapter 14, "Continuous Integration".

Setting up the starter project

Before you create a build script for Emitron, you'll need to configure the project for your Apple Developer account.

Open the **starter** project. In Xcode, follow these steps to find the code signing settings that you need to change:

1. Navigate to the project screen.
2. In the left sidebar, click on the **emitron** target.
3. Change to the **Signing & Capabilities** tab.

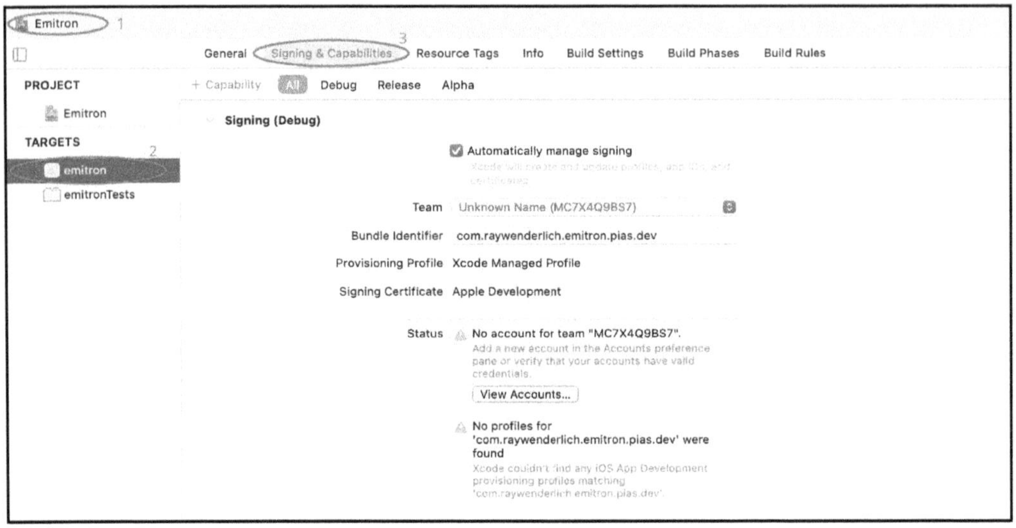

Firstly, under **Signing (Debug)**, change the **Team** to the correct team for your Apple Developer account.

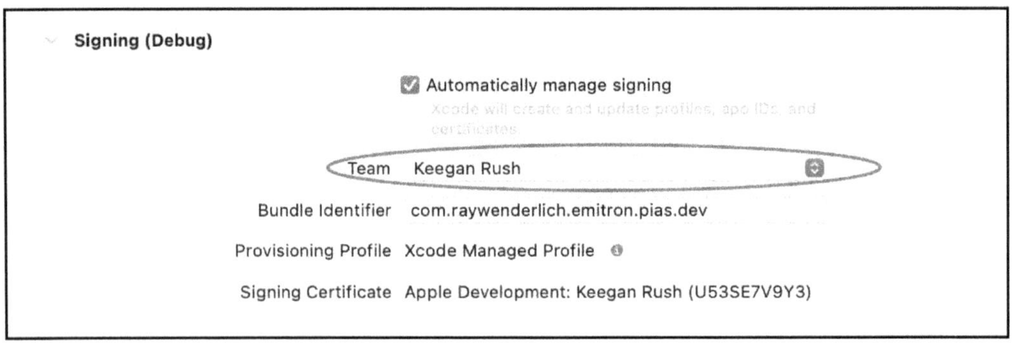

Next, under **Signing (Release)**, make sure that **Provisioning Profile** matches the profile you use to upload release builds of Emitron to App Store Connect.

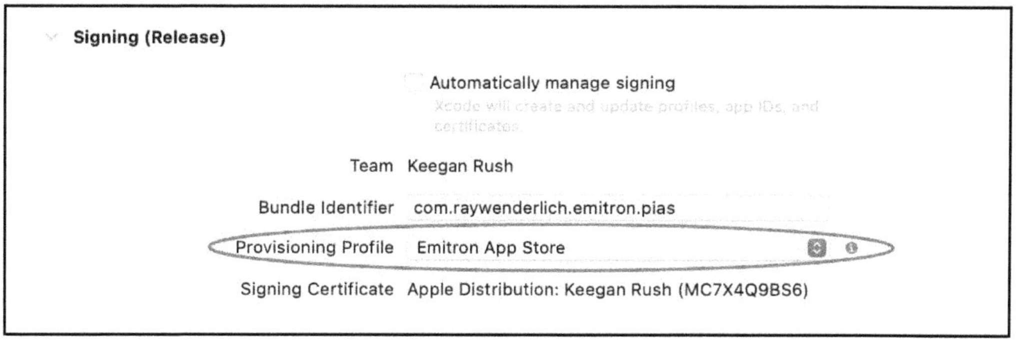

> **Note**: To learn more about provisioning profiles, or if you need a refresher on configuring them, refer to Chapter 4, "Code Signing & Provisioning".

Lastly, under **Signing (Alpha)**, change the **Team** to the correct team for your Apple Developer account. This is the same as what you did for **Signing (Debug)**.

When you're done, you won't see any more errors in the **Signing & Capabilities** tab.

Now that code signing is set up, you're ready to build Emitron on the command line.

Building with xcodebuild

You're not far away from automatic builds in the cloud that run all your tests for you. But first, at the heart of every automation script is the need to actually build your app.

Beneath Xcode's surface lies the Xcode **toolchain**, a set of tools including a compiler and debugger. When you build an app in Xcode, it's the toolchain that does the heavy lifting.

When building a project, Xcode uses a tool from the toolchain named **xcodebuild** to compile your apps.

`xcodebuild` isn't only available from within Xcode, however. All the tools in Xcode's toolchain are available for you to use via the the terminal.

Just like building an app in Xcode, using `xcodebuild` lets you build, query, analyze, test or archive any of your project's schemes from the command line.

To give `xcodebuild` a try, open a terminal window.

The starter project has an **Emitron** folder that contains **Emitron.xcodeproj**. In the terminal, `cd` to the **Emitron** folder.

Once there, call `xcodebuild` with the following command:

```
xcodebuild build -scheme Emitron
```

Here, you use `xcodebuild` to compile the Emitron scheme. This is the same as using Xcode's **Build** action, accessible by the **Product ▸ Build** menu option.

The rest of Xcode's actions are also available in `xcodebuild`.

xcodebuild syntax

When calling `xcodebuild`, you specify an **action** and a list of **options**.

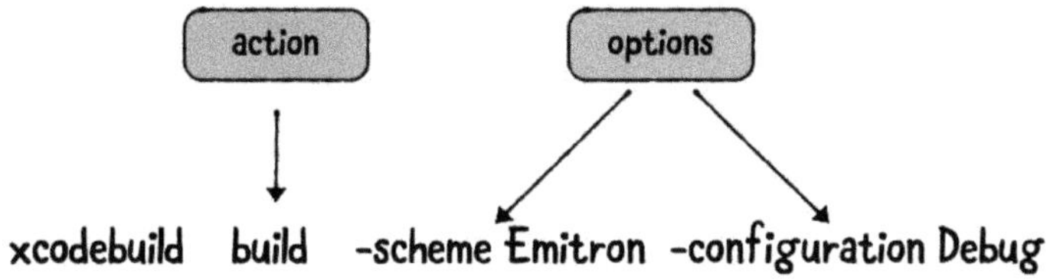

Actions

There's a variety of actions you can use with `xcodebuild`. Most of them correspond to actions available in Xcode, such as **build**, **clean**, **archive** or **test**.

Not every command uses an action – sometimes, you'll call `xcodebuild` with only a set of options.

Options

Options are like parameters you use to configure your chosen action. Earlier, you used `-scheme Emitron` to specify that `xcodebuild` should build the Emitron scheme. Here are some other available options:

- `-project` to specify the project if there's more than one.
- `-target` to build a particular target instead of a scheme.
- `-alltargets` to build all the targets in the project, instead of just one.
- `-configuration` to override the build configuration.

`xcodebuild` still has a few more tricks up its sleeves when it comes to actions and options, which you can discover by running `man xcodebuild` from your terminal.

To upload Emitron to App Store Connect, you'll need to start with the archive action, just like you'd do in Xcode.

Archiving Emitron

You've learnt how to create a regular build of Emitron, but that's not enough for your automation script. If you want to automatically upload Emitron to App Store Connect, you need to create an archive build first.

When you archive an app for distribution in Xcode, you use Xcode's **Product ▸ Archive** menu option. In `xcodebuild`, you have an equivalent **archive** action. You'll use that here to archive Emitron.

In the terminal, run the following:

```
xcodebuild archive -scheme Emitron \
  -configuration Release \
  -archivePath "Emitron.xcarchive"
```

To make things easier to read, the command you entered is split over multiple lines by adding a backslash at the end of each line, except the last.

Wait until it's done building:

This uses `xcodebuild`'s archive action to compile the Emitron scheme, using the Release configuration. Then, it archives the build into an **.xcarchive** and saves it as **Emitron.xcarchive** in the current directory.

With an archived build of Emitron, your next step is to export it as an **.ipa** destined for App Store Connect.

Exporting Emitron

So far, you've archived Emitron into an **.xcarchive** file. An **.xcarchive** isn't signed; so, it's not ready for upload to App Store Connect. To get a signed binary, you need to export your archive into an **.ipa**.

When you export an archive in Xcode, your project file determines the appropriate signing certificate and provisioning profile.

When you export an archive using `xcodebuild`, you use an **export options** file to set all the configuration you need.

Creating an export options file

Since you don't have a fancy UI to guide you through exporting an archive in `xcodebuild`, all the configuration needs to be set up front. That's where the export options file comes in.

In an export options file, you provide all the information `xcodebuild` needs to package your app, such as:

- The provisioning profile and signing certificate to use.
- Which Apple Developer team to assign this build to.
- Whether you want to package the archive for the App Store, ad-hoc, or enterprise distribution.

With all your options in the export options file, `xcodebuild` will run silently without any need to prompt you. That's exactly what you want if you'd like to go out for a coffee when waiting for a build.

Back in your terminal, run this command:

```
touch ExportOptions.plist
```

That creates a new file in the current directory named **ExportOptions.plist**.

The export options file is a **.plist**, similar to an iOS project's **Info.plist**.

Next, in your favorite text editor, open the empty **ExportOptions.plist**. Add this to its contents:

```
<!-- 1 -->
<?xml version="1.0" encoding="UTF-8"?>
<!DOCTYPE plist PUBLIC "-//Apple//DTD PLIST 1.0//EN" "http://
www.apple.com/DTDs/PropertyList-1.0.dtd">
<plist version="1.0">
<!-- 2 -->
<dict>
  <!-- 3 -->
  <key>method</key>
  <string>app-store</string>
```

```
    <!-- 4 -->
    <key>provisioningProfiles</key>
    <dict>
      <key>com.raywenderlich.emitron.pias</key>
      <string>Emitron App Store</string>
    </dict>
  </dict>
  </plist>
```

Ensure the release provisioning profile key-value pair matches the one in your developer account. This means the provisioning profile's **app identifier** and **name** have to match.

At its core, a **.plist** file is just XML. Here's what's going on in **ExportOptions.plist**:

1. Every **.plist** starts with this standard metadata.
2. The file is a key-value store of different configurations, indicated by the `dict` element.
3. The first entry in the dictionary has a key set to `method` and a value set to `app-store`. This means that `xcodebuild` will export Emitron for the App Store. The options are the same as those you get when distributing an app from Xcode.
4. Here, you set the provisioning profiles used for signing your archive. An archive can have more than one app inside, such as an iOS app bundled with a Watch app. So, you provide the provisioning profiles in the form of a dictionary with an entry for each bundle identifier in your archive.

You've created an export options file in its simplest form: with the options you specified, `xcodebuild` will package Emitron for App Store distribution with the **Emitron App Store** provisioning profile.

Exporting the archive

With an export options file, you're ready to export Emitron into an **.ipa** that you can upload to App Store Connect.

In the terminal, run this command:

```
xcodebuild -exportArchive \
  -archivePath Emitron.xcarchive \
  -exportOptionsPlist "ExportOptions.plist" \
  -exportPath .
```

Your export should succeed:

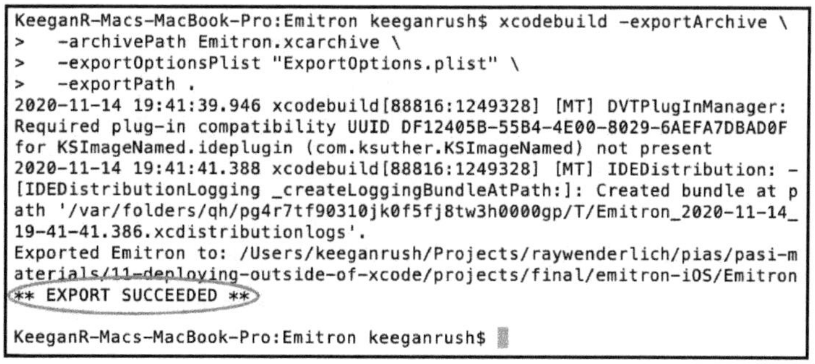

Using the `-exportArchive` option of `xcodebuild`, you've packaged an archive into an **.ipa** along with **ExportOptions.plist**. With that, you're ready to upload Emitron to App Store Connect via the command line!

Uploading Emitron to App Store Connect

Using the command line, `xcodebuild` can upload Emitron straight to App Store Connect. With one new option in **ExportOptions.plist**, `xcodebuild` will upload your **.ipa** instead of leaving it in the project folder. That means there's no need to use any other tools to upload your build.

Back in your text editor, open **ExportOptions.plist** once again.

After the `provisioningProfiles` dictionary, add this:

```
<key>destination</key>
<string>upload</string>
```

The `destination` option has two possible values: **export** or **upload**. Here, you set it to `upload` to instruct `xcodebuild` to upload your **.ipa** straight to App Store Connect.

The alternative, `export`, is the default: it'll create **raywenderlich.ipa** like earlier.

That's the only change you need to go from exporting **Emitron.xcarchive** to uploading it.

Back in the terminal, run the same `xcodebuild` command from earlier:

```
xcodebuild -exportArchive \
  -archivePath Emitron.xcarchive \
  -exportOptionsPlist "ExportOptions.plist" \
  -exportPath .
```

You may be asked to sign in to your Apple Developer account. Provide your account details if prompted to do so.

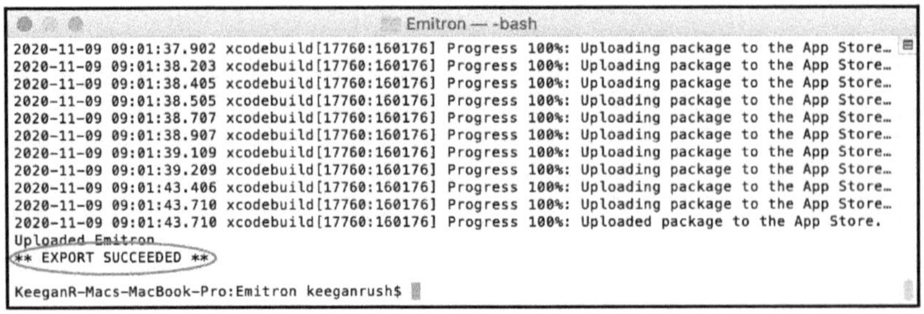

The archive will take some time to upload. Once it's done, you'll get a confirmation that Emitron was uploaded.

In App Store Connect, you'll see your new build uploaded in the Activity tab and ready for you to submit it for app review:

Great job!

> **Note**: If the upload failed with a **Redundant Binary Upload** error, read on to the next section.
>
> You need to change your project's build version. Once that's done, archive Emitron once more with the steps in the **Archiving Emitron** section and then repeat the upload again.

Now that you've uploaded a new build to App Store Connect, don't forget that you have to manually increase Emitron's build version before you upload a new build.

Bumping the build version

When you upload a build to App Store Connect, its build version has to be unique. If it isn't, you'll get a **Redundant Binary Upload** error when `xcodebuild` tries to upload the exported archive.

If you've already uploaded a build to App Store Connect, you'll need to increment Emitron's build version before uploading another.

Since you just uploaded a build with `xcodebuild`, now's a good time to bump the build version before you upload anything else.

You need to ensure that the combination of the app's **Bundle version string (short)** and the **Bundle version** hasn't already been uploaded to App Store Connect:

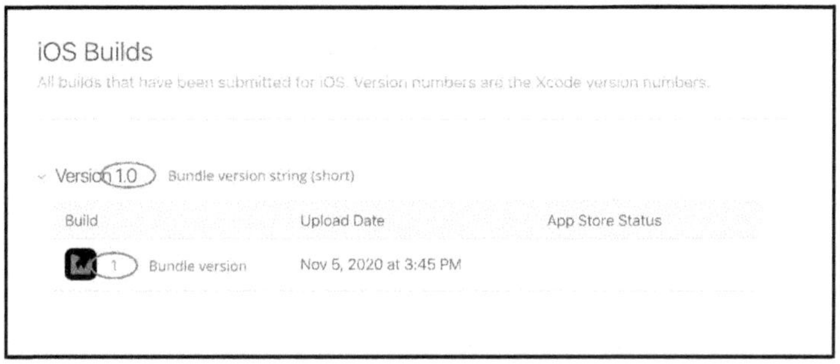

In Xcode, open **Info.plist**.

Increase the **Bundle version** entry's value by one:

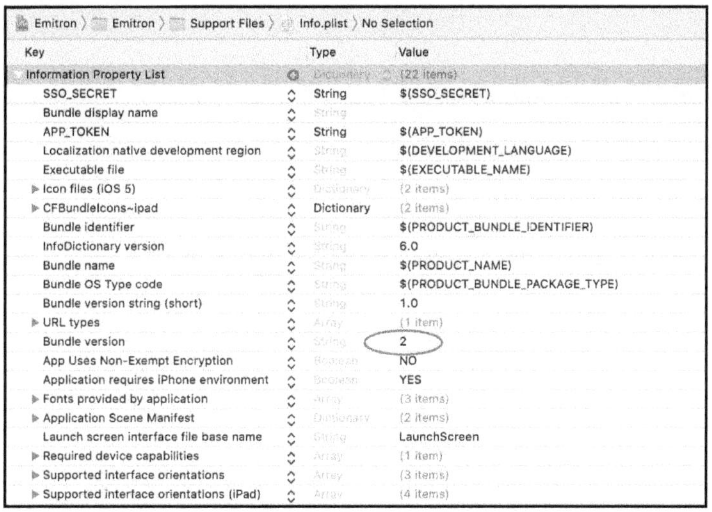

Now, you have a unique build version. This means you're ready to upload a new build to App Store Connect using the commands you learned earlier. But, wouldn't it be easier to have one simple command to run instead of remembering how to manually use `xcodebuild`?

Tying it all together

Using `xcodebuild` to manually build and upload Emitron gets you out of Xcode, but there's not much benefit beyond that. You still haven't **automated** the process.

In its current form, you have to enter the correct commands each time. That means all the dangers of human error are still there!

To truly automate Emitron's build, you need to put all the previous steps into one build script. With your build script, archiving and uploading Emitron will be easy and repeatable with one simple command.

In your terminal, run the following:

```
touch build.sh
```

This creates an empty shell script, **build.sh**. In the script, you can call `xcodebuild` just like you did on the command line.

In your text editor, open **build.sh**. Add this to its contents:

```
#!/usr/bin/env bash

# 1
xcodebuild archive -scheme Emitron \
  -configuration Release \
  -archivePath "Emitron.xcarchive"

# 2
xcodebuild -exportArchive \
  -archivePath Emitron.xcarchive \
  -exportOptionsPlist "ExportOptions.plist" \
  -exportPath .
```

At the beginning of the file is a **shebang**, which tells your computer how to execute the script. The shebang always has to be first line of the script.

The rest of the file is a combination of the commands you've used so far. Here's what's happening, step by step:

1. Archive Emitron to create **Emitron.xcarchive**.
2. Export and upload the archive to App Store Connect.

If you need to, increase the build version following the instructions in the previous section.

You've created **build.sh**, but it's just a text file at the moment. Your macOS user doesn't have the permissions to run it as a script yet.

Granting file permissions

Every file has a set of permissions that determine who can read, write or execute it. You need permission to execute **build.sh** if it's going to be of any use.

So, in the terminal, run this command:

```
chmod u+x build.sh
```

That gives permissions to the current user to execute **build.sh**.

Running the script

Now that you have the permissions to do so, run the script in the terminal:

```
./build.sh
```

Your build script kicks off `xcodebuild`, first archiving it and then uploading it to App Store Connect.

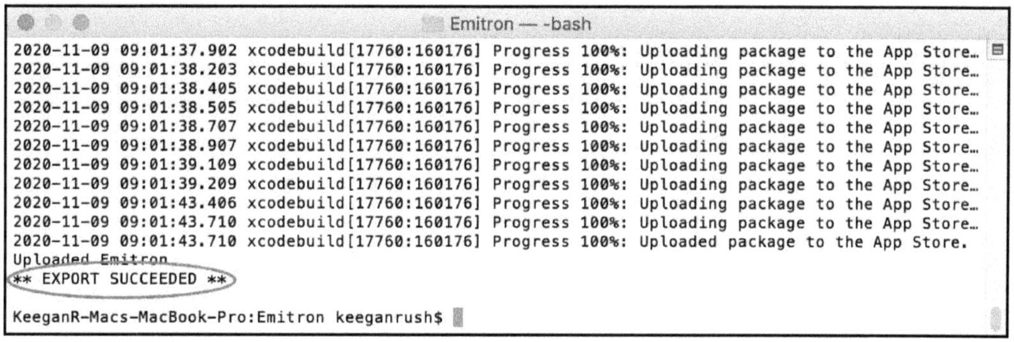

Once it's done, you'll get a confirmation that `xcodebuild` uploaded Emitron.

You'll see the build waiting for you on App Store Connect:

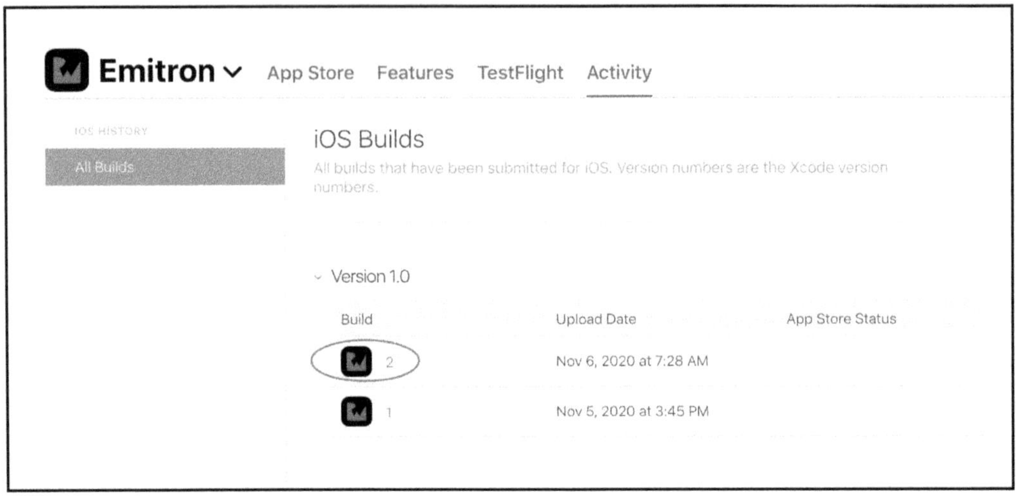

Nicely done!

More possibilities with automation

In this chapter, you learned how to build, archive, export and upload Emitron using `xcodebuild`. It's a great start, but automation can go much further than creating a build and uploading it to App Store.

Once you've uploaded your build, it's up to you to take your screenshots, manage your metadata and submit the app for review. That is unless you automate the process.

App Store Connect has an API that you can use in an automation script. You can find out more at https://apple.co/2HRAQ6u.

With the tools provided by Apple, you can go from building to submitting your app for review, all in one script. As you dive deeper into automation, your scripting work becomes a lot more complicated.

Luckily, there are tools to make automation a breeze. Read on into the next chapter to supercharge your automation with **fastlane**.

Key points

- Automation saves time, shares knowledge and prevents mistakes.
- Automating your build is the first step towards continuous integration.
- `xcodebuild` is the tool that Xcode uses to build your app. You can use it too, via the command line.
- To upload a new build to App Store Connect, you need to export an archive as an **.ipa**.
- `xcodebuild` needs an export options file to export an archive.
- By setting `destination` to `upload` in an export options file, `xcodebuild` can even upload an exported archive directly to App Store Connect.

Chapter 13: Introduction to Fastlane

By Keegan Rush

Using xcodebuild and the App Store Connect API to build and manage your app can be a lot of work. Isn't extra work what you were trying to get away from by using automation? :]

Well, you don't necessarily need to interact with xcodebuild yourself. There's a collection of open-source tools that interact the Xcode toolchain and the App Store Connect API, so you don't have to.

There are some alternatives, but the most popular approach to automating iOS builds is through the use of **fastlane**.

At its core, fastlane is a collection of Ruby scripts that make build automation easy and accessible to iOS developers. It's a collection of tools that wrap xcodebuild, the App Store Connect API and more:

- **cert** creates and maintains your signing certificates.
- **sigh** handles provisioning profiles.
- **gym** builds, signs and packages apps.
- **deliver** uploads apps, metadata and screenshots to App Store Connect.
- **pilot** uploads builds for TestFlight and handles its administration.
- **scan** runs your project's automated tests.

Those are just a few of fastlane's many actions.

Even when all you have is a superb idea for an app, fastlane can help to streamline your development process – it can even:

- Create an app record on App Store Connect.
- Manage the entire code signing process by creating provisioning profiles and signing certificates.
- Create push notification certificates.
- Take screenshots across different devices and across different languages, saving hours spent taking marketing screenshots.

If that's not enough, fastlane also comes with a rich plugin system for you to create any action your heart desires, and share it with other users.

It's because of all this that the iOS community has accepted fastlane as the go-to approach for build automation.

Next up, as a first step to working with fastlane, you'll add some simple build automation for Emitron:

1. Run unit tests with `scan`.
2. If no tests fail, prepare for code signing with `cert` and `sigh`.
3. Build Emitron for the App Store with `gym`.
4. Upload Emitron to TestFlight with `pilot`.
5. Upload builds for App Store review with `deliver`.

Strap yourself in; it's time to start living life in the `fastlane`! :]

Getting started

In this chapter, you'll be working with fastlane to upload builds to App Store Connect. To do so, you'll need to make sure that the **starter** project's app record, provisioning profile and signing certificate are correctly set up.

> **Note**: To learn more about provisioning profiles, or if you need a refresher on configuring them, refer to Chapter 4, "Code Signing & Provisioning".

To configure the starter project, refer back to the **Setting up the starter project** section in Chapter 12, "Build Automation".

> **Note**: The bundle identifier that you use for Emitron on App Store Connect should be the same as the one used throughout the book: `com.raywenderlich.emitron.pias`.

Once all of that's done, you're ready to install fastlane.

Installing fastlane

Once you've finished setting up your app record, provisioning profile and signing certificate, you'll need to get fastlane working on your computer.

There are a few ways to install fastlane. Here, you'll use a **Gemfile** and **bundler**.

Open **Terminal**. Enter the following command into Terminal:

```
sudo gem install bundler
```

Bundler is a Ruby tool that manages Ruby packages, known as **gems**.

For Terminal to gain write permission, enter your Mac's administrator account password when Terminal prompts for it.

In Terminal, change the **directory** to the starter folder's **emitron-iOS/Emitron** directory. Then, enter the following command into Terminal:

```
touch Gemfile
```

You've created a file named **Gemfile**. Open **Gemfile** in your favorite text editor. Then, add the following content to the file:

```
source "https://rubygems.org"

gem "fastlane"
```

Bundler will use **Gemfile** to track your project's gem dependencies.

Back in your terminal, run the following command:

```
bundle update
```

The `update` command triggers bundler to fetch any gems declared in your **Gemfile**.

If bundler needs `sudo` permissions, you'll be prompted for your macOS account password.

Give bundler a while to fetch fastlane and its dependencies.

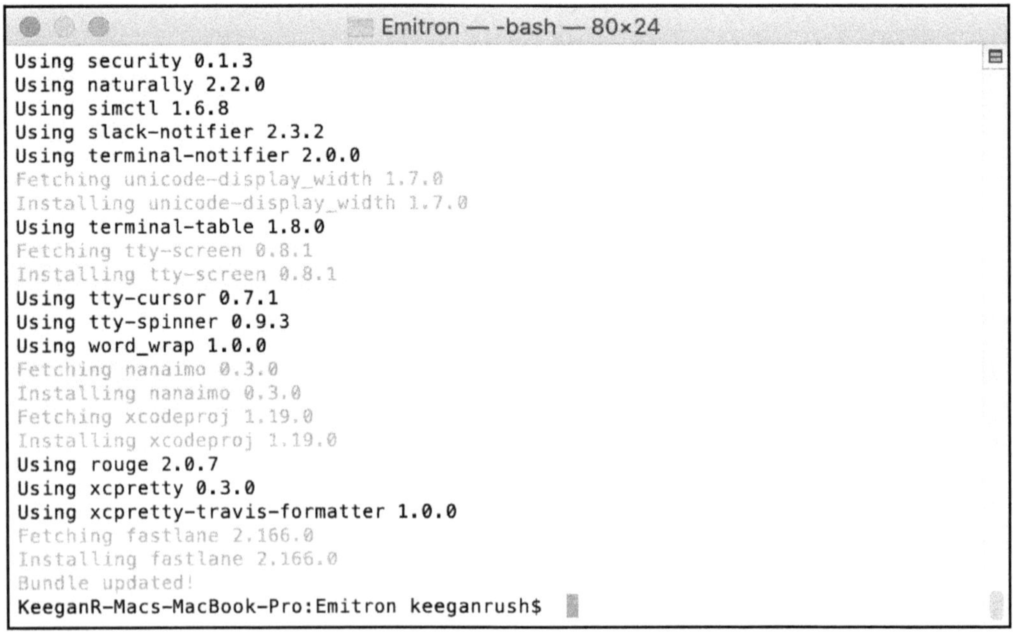

And that's it! Bundler installed the latest version of fastlane. Any time you want to update to a newer version, just run `bundle update fastlane`.

You've installed fastlane, but it won't do anything without some setup in Emitron.

Setting up fastlane

Without setting up fastlane in a specific project, it's about as useful as an empty build script. To start using fastlane, you need to give it some information about your project.

Run this command in the terminal:

```
bundle exec fastlane init
```

Since you're using a **Gemfile**, you should use `bundle exec` when using any of your Ruby gems. That means typing out `bundle exec fastlane` instead of just `fastlane` for each command. Using `bundle exec` means that you'll get the exact version of a gem that you specified in your **Gemfile**, instead of a different version installed elsewhere on your computer.

> **Note**: For any future calls to fastlane in this book, you'll just see `fastlane` instead of the full `bundle exec fastlane`. This still works, but you'll get a prompt to use the `bundle exec` form instead.

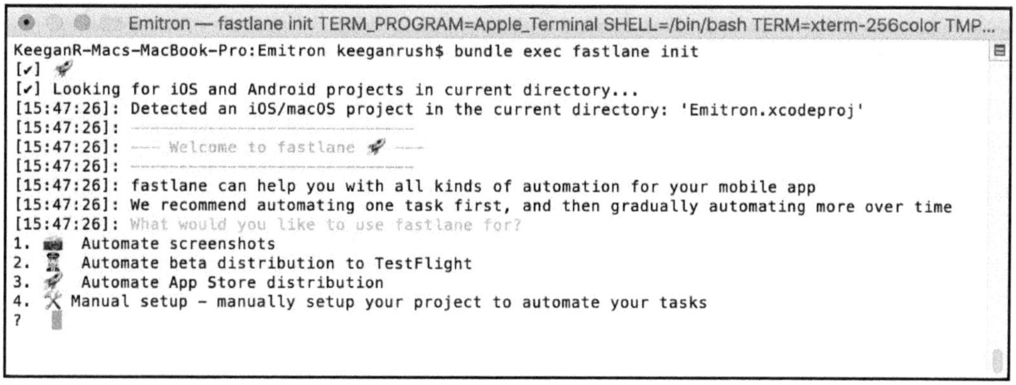

`fastlane init` guides you through your fastlane setup. Type in **4** for manual setup.

Then, press **Enter** to continue the setup.

```
Emitron — fastlane init TERM_PROGRAM=Apple_Terminal SHELL=/bin/bash TERM=xterm-256color TMP...
2.    Automate beta distribution to TestFlight
3.    Automate App Store distribution
4.   Manual setup - manually setup your project to automate your tasks
?  4
[15:50:54]: ----------------------------------------------------------
[15:50:54]: --- Setting up fastlane so you can manually configure it ---
[15:50:54]: ----------------------------------------------------------
[15:50:54]: --------------------------------------------------------
[15:50:54]: ---    Successfully generated fastlane configuration ---
[15:50:54]: --------------------------------------------------------
[15:50:54]: Generated Fastfile at path `./fastlane/Fastfile`
[15:50:54]: Generated Appfile at path `./fastlane/Appfile`
[15:50:54]: Gemfile and Gemfile.lock at path `Gemfile`
[15:50:54]: Please check the newly generated configuration files into git along with your project
[15:50:54]: This way everyone in your team can benefit from your fastlane setup
[15:50:54]: Continue by pressing Enter ⏎
```

Here, you get a confirmation that fastlane generated two files: **Fastfile** and **Appfile**.

Fastfile is the meat of fastlane where you'll write your actual build automation. Inside **Fastfile**, you'll add your own methods called **lanes**, similar to methods in Swift. Each lane you create will handle a specific task, like running tests, or preparing an alpha build.

The **Appfile** is one of many configuration files that you can use with fastlane. By putting app-specific metadata in **Appfile**, **Fastfile** stays neat and tidy. You'll find this pattern throughout fastlane, such as a **Gymfile** for use with the `gym` action and a **Scanfile** for use with `scan`.

fastlane will give you its own short tutorial about how it works. Read on and keep pressing **Enter** until `fastline init` finishes.

```
Emitron — -bash
[15:58:38]: Continue by pressing Enter ⏎

[15:58:52]: --------------------------------
[15:58:52]: --- Where to go from here? ---
[15:58:52]: --------------------------------
[15:58:52]:    Learn more about how to automatically generate localized App Store screenshots:
[15:58:52]:            https://docs.fastlane.tools/getting-started/ios/screenshots/
[15:58:52]:    Learn more about distribution to beta testing services:
[15:58:52]:            https://docs.fastlane.tools/getting-started/ios/beta-deployment/
[15:58:52]:    Learn more about how to automate the App Store release process:
[15:58:52]:            https://docs.fastlane.tools/getting-started/ios/appstore-deployment/
[15:58:52]:    Learn more about how to setup code signing with fastlane
[15:58:52]:            https://docs.fastlane.tools/codesigning/getting-started/
[15:58:52]:
[15:58:52]: To try your new fastlane setup, just enter and run
[15:58:52]: $ fastlane custom_lane
KeeganR-Macs-MacBook-Pro:Emitron keeganrush$
```

With that, you've fully configured fastlane and you're ready to start using it to build and upload Emitron to TestFlight and the App Store.

Building Emitron

Before worrying about uploading Emitron to App Store Connect for TestFlight or the App Store, you'll first use fastlane to automate a simple build. You'll gain familiarity in configuring a project for an automated build using fastlane.

In Emitron's project folder, you'll find a brand new **fastlane** subfolder. This folder contains everything to do with fastlane, including your new **Fastfile** and **Appfile**.

Open **Fastfile** in a text editor. Replace its contents with this:

```
# 1
ENV["FASTLANE_XCODEBUILD_SETTINGS_TIMEOUT"] = "600"
# 2
default_platform(:ios)
# 3
platform :ios do
  # 4
  lane :build do
    scan
  end
end
```

You've added one lane to **Fastfile** named `build`. The purpose of this lane is to build and archive Emitron, if it passes all of the project's unit tests.

Here's what **Fastfile** does, step by step:

1. As of the time of writing of this book, fastlane has a slight problem with projects using Swift Package Manager. When building your project, there's a chance that fastlane will time out while loading Swift package dependencies. This sets the timeout to ten minutes in order to provide ample time for resolving dependencies.

2. All lanes in fastlane are categorized by platform. Here, you specify that fastlane should assume that iOS is the chosen platform. With this, you don't have to specify a platform manually when running your lane.

3. Emitron is an iOS project, so you use `platform: ios` for the one and only platform section. You can think of this section as a class in Swift code.

4. Inside a platform, you add lanes. Here, you're creating a lane named `build`. The `build` lane has only one action at the moment: `scan`.

The `scan` action runs your project's test target. It's the same as the **Test** action in Xcode. It's a good first step, and you'll build on it later.

With **Fastfile** in hand, you're finally ready to take fastlane for a spin.

In the terminal, run this command:

```
fastlane build
```

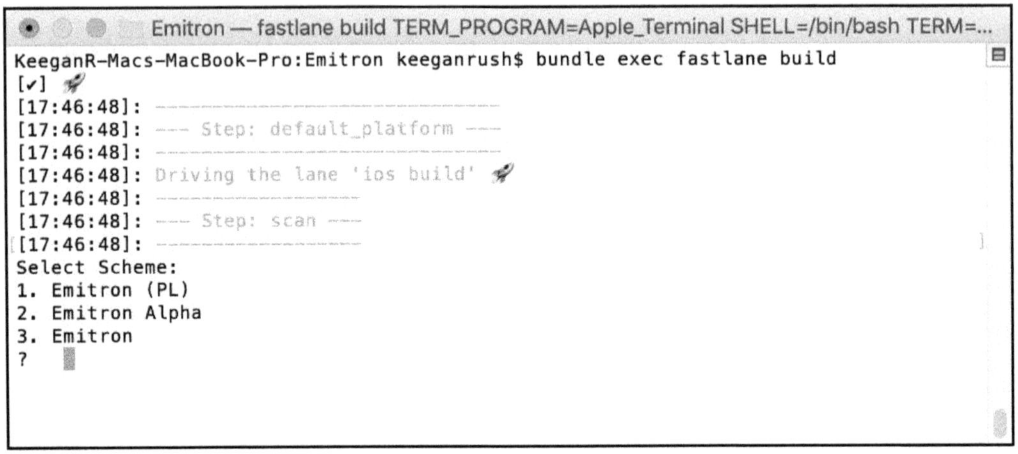

Fastlane kicks off your `build` lane, which runs `scan`.

Scan doesn't know which scheme to build for testing, so you get a prompt. Enter **3** for the Emitron scheme. Press **Enter** to confirm your selection.

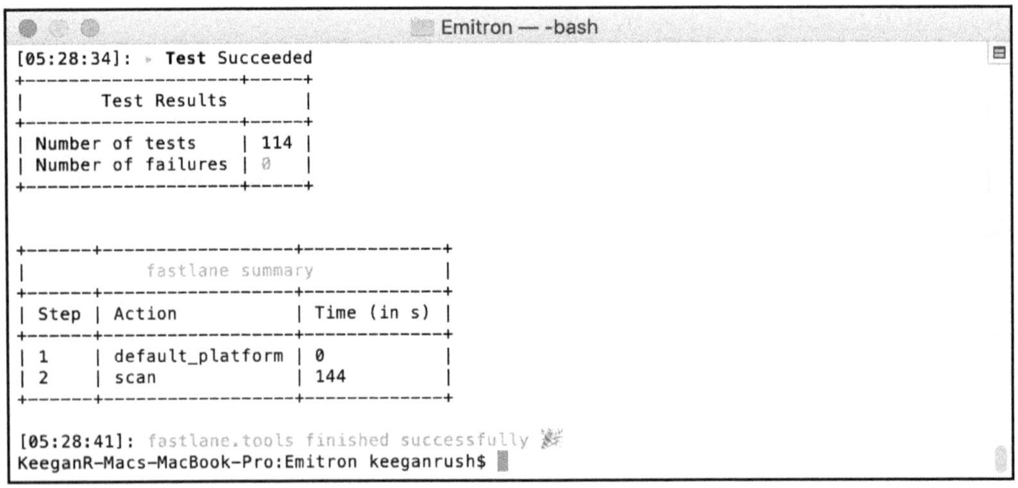

After a couple of minutes, you'll get a confirmation that fastlane has finished running your lane. Great work!

Wouldn't it be nicer if `scan` didn't have to prompt you for the scheme name? By configuring `scan` with all the details on how to test Emitron, it can run silently without any need for your input.

Configuring scan

In fastlane's current state, there are no explicit directions on *how* `scan` should test Emitron.

Fastlane is built around sensible defaults, and that can get you most of the way there.

When fastlane needs more context, there are three ways to specify an action's behavior:

1. By responding to prompts when running your lane.
2. By adding parameters when calling an action in **Fastfile**.
3. Through the use of an action's configuration file. For example, **Scanfile** for the `scan` action.

If you don't give enough instruction to `scan` on what it should do, you'll get prompts to provide more info in the terminal. That's not ideal for automation, because it opens the process up to human errors.

To avoid prompts, you can store configurations in **Scanfile**. This way, any calls to `scan` will use the values in **Scanfile**.

If you need to override what's in **Scanfile**, you can do it by using parameters in **Fastfile**. The syntax is similar to a regular Swift method, for example:

```
scan(scheme: "Emitron", clean: true)
```

To get started with **Scanfile**, run this command in the terminal:

```
fastlane scan init
```

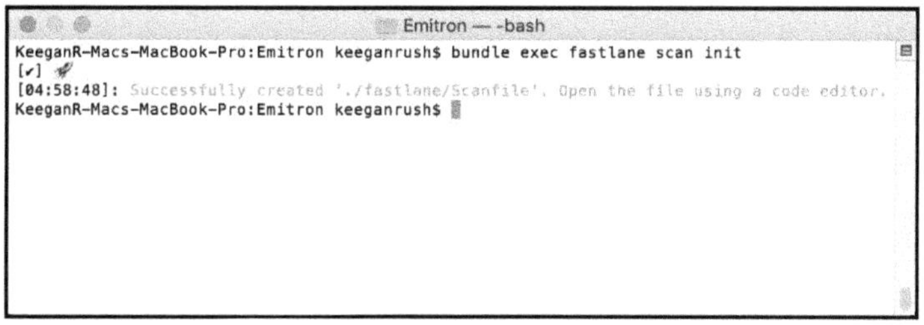

That creates **Scanfile** alongside **Appfile** and **Fastfile**.

In your text editor, open **Scanfile**. Replace its contents with this:

```
# 1
scheme("Emitron")
# 2
device("iPhone 12 Pro")
```

Whenever you use `scan` in **Fastfile**, it'll use **Scanfile** to set its behavior. Each row in **Scanfile** is a parameter to `scan`.

Here's what's happening:

1. Build the Emitron scheme.
2. Run tests on the iPhone 12 Pro.

With that, you're ready to run your first lane.

In the terminal, run the `build` once more:

```
fastlane build
```

This time, you won't be prompted to choose a scheme.

Give it a couple of minutes, and when it's done, you'll get the same confirmation from before:

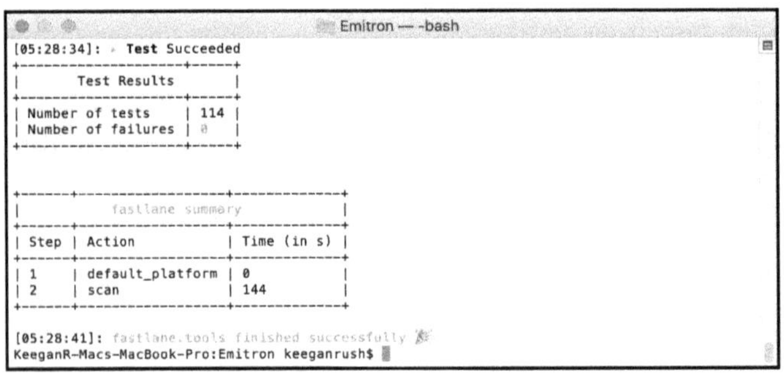

With your tests running smoothly, you're ready to expand upon the `build` lane for further automation.

Signing and building

From code signing to app archiving, the process is infamous for causing developers headaches. You can use fastlane can automate that minus the headaches.

Starting your lane with `scan` is a great safety check before building Emitron for the App Store. After running tests, your `build` lane can compile a release build of Emitron.

Back in **Fastfile**, add the following to the `build` lane just after your call to `scan`:

```
cert
sigh
gym
```

See how easy it is to call fastlane actions?

The code you added doesn't just build Emitron; it also sets up your signing certificate and provisioning profile.

Here's what each action does, step by step:

- **cert** takes care of everything to do with signing certificates. Using it here will sign your app with an existing signing certificate. If you don't have a valid certificate on your computer, `cert` will actually do the work of creating one for you!
- A close companion of `cert`, **sigh** is aptly named after the sound all iOS developers make when dealing with provisioning profiles. `sigh` can create new provisioning profiles or download an applicable one from the Apple Developer portal. As you have it here, `sigh` will download the valid provisioning profile that you've already set up in the Apple Developer portal. Combined with `cert` in your lane, `sigh` is the last step needed to complete your code signing setup.
- **gym** is the workhorse that builds your app and packages it into an **.ipa**, ready to upload to the App Store. Instead of mucking about with xcodebuild, it's as easy as `gym`!

> **Note**: When you use `gym` to build Emitron, it'll sign the build using the provisioning profile specified in Xcode's **Signing & Capabilities** settings.
>
> It's important that you've set up your project correctly, so that the profile specified in Xcode matches the valid profile in the Apple Developer portal. Take a look at **Setting up the starter project** in Chapter 12, "Build Automation" for more info.

Your completed `build` lane will run tests, prepare the appropriate certificate and provisioning profile, build Emitron, and finally package it for distribution.

Before you take the lane out for a test drive, you need to add some configuration, similar to what you did for `scan`.

Configuring code signing

`cert` and `sigh` both need a bit more context to function. Each of them takes their configuration from **Appfile**, the configuration file for project metadata.

Open **Appfile** in your text editor.

Replace its contents with this:

```
app_identifier("com.raywenderlich.emitron.pias")
apple_id("keeganrush@gmail.com")
itc_team_name("Keegan Rush")
team_id("MC7X4Q9BS6")
```

You need to replace the values with your own values.

Once again, each line is a parameter ready for use in your **Fastfile**. Here's what each one does:

- **app_identifier** is your bundle identifier, used to tell `sigh` which provisioning profile to prepare.
- **apple_id** is the email associated with your Apple Developer account. You'll need to sign in when running `cert` and `sigh`.
- **itc_team_name** is the name of your Apple Developer team, which you can find in your Apple Developer account details.
- **team_id** is the ID of your Apple Developer team.

For `apple_id`, just use the email address that you use to sign in to your Apple Developer account.

To find your team name and ID, follow these steps:

1. In your web browser, navigate to developer.apple.com.
2. Sign in if you haven't already.
3. Click **Account** in the top bar.
4. Click **Membership** in the sidebar under **Program Resources**.

See image below:

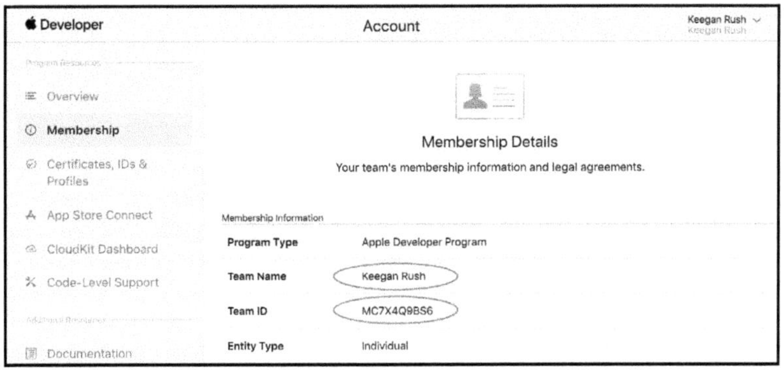

In **Appfile**, replace `itc_team_name` and `team_id` with the correct values from your membership information:

- Use your value for **Team Name** as the value for `itc_team_name`.
- Use your value for **Team ID** as the value for `team_id`.

With those values in **Appfile**, both `cert` and `sigh` can run silently. You'll still be prompted by fastlane when `gym` runs, however – unless you set up a **Gymfile** to provide configuration.

Configuring gym

To hand off the iOS apps build and package processes to fastlane, you'll use `gym`. Integrating `gym` into your automation flow makes generating a signed `ipa` a breeze. `gym` uses the `cert` and `sigh` configurations you've setup earlier to sign your `ipa`.

In your terminal, run the following:

```
fastlane gym init
```

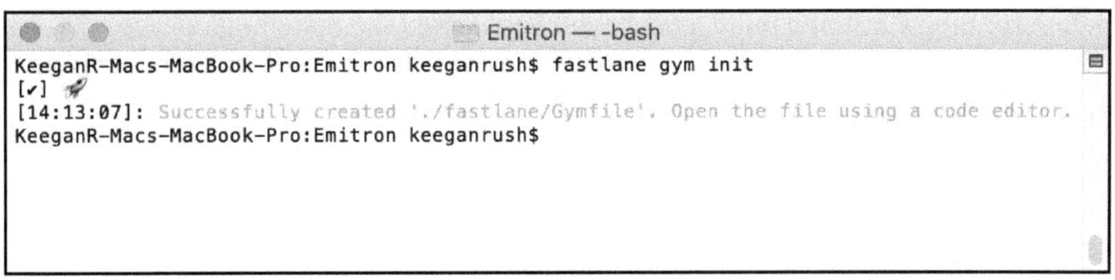

Similar to when you set up `scan`, this creates a **Gymfile** in the **fastlane** folder.

Open **Gymfile** in your text editor, and replace its contents with this:

```
# 1
scheme("Emitron")
# 2
clean(true)
# 3
output_directory("./")
# 4
export_method("app-store")
```

Here's how **Gymfile** instructs gym to build Emitron:

1. Build the Emitron scheme.
2. Clean the project before building.
3. Put the generated archive in the current folder, rather than in Xcode's Derived Data folder.
4. Export the archive for uploading to the App Store rather than as an ad-hoc or development build.

And that's it! You're ready to try out your new additions to the `build` lane.

Running the completed lane

With the actions you added, the `build` lane will now:

1. Run tests.
2. Prepare your code signing certificate.
3. Prepare the relevant provisioning profile.
4. Build, sign and package Emitron.

Before running a fastlane build, ensure you've selected the matching release **provisioning profile** and **bundle identifier** in the starter project as in the **Appfile**.

Back in the terminal, run `build` once more:

```
fastlane build
```

Fastlane executes each of your actions in order, starting with `scan`.

Once your tests have passed, fastlane moves on to `cert`. Here, you'll get prompted for your password to your Apple Developer account:

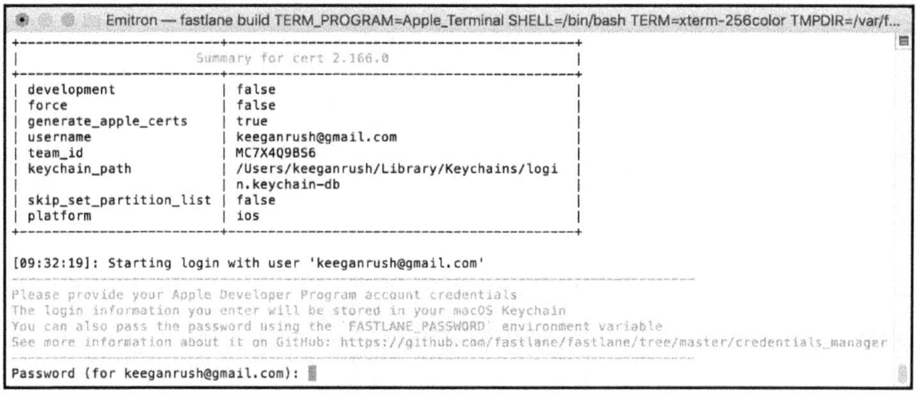

There are other ways to provide the password, such as storing it as an environment variable named `FASTLANE_PASSWORD`. Most importantly, remember to manage your secrets well and don't add your password to Git!

For now, enter your password in the terminal and press **Enter**.

Once you're signed in, `cert` and `sigh` will carry on without a hitch.

Finally, fastlane moves on to `gym`. Give it a few minutes to build Emitron.

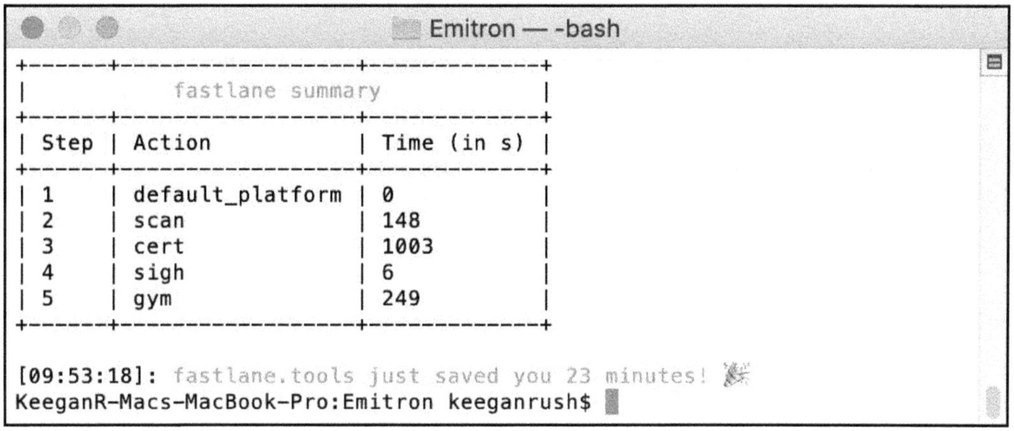

Once it's done, you'll get a summary of your lane and an estimation of the time you just saved by automating your workflow. With twenty-three minutes saved, that's cause for celebration!

In the terminal, get a listing of the contents of the Emitron project folder:

```
ls
```

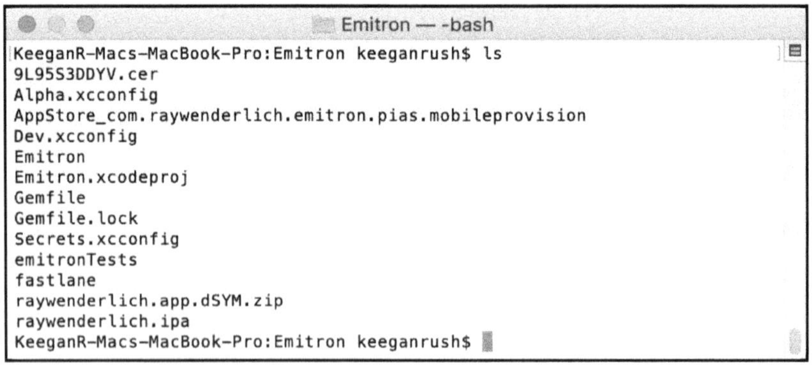

The output of your `build` lane, **raywenderlich.ipa**, is patiently waiting to be uploaded to App Store Connect.

Uploading to App Store Connect

When uploading to App Store Connect, you can choose to upload an app specifically for TestFlight or App Store review. To upload archived apps for their respective purposes, you'll create two new lanes: alpha lane using Emitron's alpha build and release lane using Emitron's release build.

Creating the alpha lane

In **Fastfile**, add the following after the end of the `build` lane:

```
lane :alpha do
  # 1
  build
  # 2
  pilot
  # 3
  increment_build_number
end
```

This creates a lane to upload alpha builds to TestFlight. Here's what's happening, step by step:

1. Run your `build` lane to build, sign and package Emitron.
2. Run fastlane's `pilot` action to upload Emitron to TestFlight.
3. Increment the build number, rather than bumping the bundle version in **Info.plist** manually. This step is last on purpose. If any of the previous steps fail, the build number stays the same.

Here, you're using the `pilot` action solely for uploading Emitron, but it can do much more. All of your TestFlight administration can be done using fastlane, including managing testers and distributing the builds you're uploading.

`pilot` doesn't need any further information because it gets everything it needs from **Appfile**. That's the power of fastlane's easy configuration.

If `pilot` successfully uploads the build, `increment_build_number` will then bump up Emitron's build number to prevent errors on the next upload.

Incrementing the build number

When uploading a build to App Store Connect, one particular error plagues developers more than any other. If you happened to forget to change your app's build version, you'll be greeted with a familiar **Redundant Binary Upload** error.

Thankfully, with fastlane, your days of needing to go to **Info.plist** in order to bump a build version before archiving and uploading a new build are over.

Fastlane increments build numbers with the aptly named `increment_build_number` action. To set it up, you'll need to make some changes to Emitron's build settings.

Setting up increment_build_number

Fastlane can't automatically bump your build number without changing how your project's versioning works.

In Xcode, follow these steps to find the build settings that you need to change:

1. Navigate to the project screen.
2. In the left sidebar, click on the **emitron** target.
3. Change to the **Build Settings** tab.
4. In the search bar, search for **versioning**.

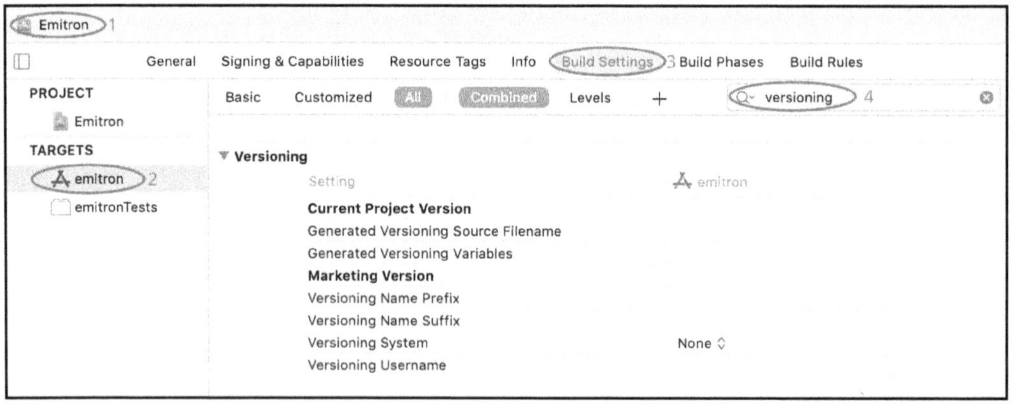

Here, you need to make two changes to prepare Emitron for automatic versioning.

First, set the **Current Project Version** to your app's current **bundle version**.

You'll find the bundle version in **Info.plist**:

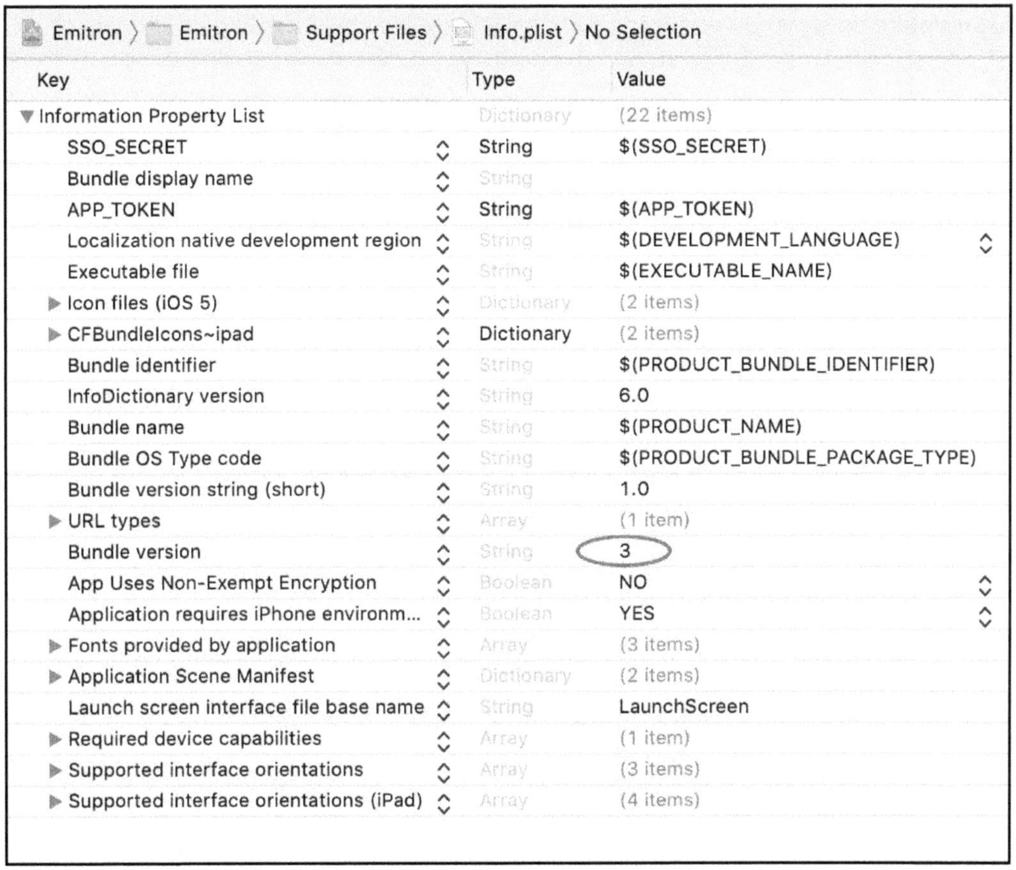

Note: It's important that the number you're using for the **Current Project Version** and the **bundle version** is unique, meaning that you haven't uploaded any builds to App Store Connect with that same version. Have a look at the **Bumping the build version** section in Chapter 12, "Build Automation" for more info.

If you need to set the **Current Project Version** and the **bundle version** to a unique value, do that now.

Lastly, change the **Versioning System** build setting to **Apple Generic**.

After you're done, your versioning settings will look something like this:

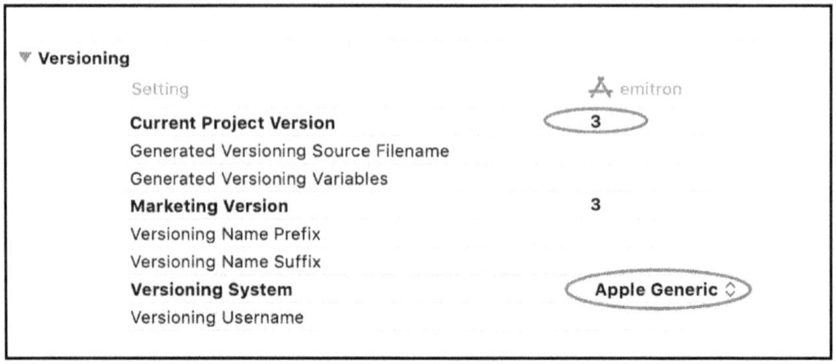

From now on, your Current Project Version and bundle version will stay in sync. Every time you run the `alpha` or `release` lanes in **Fastfile**, both the Current Project Version and the bundle version will increase by one.

Now that you've set up your project versioning, that's all the configuration you need to upload a new build to TestFlight.

Before trying out your new lane, you'll need to generate an **app-specific password** if you don't have one already.

Creating an app-specific password

If you want to upload an iOS app to App Store Connect from outside of Xcode or xcodebuild, you'll need to generate an app-specific password. Rather than signing in with your Apple Developer account's usual username and password, any tools that need access to your developer account *must* sign in using an app-specific password. If you don't have one, and try to use your Apple ID's regular password instead, `pilot` will fail when trying to upload Emitron!

To create an app-specific password, follow the instructions on Apple's **Using app-specific passwords** page: https://support.apple.com/en-us/HT204397. Keep your password somewhere safe; you can generate new passwords easily, but you can't view an old one.

With that password, your account is secure and ready to upload a new build via fastlane.

Running the alpha lane

To upload a new build to TestFlight, all you need to do is to run the `alpha` lane.

In the terminal, run the following command:

```
fastlane alpha
```

Fastlane runs your tests, builds Emitron and prepares to upload it to App Store Connect. Once the build is ready, `pilot` will ask you to sign in using your app-specific password.

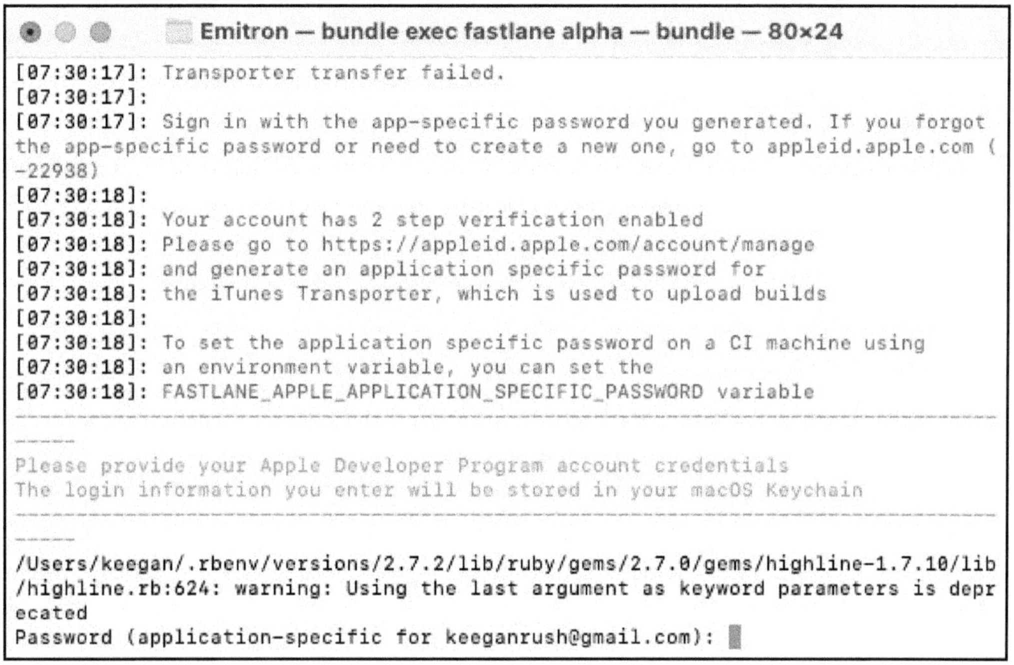

Enter your app-specific password when prompted.

Wait a little longer while fastlane uploads Emitron and Apple processes the new build.

See image below:

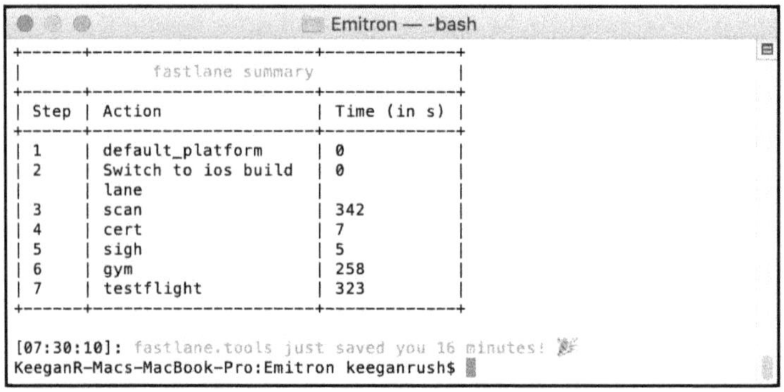

Give it a moment, and you'll get the familiar confirmation that fastlane ran your lane successfully.

Fastlane uploaded your build to App Store Connect, but the `pilot` action doesn't end there. With `pilot`, you can also upload a changelog and all other metadata needed to submit your app for external testing.

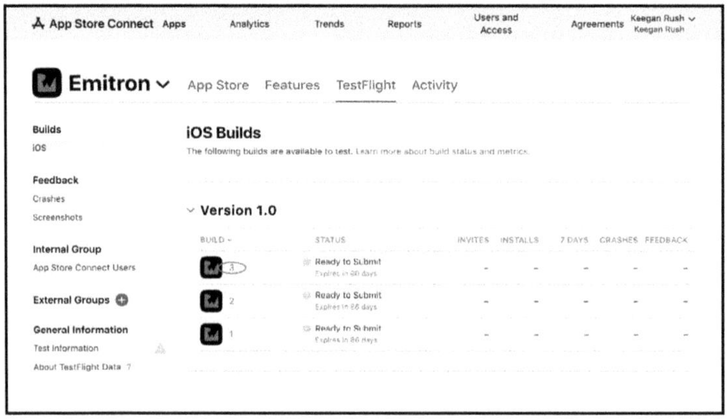

For now, if you have any internal testers on TestFlight, the build that fastlane just uploaded will be ready and available for them to test. For the apps you share with external testers, you can even have `pilot` submit a beta build for review!

> **Note**: If fastlane fails with the **Redundant Binary Upload** error, it means your build number still isn't unique.
>
> Increase the project's **Current Project Version** once more and try again.

When you're done testing the alpha build of the app, you'll want to upload a release build.

Creating the release lane

To upload a release build of Emitron, you'll make a new lane similar to `alpha`.

Back in **Fastfile**, add this after the end of the `alpha` lane:

```
lane :release do
  # 1
  build
  # 2
  deliver
  # 3
  increment_build_number
end
```

This new `release` lane is structurally similar to the `alpha` lane. Here's what's going on:

1. Use the `build` lane to compile, sign and package Emitron.
2. Use fastlane's `deliver` action to upload and prepare a release build.
3. Bump the bundle version up by one to prepare for the next build.

`deliver` goes far beyond uploading your build. You can use `deliver` to upload App Store metadata and screenshots as well, which will fill in everything you need to submit a new app for App Store review. In fact, `deliver` can go as far as submitting your build for review!

There's a little bit of configuration to handle before running `deliver`.

Configuring deliver

In the terminal, run the following:

```
fastlane deliver init
```

Fastlane creates a **Deliverfile**, following the same pattern you're used to for the other actions. Also, `deliver init` creates two new folders inside the **fastlane** folder: **metadata** and **screenshots**.

Inside **metadata**, you'll find subfolders and text files corresponding to the app metadata you need to fill in before submitting your app for review.

If you're using the `snapshot` action to take screenshots, or if you have your own, then the **screenshots** folder is where you'll keep the screenshots that `deliver` should upload.

For Emitron, you won't use `deliver` to upload metadata or screenshots. Because of this, you'll have to instruct `deliver` to skip the upload of metadata and screenshots.

In your text editor, open the newly created **Deliverfile**. Replace its contents with this:

```
# 1
skip_metadata(true)
# 2
skip_screenshots(true)
# 3
force(true)
```

Here's what's going on, step by step:

1. Tell `deliver` to skip uploading metadata, essentially ignoring the contents of the **metadata** folder.
2. Similar to `skip_metadata`, skip uploading screenshots in the **screenshots** folder.
3. Usually, running `deliver` will open a review page in your web browser before uploading screenshots and metadata. Setting `force` to `true` skips the review page, since you're only uploading the app. This has the added benefit of running `deliver` silently, without any user prompts.

Running the release lane

In the terminal, run your new `release` lane:

```
fastlane release
```

Wait for your lane to complete.

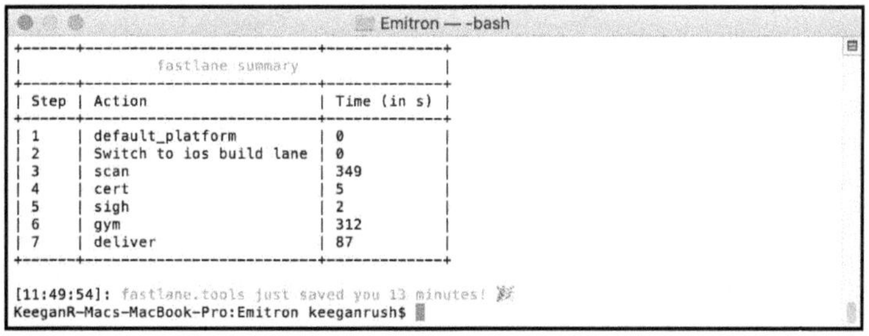

Once it's done, you'll see that familiar confirmation.

In App Store Connect, you'll see your new build uploaded and ready for you to submit it for App review:

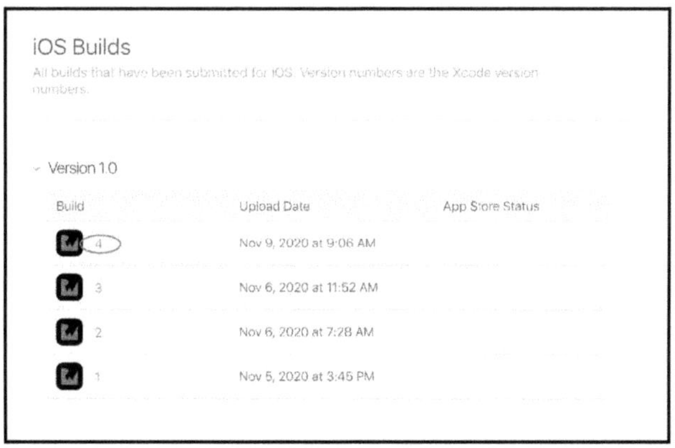

Pause for a moment; enjoy the warm, fuzzy feeling of knowing how much time you've just saved with automation.

You're off to the races with fastlane!

More on fastlane

In this chapter, you've come a long way: from being restricted to manual builds in Xcode to an automated build pipeline with fastlane.

To do so, you only used a handful of actions:

- `scan`
- `cert`
- `sigh`
- `gym`
- `pilot`
- `deliver`

However, there's a lot more to fastlane. There are still more actions to learn about, some of which will help you to automate the perfect build pipeline for your app:

- **produce** creates new app records on App Store Connect.
- **snapshot** takes beautiful App Store screenshots for different devices and languages.
- **frameit** sizes screenshots and puts them in marketing frames.
- **pem** manages push notification profiles.
- **boarding** invites beta testers.
- **match** is an innovative new approach to code signing.

That's a lot of functionality in one tool! In fact, fastlane isn't only good for automating builds. In my opinion, it's much easier to create apps, manage code signing and more with fastlane than it is via the App Store Connect site.

To learn more about these and everything else on offer, have a look at docs.fastlane.tools.

Key points

- Fastlane acts as a wrapper for `xcodebuild` and the App Store Connect API.
- Fastlane can be broken down into a structure of platforms, lanes and actions.
- By using the vast variety of actions, fastlane can streamline your entire build process and make other project setups much easier.
- Most fastlane actions are configurable using one of fastlane's various configuration files.

Chapter 14: Continuous Integration

By Keegan Rush

Automation makes a developer's life so much easier. One benefit of automation is that it removes some of the capacity for human errors. When your build script records all the steps for distribution, you're much less likely to archive the app on the wrong Git branch or with the wrong build configuration.

So far, the automation you've explored is great for your own personal use. But working as a team, while filled with benefits, comes with its own set of problems.

In a team, coordinating work between developers can be as much work as the programming itself. Combining, or **integrating**, the work of each developer is a challenge.

Continuous integration (CI) is the development practice of integrating the team's work early and often.

Rather than waiting weeks or months for the team to complete large chunks of work, CI makes quick work of team coordination by integrating all code in one central location. By frequently running unit tests to ensure that integration is successful, CI keeps the team clued in to the state of the app's codebase.

> **Note**: This chapter assumes some basic knowledge of Git and the command line, as well as your own GitHub account.

More CI benefits

Effortless integration is the first and foremost benefit of CI, but the advantages don't end there. Here are some other important benefits.

Detecting problems early

Often, when someone refers to continuous integration, they're referring to **CI services**. Developers implement continuous integration through the use of a CI service that provides a **build server**. While you can roll your continuous integration solution, it's much easier with a service.

Rather than running automated tests on your computer when you feel like it, continuous integration means running the tests on a build server every time the code changes. If a developer pushes code to GitHub that causes the tests to fail, also known as **breaking the build**, your CI lets you know immediately.

Using continuous integration, you can automatically run your build script every time you finish a feature or commit code to GitHub.

If you trigger your CI service to run tests on every new commit, you never need to backtrack to find the cause when something goes wrong. If all the tests pass on one commit but fail on the next, you know exactly where to look to fix the broken build.

It's great that your tests are running early and often, but another benefit of CI is *where* your tests are running.

Providing a single source of truth

CI services leave your personal computer out of the equation. All you need to do is push your latest code to GitHub, and CI will build your app and run your tests *in the cloud*.

Not only can you step out for a coffee while your app is building, but with CI, you can pack up your laptop and take it with you. This is a big deal because a developer's computer isn't always the most stable.

Locally, you may be running a beta version of macOS and Xcode, or the latest and greatest fastlane build. This can be a problem, however, when it comes time to run your release build. An app built on one version of Xcode might show different behavior when a different Xcode version builds it.

That's why your CI server acts as your **single source of truth**. Continuous integration provides you with a server that's perfectly configured to build your app. The versions of macOS, Xcode and any other dependencies stay consistent.

If your computer has problems building the app, take a look at the state of the build on the CI server. If the build is broken, then you can track down which commit broke the build to fix things. But, if the build passes — meaning the app compiles successfully and all tests pass — then the problem probably lies with your computer.

A CI server makes it possible to merge your latest work into the main branch often. You have one central place that tells you if the integration succeeded or failed.

So, you know why you might want to set up CI for your app, but how does it work? To understand the process, you'll learn about the components that embody this development practice.

CI components

Continuous integration works through the combination of a **build server**, **jobs** and **triggers**.

The **build server** is the central location where CI does its work. It prepares release builds or runs tests to report on the state of the app.

A **job** is any operation that you want to perform on the build server. Running your build script on the CI server is an example of a job. You could have one job to run unit tests, another to upload a build to App Store Connect and another to email you with the result.

The build server won't do anything until a **trigger** tells it to kick into gear. When a trigger fires, the CI server will execute one or more jobs.

When you're working on your computer, you run an automation script by calling it in the terminal. With CI, you don't run anything yourself. Instead, you set up triggers that run your jobs when certain events happen. For example, you can create a trigger that runs on the creation of a pull request, when pushing code to GitHub or even at a certain time of day.

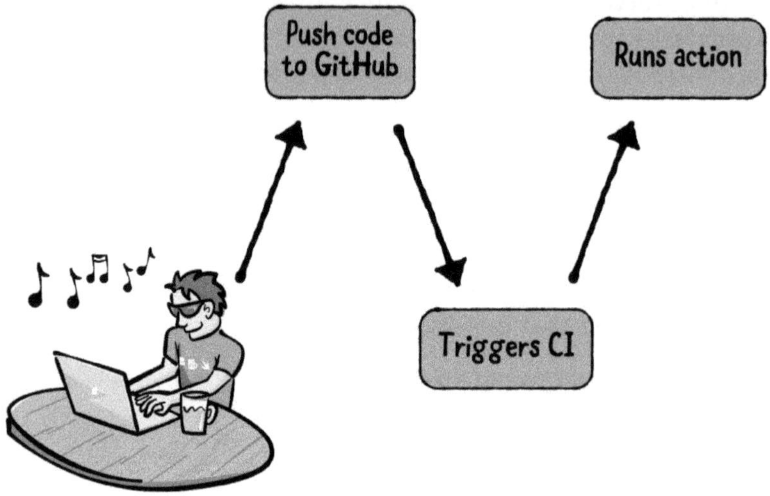

Example of a CI workflow

In the example above, pushing code to GitHub is an event that executes a trigger on your continuous integration server. That trigger initiates a job, which could be running your tests, creating a new release build, sending a Slack message or anything in between.

Luckily, you don't have to write the code to implement jobs and triggers. There are plenty of CI providers that handle that for you.

The mechanics of CI stays consistent between jobs and triggers. Depending on your needs, however, there are different types of build servers to choose from when picking a CI provider for your project.

Different types of CI

Roughly speaking, CI providers come in three different flavors: full service, managed and manual.

Full-service CI

This is the most convenient option of the three. With a full-service CI provider, you get a simple point-and-click interface. The interface guides you through setting up your build to deploying it to TestFlight or elsewhere.

Full-service CIs are easy to use, but they aren't very customizable. If you have complicated requirements, they might not fit your needs.

Two examples of full-service providers are Bitrise: https://www.bitrise.io/ and Microsoft's App Center: https://appcenter.ms/.

Managed CI

Managed CI straddles the line between guided point-and-click options and full customization. A managed CI service handles the hardware for you in the cloud. All you need to do is provide a build script, usually using `fastlane` or `xcodebuild`.

Managed CI is a good option if you have a solid understanding of deploying apps, because you'll have to do the work of building and signing the app yourself.

Two popular examples are CircleCI: https://circleci.com/ and GitHub Actions: https://Github.com/features/actions.

Manual CI

These services provide the most opportunity for customization. In addition to handling app building and deployment, you'll also need to manage your own build server.

Manual CI services are the cheapest of the options, but managing a build server can be a full-time job in itself. For this reason, manual CI tends to be the domain of larger companies that demand full control over the build and distribution of their apps.

The most popular option for manual CI is Travis CI: https://travis-ci.org/. For iOS, you also have the option of Xcode Server.

Implementing your first CI

Now that you know what continuous integration does and how it works, it's time to jump in by implementing CI in the Emitron project.

As you've seen, there are numerous CI providers to choose from. In this chapter, you'll work with **GitHub Actions**, a managed CI system. You'll create a repository for Emitron on GitHub and connect it to GitHub Actions to implement your first CI pipeline.

Creating a GitHub repository

Any project that uses CI needs a version control system such as Git. Without it, there's no easy way for your CI server to integrate everyone's changes.

To get started with CI, you'll first create a Git repository and upload the Emitron app to GitHub.

In your browser, open https://github.com/. If you're not signed in to your GitHub account, sign in now.

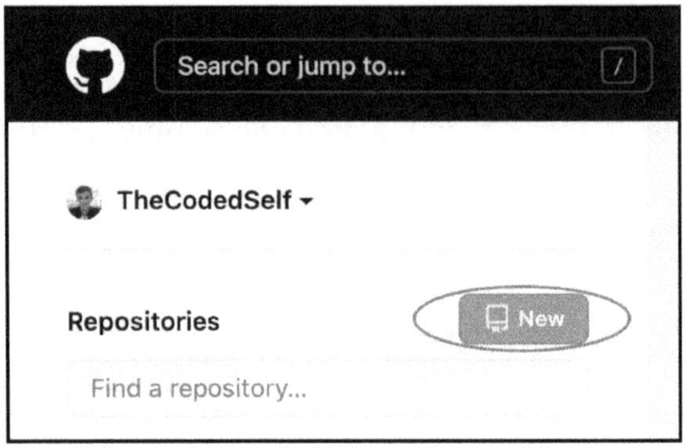

In the left sidebar, click the **New** button to create a new repository.

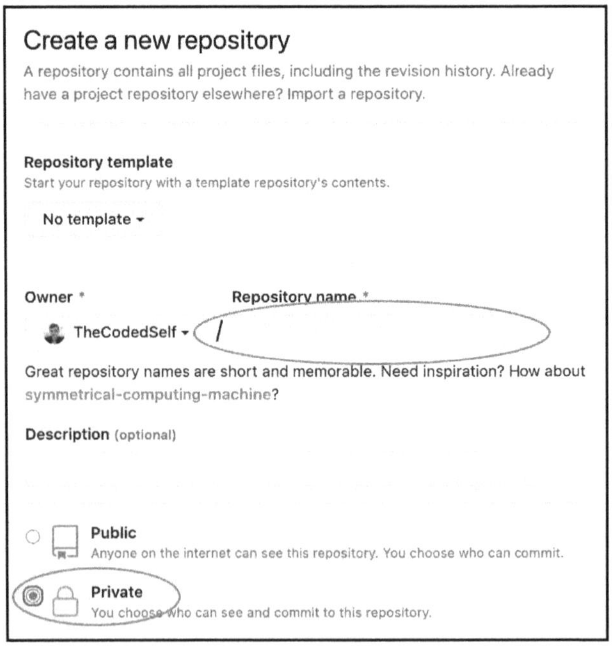

Set the repository name to **emitron**. Mark the repository as **private**, since it's just for you.

Next, click **Create repository**.

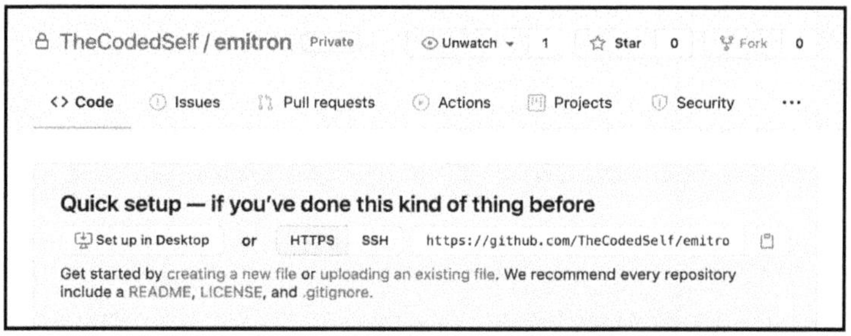

You'll need the Emitron repository page later, so keep it open for now.

At the moment, you have an empty repository. You'll add Emitron's project code to it next.

Uploading Emitron

To upload Emitron's project code to your empty repository, you need to initialize Git within Emitron's project folder on your machine.

Open a terminal window. Then, `cd` to the **Emitron** folder within the starter project.

Once there, run the following command in the terminal:

```
git init
```

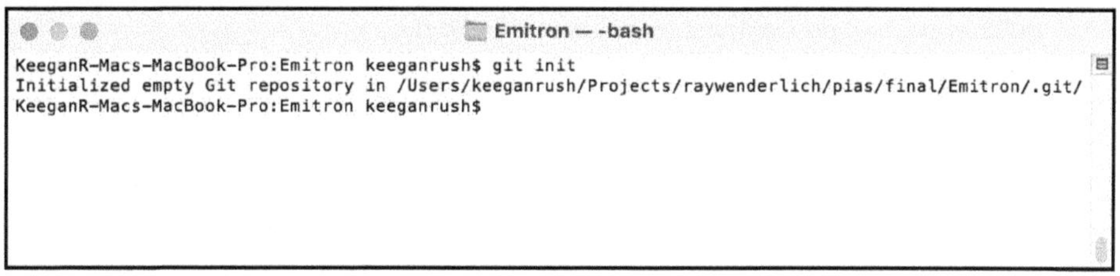

This initializes Git within the Emitron project.

Next, run this command:

```
git add . && git commit -m "Initial commit"
```

See below:

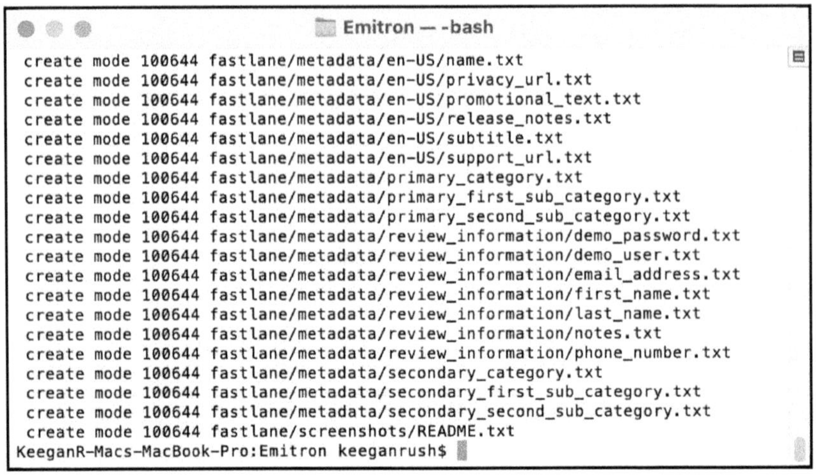

You've now added the entire Emitron folder to your new Git repository and committed it. With that, you've set up your repository locally.

To upload it to GitHub, you need to point your local repository to the one you created on GitHub. Back in your browser, you should still have the page open for your empty repository. There, you'll find the repository's URL:

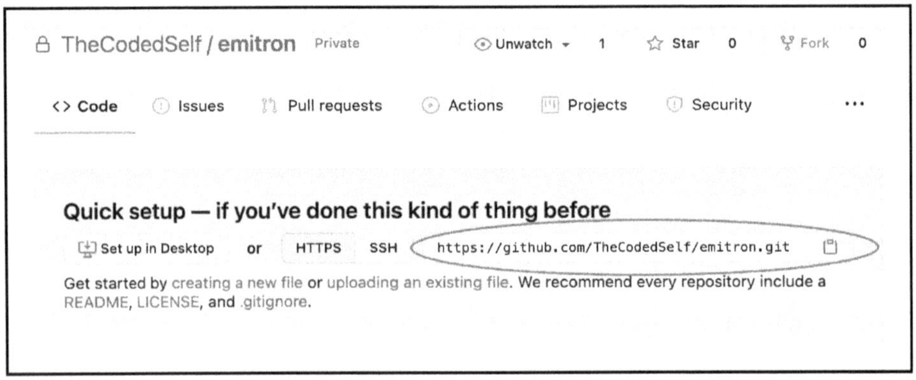

Copy your repository's URL. You'll need it to upload your local repository to GitHub.

Open your terminal window again. Run this command, replacing my repository's URL with your own:

```
git remote add origin \
  https://github.com/TheCodedSelf/emitron.git
```

> **Note**: To make things easier to read, the backslash at the end of the first line splits the command you entered into two lines.

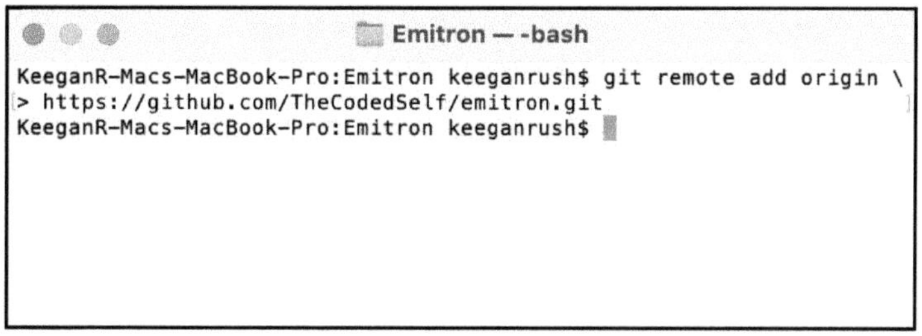

Before uploading the project to GitHub, you have one final step to complete. Git repositories have a history of setting the name of the main branch to `master`. However, GitHub uses the more inclusive `main` as its primary branch name.

Run this command to update your branch:

```
git branch -M main
```

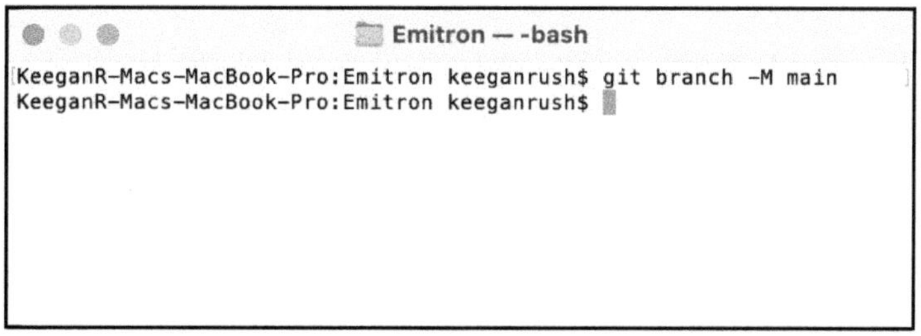

This updates your branch name from `master` to `main` to match GitHub's conventions.Finally, you're ready to upload Emitron. Run this last command:

```
git push -u origin main
```

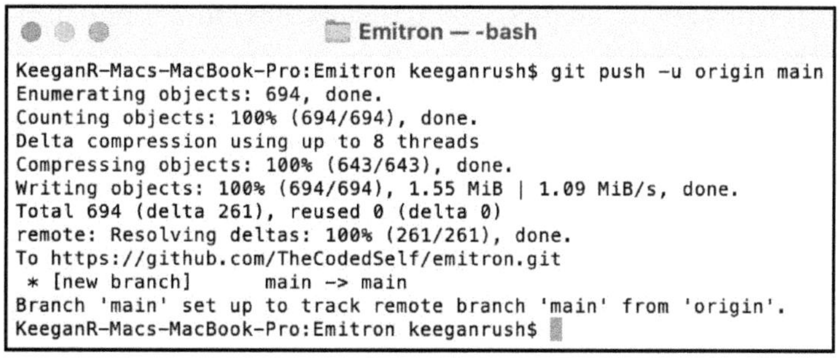

With that, you've uploaded Emitron to GitHub.

Back in your browser, refresh the repository page:

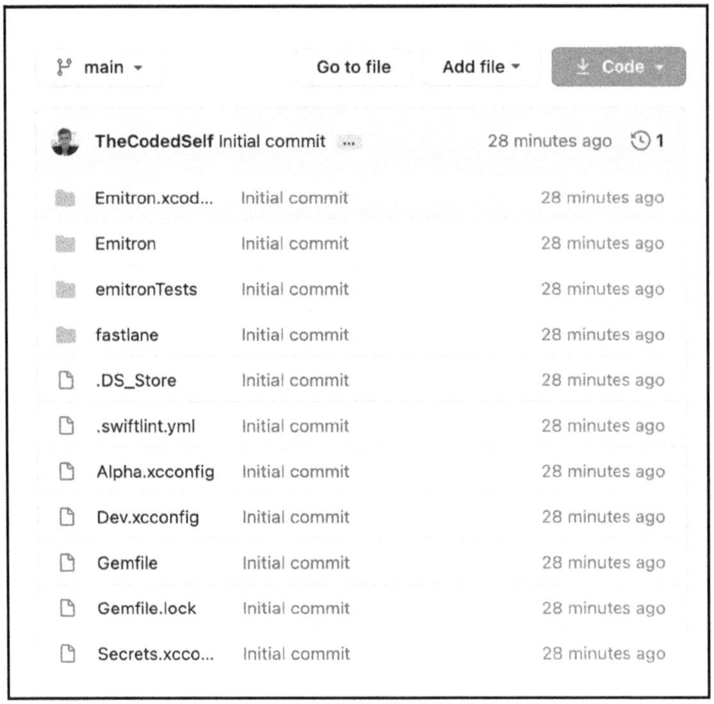

There it is, all your project code is on GitHub and ready for continuous integration!

Setting up GitHub Actions

Since your project is already on GitHub, GitHub Actions is a convenient solution for CI. Since you already have a GitHub account, you won't need to sign up for any other third-party accounts.

To use GitHub Actions for CI, all you need is a **workflow** folder in your repository with one or more workflows.

In GitHub Actions, a **workflow** is a list of jobs that should run, as well as a trigger that executes them. You define workflows as **.yml** files in a **.github/workflows** directory in your repository.

In your terminal, create the **workflows** folder for GitHub Actions.

```
mkdir .github && mkdir .github/workflows
```

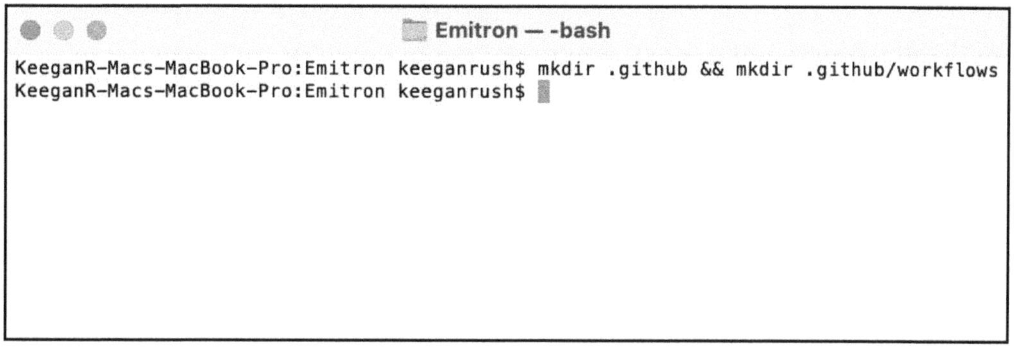

Note: Your terminal's active folder should be the same as the root folder for your GitHub repository.

GitHub uses the **.github** folder for any project configuration, such as your workflows. This command creates the **.github** folder and then a **workflows** folder within it.

Creating a workflow

Next, run this to create your first workflow file:

```
touch .github/workflows/run-tests.yml
```

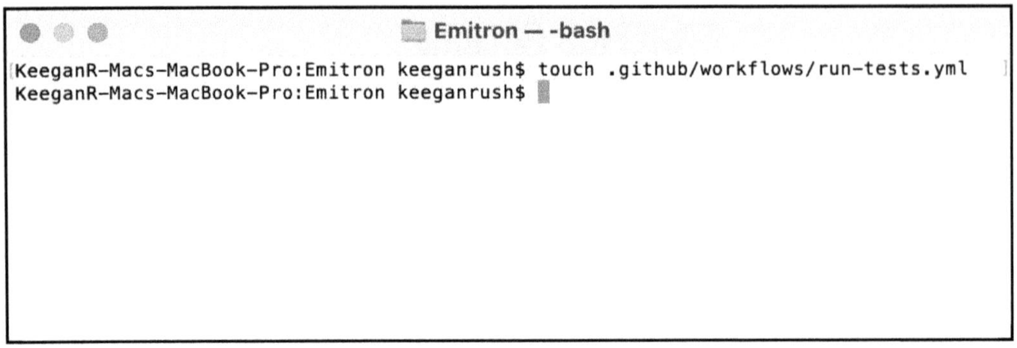

This creates an empty workflow named **run-tests.yml**.

To see hidden files in Finder, press **Command-Shift-.** (i.e., Command-Shift-Period).

Open **run-tests.yml** in your favorite text editor. Replace its contents with the following:

```
# 1
name: Run tests

# 2
on:
  push

# 3
jobs:
  build:
    runs-on: macos-latest
    # 4
    steps:
    # 5
    - uses: actions/checkout@v2
    # 6
    - name: Install fastlane
      run: |
        bundle install
    # 7
    - name: Execute fastlane
      run: |
        bundle exec fastlane test
```

Your first workflow will instruct GitHub Actions to build Emitron and run its set of automated tests using fastlane. Here's what's happening, step by step:

1. Set the name of your workflow to **Run tests**. You'll see this name in GitHub when your workflow runs.
2. Use the `on` keyword to specify your trigger. This workflow runs when a new commit is **pushed** to your repository.
3. Under `jobs`, you declare all the jobs that should run when triggering this workflow. Your new workflow has only one job named `build`.
4. Each `job` has a list of `steps`.
5. The first step is an **action** that GitHub provides. Actions are reusable pieces of code that you can use in your jobs. Here, you use the `checkout` action to check out your repository on the build server. Your repository isn't even on the build server until you use `checkout`!
6. When you want to do something that isn't available in `action`, you define a custom step with the **name** and **run** keywords. `name` is the name of your step and `run` is the command that the build server will run when the step executes. This step uses Bundler to install dependencies and make fastlane available on the build server.
7. Lastly, you have the meat of your workflow. The final step uses fastlane to run Emitron's `test` lane. This will run Emitron's test suite. If all tests succeed, your workflow will end successfully, and you'll have a green build. If not, you'll up with a red (failed) build.

You'll notice that the workflow starts with the basics: checking out the repository and installing dependencies. This happens every time your workflow executes.

Transient builds

Usually, CI servers are **transient**. Whenever GitHub Actions runs one of your workflows, the build server starts in a clean state. Each time a workflow runs, you need to fetch the repository with `checkout` and install any dependencies you need, such as fastlane.

This might seem like an extra bit of work, but it's a good thing. The reason that CI helps you to ensure a consistent build is because you must be explicit about what your workflow needs to run successfully.

With your new workflow file, you've done everything you need to set up GitHub Actions. However, everything you've done so far only exists locally on your computer. To see CI in action, you need to push your changes to GitHub.

Running the workflow

In your terminal window, run this command:

```
git add .github/workflows/run-tests.yml
```

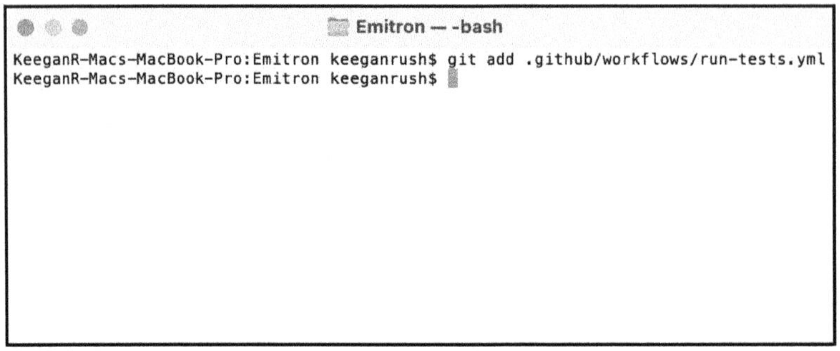

This prepares your workflow so you can commit it. Next, commit the file:

```
git commit -m "Add first workflow"
```

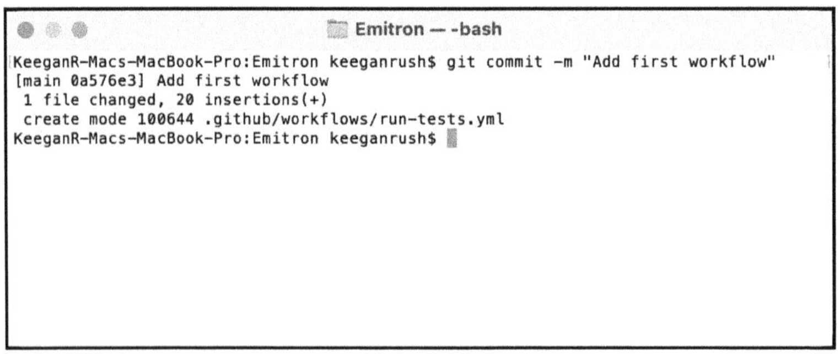

Finally, you're ready to upload your changes. Run this:

```
git push -u origin main
```

See below:

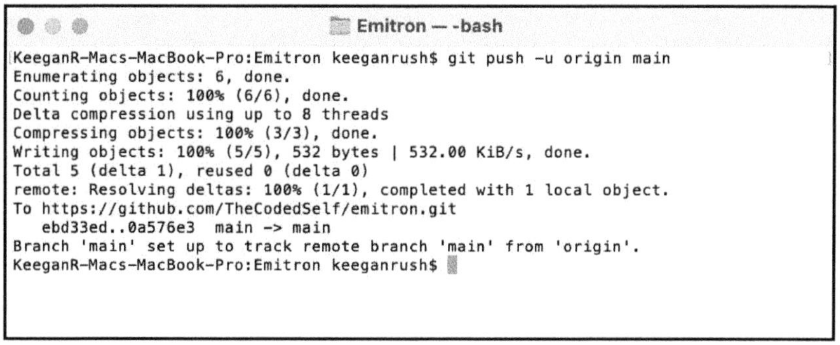

With that, you've uploaded your new workflow to the **main** branch in your GitHub repository. The workflow is set to trigger when you push a new commit, so you should have a build running in GitHub Actions right now.

Viewing the results

Back in your browser, navigate to your GitHub repository.

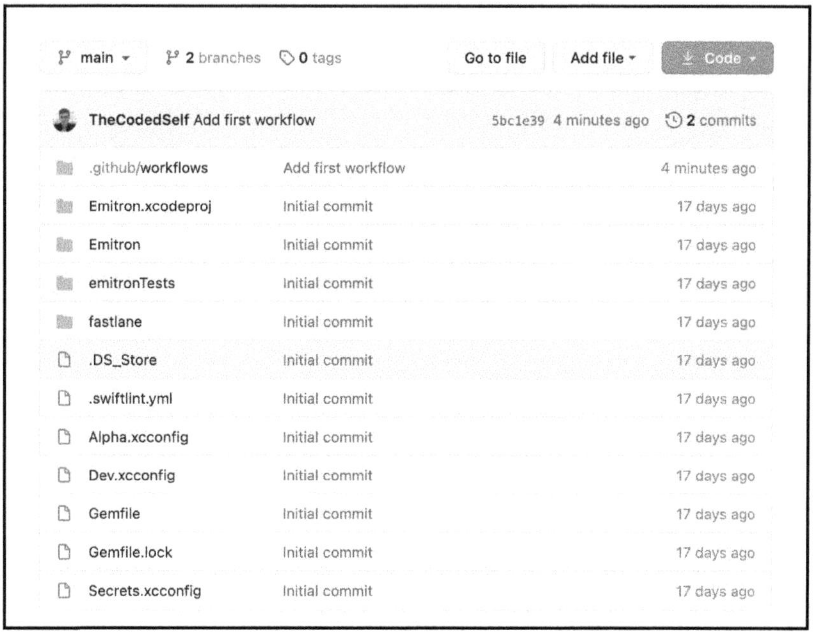

Click the **Actions** tab.

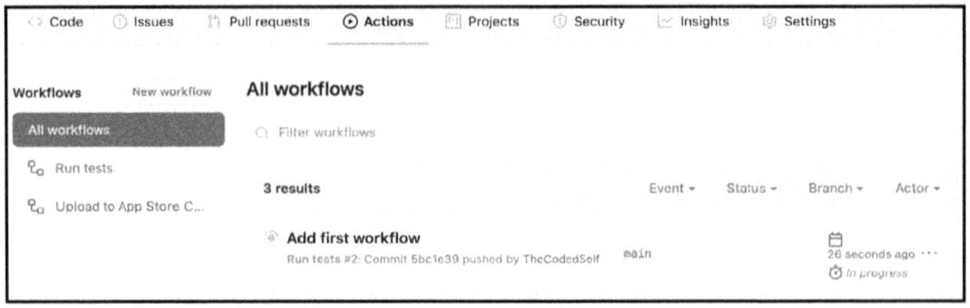

Here, you see an entry for the **Run tests** workflow executing the **Add first workflow** commit. On this screen, you'll see all the different workflows that you or other developers run for any commits in the repository.

Click **Add first workflow** to open the running build. Give it some time to finish successfully:

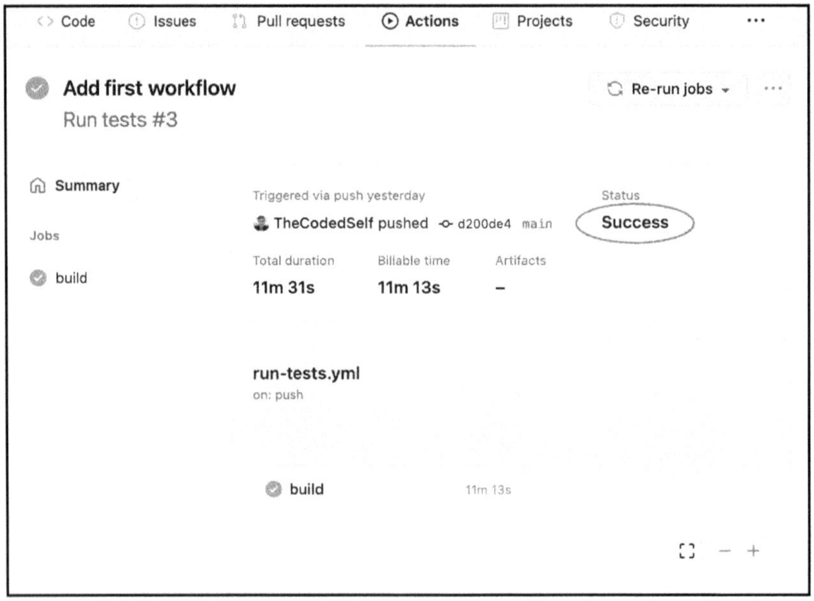

Great job!

On this screen, you'll see the results of all the jobs in your workflow. **Run tests** has only one job, **build**, so that's all you see here.

In the left sidebar, under **Jobs**, click **build**.

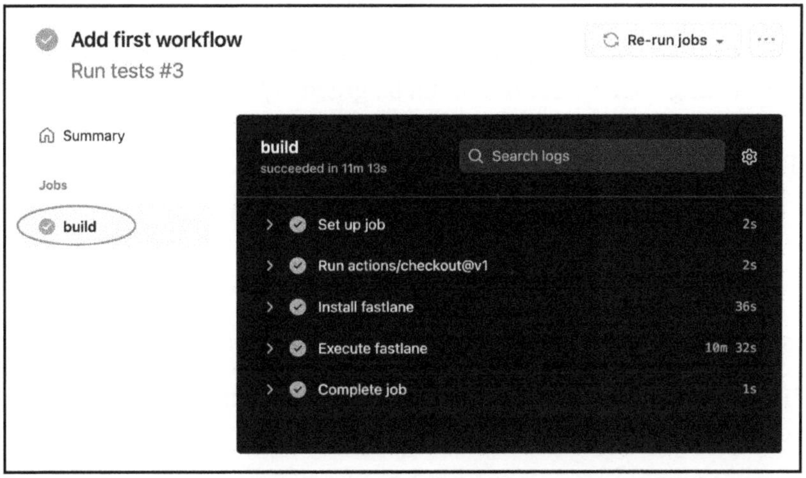

The job summary tells you how long each step took to execute. You can also view the logs for each step — something that comes in handy if you're trying to figure out why a build failed.

Click **Execute fastlane** to view the logs. Scroll almost all the way to the bottom, somewhere around line 860. Here, you'll see the results that fastlane prints to the console after running Emitron's tests:

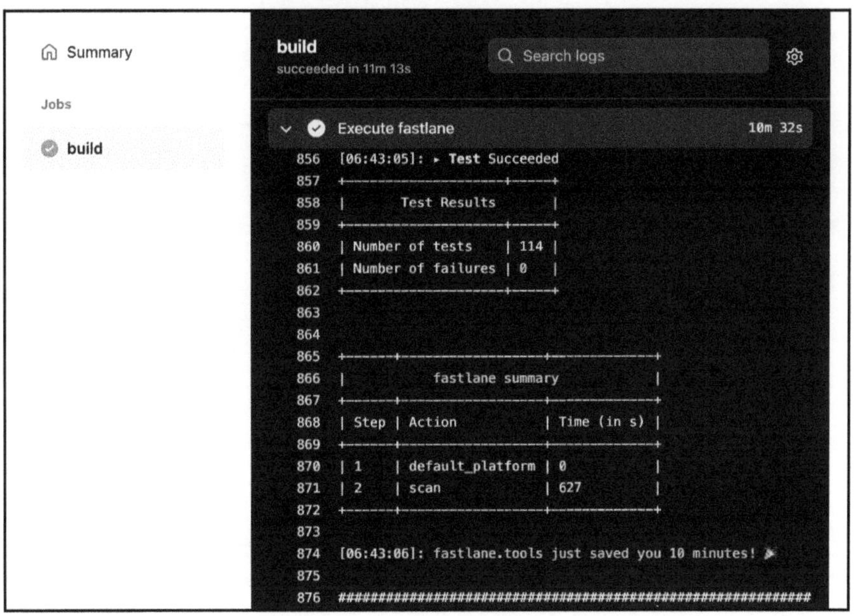

You've successfully set up your first build on CI. With this, any developers can see if the tests are successful whenever they push code.

If the workflow fails, either because Emitron doesn't compile or because a test fails, treat it as a warning sign. CI builds should be green *before* integrating different branches. That way, it's much more likely that your main branch will build and work as you expect.

Key points

- CI helps you easily integrate the work of many developers.
- By paying attention to public build status, you can catch failing tests early, before they become a problem.
- Your CI server becomes a single source of truth that you can rely on if things aren't working locally.
- A workflow is the combination of a trigger with one or more jobs.
- CI services can be full service, managed or manual.

Where to go from here?

In this chapter, you explored the benefits and practices behind continuous integration. You also created your first CI workflow, which runs Emitron's tests and reports back on the state of the build.

Continuous integration is all about making the development process easier when working as a team. A workflow that simply runs your tests and publishes a build status for the team is enough to achieve smoother integration.

The lessons you've learned in this chapter, by implementing Emitron's **Run tests** workflow, are the building blocks towards something even bigger: **continuous delivery**.

Your builds on your CI server don't need to stop after running tests. Continuous delivery (CD) takes a successful build, archives it and publishes it to TestFlight or elsewhere.

Thanks to code signing, iOS apps come with unique challenges when trying to publish an app via a CI workflow. With all the lessons you've learned so far, you're prepared to take on the challenge of continuous delivery!

In the next chapter, you'll look at some case studies of how successful companies use App Store Connect, code signing, automation and CI/CD to publish apps in the real world.

Chapter 15: Publishing in the Real World

By Keegan Rush

By this point, you've come quite a distance on your app distribution journey. You know how to deploy your app on TestFlight and the App Store, and you're well-versed in the process of automation. Distributing Emitron has been straightforward, without too many problems along the way — but that's not always the case with app distribution.

In the diverse world of iOS app distribution, you'll find companies of varying sizes and differing needs. Some companies build similar apps for many clients with client-specific branding. Others have a strong need for security and testing, such as large banks. Here, you'll typically find a slow and strict release cycle. Small startups, on the other hand, are more comfortable with playing fast and loose with their releases.

In this final chapter, you'll reference everything you've learned so far. You'll test your new skills by exploring the needs of different organizations. Each section in this chapter is dedicated to problems that different companies face in the real world. So, get ready, it's time to put what you've learned into practice!

White labeling

How do you order a pizza from your favorite pizza place? You'll find many popular pizza restaurants in every neighborhood, and they all share common needs. Every restaurant needs to manage stock, process payments and receive orders.

As an app developer, there's an opportunity lying in those overlapping requirements. Since all pizza restaurants have the same needs, wouldn't it be easy to build the same app for each restaurant? You'd only need to change the branding: the app's icon, name and possibly some aspects of the design.

A **white-label** app is a generic app that you recompile and rebrand to fit the client's needs. You could create apps for all the pizza places in your city by making a single, generic pizza restaurant app and then white labeling it for each specific client.

Using what you learned in Chapter 9, "Build Customizations", white labeling is a breeze.

White labeling with build configurations

In Chapter 9, "Build Customizations", you set up different build configurations for Emitron to create dev, beta and release builds. You use a similar trick for white labeling.

Say you have two clients that both want a pizza restaurant app, one named **Paulie's Pizza** and another named **Cheesy Dining**. There'll be some differences between the two such as:

- App icon
- Bundle identifier
- App name
- Restaurant name

These are all bits of information that you can update with build configurations. First, create two build configurations, one for each restaurant. Then, use the configurations to swap out values for branding unique to each restaurant for every build. In Chapter 10, "Advanced Build Configurations", you learned how to use build configuration files, which make this job easier.

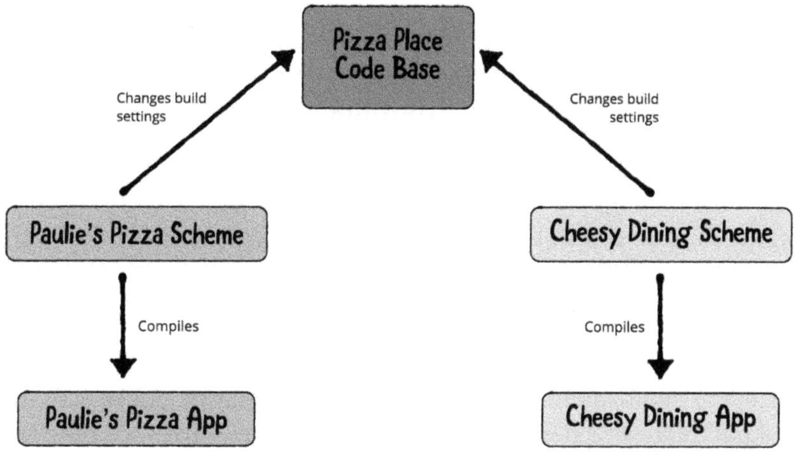

Once you have your build configurations set with the correct values, you can put them into use by creating one schema for Paulie's Pizza and another for Cheesy Dining. To build the app for either client, just build the appropriate schema. You consider each schema as its own separate app, which you release on the App Store using what you learned in Chapter 3, "Submitting Your First App for Review".

Fast deployments

When you're part of a small, scrappy startup, time to market is critically important. If you've completed work that brings value to your users, it's best to get it into their hands as soon as you can. That means getting new features through the **software development lifecycle** as quickly as possible, from idea to implementation, testing and, finally, release.

While you *could* just make it a personal goal of yours to always be on the ball, providing new builds to testers as soon as the code is on GitHub, it makes more practical sense to take advantage of **automation** and all its benefits. In Chapter 12, "Build Automation", you learned all about automation. By reducing the effort it takes to compile and archive your app, you make it easy to publish frequent builds.

With a build in hand, you still need to deliver it to testers. You can automate this step, too. In Chapter 14, "Continuous Integration", you learned how to build your app in the cloud with GitHub Action's jobs and triggers. On that note, you can take GitHub Actions even further by implementing continuous delivery.

Continuous delivery

While continuous integration helps you merge the team's work and provide feedback on the build through automated tests, **continuous delivery** supports build distribution to testers.

Continuous delivery builds on the foundations of continuous integration — you just add more jobs to your existing workflows to distribute the build. On iOS, this means including the appropriate code signing and provisioning. Thanks to Chapter 4, "Code Signing & Provisioning", you have the tools you need to sign and distribute your builds.

For the fastest of deployments, you'll start with a trigger that kicks off a build whenever a pull request is merged into the main branch. That way, once a developer completes a feature and merges it, the CI/CD server will provide a new build for testers. Your workflow will then build the app, sign it and distribute it to TestFlight (see Chapter 6, "TestFlight") or the platform of your choice.

With continuous deployment publishing your builds after every merged pull request, you can focus on the code and let automation do the busy work for you. And, when you're ready, your build is already waiting to be released to the excited hands of your users.

Smooth app reviews

Continuous delivery provides a stable, predictable build pipeline. Sometimes, however, building your app is only half the battle.

To ensure quick time to market, you need to get ready for App Review, too. Refer to Chapter 7, "Preparing for App Review", to brush up on the App Store guidelines and to know what to do when something goes wrong.

Frequent updates

A helpful addition to your CI/CD pipeline is a job that shares the build's state. You can accomplish this in a few ways:

- Send an email at the end of the build.
- Send a Slack message to a dedicated channel in your organization.
- Show the current build state in a physical **build screen** in your office.

If you see a red build status coming through in a status update, make sure to fix the build to keep your deployments running regularly!

Different environments

While some companies value quick releases, others have a stronger need for extensive testing. Companies dealing with sensitive information, such as banks and other financial institutions, go through rigorous testing cycles. Releases are larger and can take months to reach the App Store.

Usually, when working with such sensitive data, you don't test on the production server at all. This prevents any mistakes from happening in the same environment that customers rely on for their day-to-day work. Instead, multiple back-end environments allow developers and testers to play around with zero risk to the client's production database.

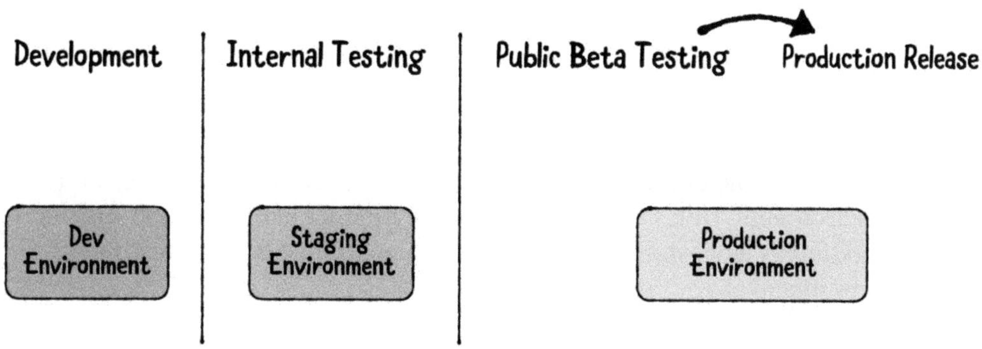

Swap out your API to protect client data during testing.

A common pattern to use with multiple back-end environments is to have three servers:

1. Development
2. Staging
3. Production

Once a build passes initial testing on the Development environment, the team makes the build available on the Staging environment. Then, once the build is ready for release, the team switches it to the Production environment.

Implementing different environments

To swap out the environment, you'll make use of build configurations, similar to the approach you use for white labeling.

First, you'll create build configurations for each environment you have.

> **Note**: If you're using the **development, staging and production** approach outlined above, you only need to create one build configuration: **staging**. The `debug` configuration uses your `development` environment and `release` uses `production`.

Then, create a new build setting for the app environment, which you'll set to the URL for your environment. For example, `https://staging.emitron.com/api` for Emitron's Staging environment, `https://dev.emitron.com/api` for Development, and so on.

In Chapter 11, "Managing Secrets", you learned how to reference build settings in code. You'll need to follow that approach so you can access your environment URL. Finally, use that URL to make any API calls.

You can also change the bundle identifier so one device can install apps for more than one environment. Don't forget to change the product name and app icon for builds on a different environment. Otherwise, you might just do your testing on Production by mistake!

Alternative hosting

While TestFlight is a remarkably convenient option for testing alpha builds, it isn't the only choice available. Other platforms, such as AppCenter and Bitrise, also host builds for internal distribution. AppCenter facilitates analytics and crash reporting as well, making it a convenient solution for managing your app.

Companies that place a premium on security aren't always comfortable hosting their builds on third-party solutions, including Apple's TestFlight. Some choose to use **ad-hoc distribution** and manually host their builds on an internal company website.

See Chapter 5, "Internal Distribution", for more on ad-hoc and enterprise builds.

One app, many teams

Besides rigorous testing, large companies face another problem that can be solved with your newfound understanding of app distribution: the coordination of **large teams**. There's a limit to how many iOS developers you can put in a room to work on the same app. With too many developers on one team, the team becomes increasingly prone to communication and coordination problems.

Continuous integration alleviates many of these problems. Even with continuous integration in place, however, you'll find it challenging to grow a team past a certain point.

Does that mean you can only have a handful of developers working on the same app? Not at all! One strategy that larger organizations apply is to use *multiple* teams of developers and testers to work on an app. Each team is self-organized and responsible for a certain feature or section of the app.

However, when multiple teams work on the same codebase, you still need to worry about merge conflicts and broken builds. So, there's still not enough separation to ease the coordination issues of working with so many developers.

Rather than working together on the same codebase, each team can develop their proprietary codebase and avoid conflicts by using **frameworks**.

Building with frameworks

Leveraging frameworks is a great strategy to share code with others. In this context, each team builds its own framework to integrate into the main app. The codebase for the main app is, for the most part, an empty shell that integrates each framework.

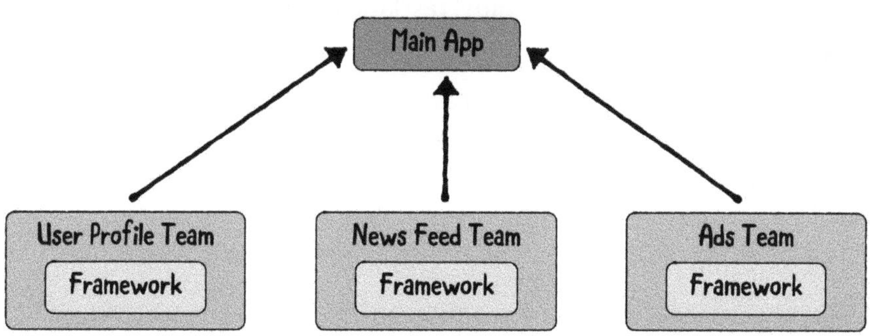

An example of a social media app. Each team builds a framework and the main app depends on those frameworks.

For any code that needs to be shared between teams, you just use — you guessed it — another framework!

When it's time to build the main app for testing and distribution, a CI/CD server compiles the main codebase. The build script pulls in stable versions of each team's frameworks through a dependency manager like Swift Package Manager or CocoaPods.

This approach lets teams work independently of each other. It also dramatically reduces the compile time in large apps because a team is only ever compiling its own framework. That framework then links to stable versions of any other frameworks it depends upon.

Multiple platforms

Besides sharing between teams on the same iOS app, you can use frameworks to share code between platforms — for example, between the iOS, iPadOS, macOS, tvOS and watchOS team. To take things further, you can also create a framework to share code between an iOS and Android app.

To do so, you'll need to step out of your Swift comfort zone. Cross-platform frameworks are often written in C or C++, but you can also use a modern language like Rust, if your C++ is a little rusty itself. :]

Automating with fastlane

Distributing an app takes a great deal of work, but it doesn't need to be that way every time. In Chapter 13, "Introduction to Fastlane", you learned how to use fastlane to automate your build. Actually, fastlane can do a whole lot more than just building your app.

Fastlane's utility begins before you've written a single line of code. You can use fastlane to create an app record in App Store Connect, just as you learned in Chapter 2, "Your First App in the App Store". You can manage all of your app's metadata, including:

- Review information
- Name, description and subtitle
- Copyright details

Once you've built your app, you still need to do a lot of manual work. You need to upload the appropriate screenshots for a number of different devices to App Store Connect. What's more, if you've localized your app into different languages, you'll need screenshots for each of those languages, too!

Thankfully, taking screenshots is a breeze with fastlane. Its **snapshot** action hooks into your UI tests to take screenshots for you.

With fastlane, you can go from compiling, to submitting your app for review, to publishing it on the App Store, all from the command line. That is, if you're brave enough! :]

After release

For many developers, one of the hardest aspects of app development has nothing to do with writing code.

If you're an indie developer releasing your own app, you have to manage every aspect of your app's successful release on your own. That means marketing, support, product management and more.

Some snazzy screenshots and an app preview video can entice people to download your app. Besides that, learning a bit about **App Store Optimization** is a great first step to promoting your app in the App Store. You may also want to focus your efforts elsewhere with a spirited campaign of **inbound marketing**.

Take a look at Chapter 8, "App Approved! (Now what?)", to get started on supporting your app after release. Beyond that, you may want to start using organization tools like **Trello**: https://trello.com/ and **Notion**: https://www.notion.so/ to plan and track your strategy.

Key points

- Different companies face different challenges. You can use the knowledge gained in this book to help solve them.
- White labeling lets you reuse the same code base for multiple clients.
- When time to market is a key factor, invest time in automating daily builds.
- For rigorous testing, consider setting up multiple environments.
- TestFlight is a convenient hosting solution for test builds, but some companies host their in-house builds for added security.
- Teams can share code using frameworks.
- Fastlane has a lot to offer in the world of automation, even from the first day of coding out a new idea.
- Your journey doesn't end once your app is released. Managing your app is as important as writing the code.

Chapter 16: Where to Go From Here?

By Keegan Rush

Congratulations on finishing “iOS App Distribution & Best Practices”!

This book has a wide target audience: if you’re a non-developer, this book taught you how to get your team’s code published. As an iOS developer involved in the release pipeline, you’ll have significantly fewer code signing frustrations. You’ve learned exactly what it takes to distribute and manage an iOS app.

In this book, you learned how the App Store is a game-changer in the field of software distribution and how you can be a part of the excitement. To start, you went over the simple process of submitting your first app for review.

Next, you went into the depths of code signing and provisioning. You prepared yourself to tackle any challenges you might face when releasing an app.

However, the journey doesn’t end once you’ve submitted your app. The book also touches on managing your app after a release.

In the second half of the book, you gained a deeper understanding of how Xcode builds your app. You learned about targets, schemes and build settings, and how you can configure them to create the ideal release pipeline.

Speaking of the ideal release pipeline, you learned about app distribution best practices. You stepped out of Xcode with build configuration files and used them for secret management. Stepping out of Xcode was the beginning of your automation journey, which began with `xcodebuild` on the command line and ended with running fastlane on a continuous integration server.

Twelve-Factor App Methodology

Many of the best practices described by this book are inspired by the **Twelve-Factor App Methodology**: https://12factor.net/.

Designed primarily for web apps, the methodology covers the separation of your app's code with its configuration and dependencies. Its practices make sure that apps are easily testable and deployable.

While not all aspects of the twelve-factor methodology apply to iOS, referring to it for guidance will help you prepare the ideal release pipeline.

DevOps

Many of the topics covered in this book delve into the practice of **DevOps**.

DevOps, a portmanteau of *development* and *operations*, is a set of practices that focus on providing high-quality software, easily and quickly. Think of it as the antithesis of spending your Friday afternoons battling with code signing and deployment.

With everything you've learned in this book, you're well on your way to becoming your company's go-to DevOps specialist.

Becoming the next fastlane

While you're learning more about DevOps for iOS, you'll surely become acquainted with fastlane.

Fastlane uses the **App Store Connect API**: https://apple.co/3aO2dcp to get and set your build's metadata, manage testers and more. The App Store Connect API is available to owners of an Apple Developer Program membership.

Maybe fastlane inspired you to build your own tool — or perhaps you've noticed some room for improvement? If you want your tool to become the very next fastlane, saving countless hours for developers worldwide, you know where to start. :]

Beyond publication

If you're releasing your own app, some of the hardest challenges have nothing to do with code.

To make sure all your potential users can discover your app, you need to invest a considerable amount of time into marketing and promoting it. You'll need a website or a landing page at the least.

An **app preview video** to go along with your snazzy screenshots can also help marketing.

Once users have found and downloaded your app, it's essential to follow up. Do so by collecting analytics, soliciting feedback and conducting user research.

Conclusion

I hope that you enjoyed your journey to App Store mastery and that you feel more comfortable with the release process. If you have any questions, comments or suggestions, please stop by our forums at https://forums.raywenderlich.com.

Thank you again for purchasing this book. Your continued support is what makes the tutorials, books, videos, conferences and other things we do at raywenderlich.com possible, and we truly appreciate it!

– Keegan, Pietro, Jayven, Jordan, Manda, Sandra and Soheil.

The *iOS App Distribution & Best Practices* team

17 Conclusion

In this book, you learned how the App Store is a game-changer in the field of software distribution and how you can be a part of the excitement. You went over the simple process of submitting your first app for review, and deep dived into the intricacies of code signing. You prepared yourself to tackle any challenges you might face when releasing an app.

However, the journey doesn't end once you've submitted your app. The book also touches on managing your app after a release. You gained a deeper understanding of how Xcode builds your app. You learned about targets, schemes and build settings, and how you can configure them to create the ideal release pipeline.

We hope that you enjoyed your journey to App Store mastery and that you feel more comfortable with the release process. If you have any questions, comments or suggestions, please stop by our forums at https://forums.raywenderlich.com.

Thank you again for purchasing this book. Your continued support is what makes the tutorials, books, videos, conferences and other things we do at raywenderlich.com possible, and we truly appreciate it!

– Keegan, Pietro, Jayven, Jordan, Manda, Sandra and Soheil.

The *iOS App Distribution & Best Practices* team

Section II: Appendices

Appendix A: TestFlight

By Pietro Rea

Unlike other types of internal distribution, there's no special "TestFlight build" separate from a finalized App Store build. TestFlight requires a **distribution build**. This Appendix walks you through creating a distribution build and uploading it to App Store Connect.

Before moving on, make sure you have the following set up already:

1. An **Apple ID** enrolled in Apple's developer program. You also need to be logged into Xcode with the same Apple ID.
2. An **App ID** registered in Apple's developer portal for the raywenderlich.com app.
3. A **distribution certificate** registered in the developer portal and saved to Keychain Access on your Mac.
4. An **App Store distribution provisioning profile** registered in the developer portal and registered with Xcode.
5. An **iOS device** running iOS 13.4 or newer to match the sample app's deployment target.

Open the starter folder for Chapter 6 and double-click **Emitron.xcodeproj** in the **starter** folder to open the project in Xcode.

Open the **Signing & Capabilities** tab for the **emitron** target. Scroll down to **Signing (Release)** and change **Bundle Identifier** to the one you registered in the developer portal back in Chapter 3, "Submitting Your First App for Review".

Bundle identifiers are unique across Apple's platforms, so your bundle identifier will be different in your case.

Next, open the **Build Settings**. Scroll down to the **Signing** section. For the following three build settings, click the disclosure icon (it looks like a ">") and modify the build setting for the **Release** build configuration:

1. Change **Code Signing Identity** to **Apple Distribution**.
2. Change **Development Team** to the team you're logged into.
3. Change **Provisioning Profile** to **Emitron Distribution Provisioning Profile** or the name of your distribution provisioning profile if it's different.

Your build settings should look like those in the next screenshot. Remember that your team name will be different from the one below.

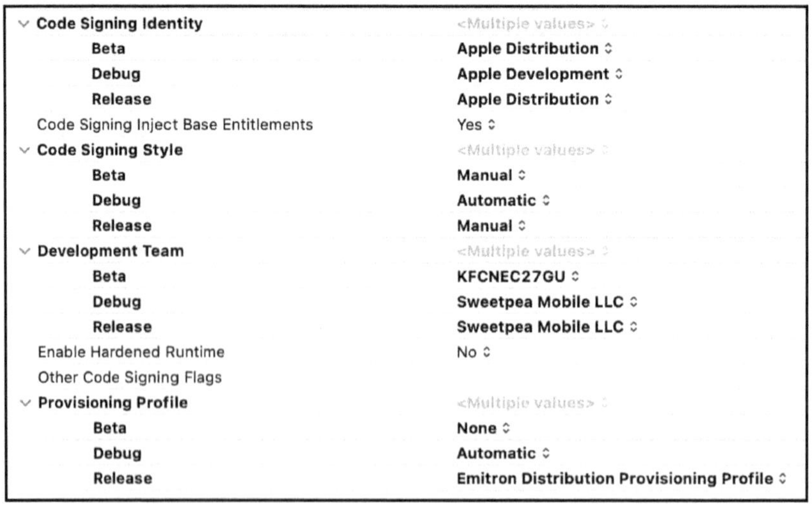

Time to create the build. In Xcode, choose **Any iOS Device (arm64)** as the build destination. Select **Product ▸ Archive** from the menu to start the build process.

Organizer appears once Xcode finishes building. The top entry is the archive you just finished building.

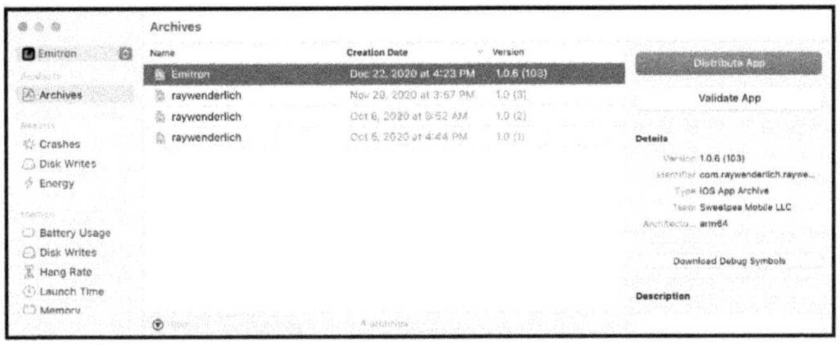

Click **Distribute**. On the next screen, select **App Store Connect** as the distribution method. TestFlight's backend systems all live in App Store Connect. That's why you don't see a special TestFlight option on this screen. Click **Next**.

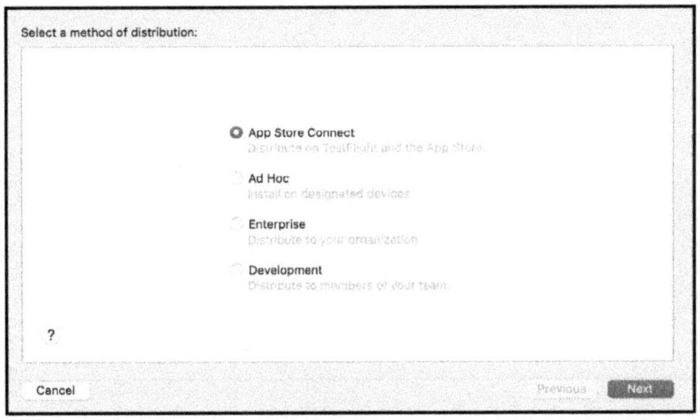

Select **Upload** to send the build to App Store Connect. Click **Next**.

Leave the checkboxes for bitcode and symbols selected. Click **Next**.

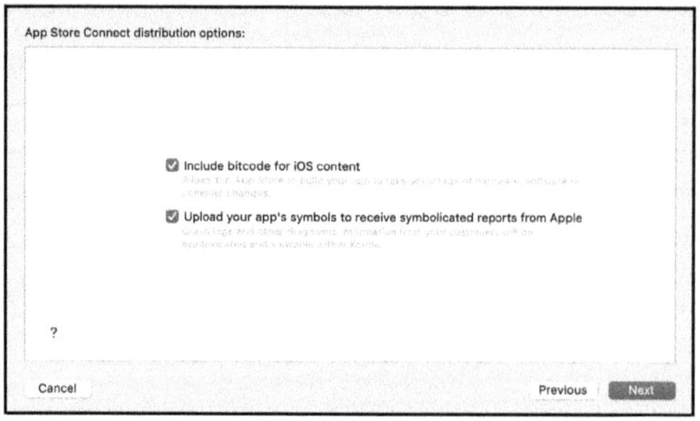

On the following screen leave the default distribution certificate selected. Next to **raywenderlich.app**, click the dropdown and select **Emitron Distribution Provisioning Profile**. Click **Next**.

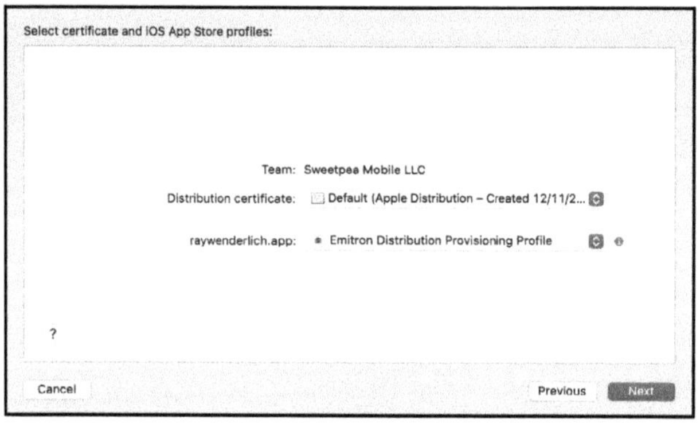

The next screen is a summary screen. Click **Upload.** Finally you see a confirmation screen saying that the upload completed successfully.

Appendix B: Release Page & Checklist

By Pietro Rea

This appendix contains a sample release page for a fictional release of Math Ninja HD, the sample app for Chapter 8, "App Approved! (Now What?)".

Only the last section is the "release checklist". The first two sections include information about the release that's often helpful to document for future reference.

Release Info

- **App Version**: v.1.3
- **Date submitted for review**: TBD
- **Date released to the public**: TBD
- **Description (internal)**: This release includes bug fixes and makes the final boss of the game, Tomato-San, much harder to beat. Most importantly, we updated the corner radius for all of our buttons based on feedback from our TestFlight beta testers.

Before submission

1. Create new app version in App Store Connect.
2. Attach release notes from Aman (product manager).
3. Attach new app screenshots from Wyeth (graphic designer).
4. Set version release mode to "manual".
5. Double-check if we need to reset ratings with this release.
6. Verify keywords, metadata & territories can remain the same.
7. Submit to App Review.

Release checklist

1. Verify all backend dependencies are in production. For this release: **ninja-service**, **arithmetic-service** and **microservice-discovery-service**.
2. Verify all relevant feature flags for the back-end are toggled on.
3. Verify all relevant feature flags for the app are toggled on.
4. Redeem promo code for this version & perform smoke tests.
5. Verify debug menu doesn't show up in pre-release build.
6. Release new version in App Store Connect.
7. Tag release branch in git (`git tag v1.3.0`) and push to GitHub.
8. Merge `release` branch into `main` branch. Push to GitHub.
9. Create a new release in GitHub with the tag you just created.
10. Close release in JIRA, our ticket management tool.
11. Post in `#team-turboprop` and `#general` in Slack that we're live.
12. Notify Genevieve about the release (PR director).
13. Notify TestFlight external testers about the release.

www.ingramcontent.com/pod-product-compliance
Ingram Content Group UK Ltd.
Pitfield, Milton Keynes, MK11 3LW, UK
UKHW051447290926
15471UKWH00008B/1072

9 781950 325153